HALF BAKED
HARVEST
cookbook

HALF BAKED
HARVEST
cookbook

RECIPES *from* MY BARN *in the* MOUNTAINS

TIEGHAN GERARD

CLARKSON POTTER/PUBLISHERS
NEW YORK

To all my Half Baked Harvest readers, this book is dedicated to you. Without you there would be no cookbook. Thank you for reading daily and for your never-ending support. I love you guys.

And to my family, you are all my best friends and my greatest motivation in life. Thank you for trying all of my recipes, even the ones with "green stuff," and for putting up with me throughout this crazy process of writing a cookbook!

Contents

The Beginning

FOR AS LONG AS I CAN REMEMBER, I HAVE LOVED CREATING THINGS. When I was little, I would spend countless weekends working on craft projects, making photo collages from magazine cutouts, rearranging my bedroom, or helping my grandma set up for parties. Never was I not doing something. For the longest time, I had always said that I was going to grow up to be a fashion stylist. I loved clothes, but even more than that, I loved putting pieces together to make them pretty. I get this from my nonnie, who taught me all I know about tablescapes, entertaining, and making one heck of a Dutch Baby (page 29). It wasn't until I was fourteen or fifteen that I started to get into cooking, but once I started, I never stopped . . . clearly.

Let me back up. I am one of seven kids. Yes, I did say seven, and yes, we all have the same mom and dad. For most of my life, I was the only girl of the bunch—my little sister, Asher, wasn't born until I was fifteen. This meant my early years were spent as one of the biggest tomboys around. Dirt bikes, snowboarding, swimming in the lake. My mom put me in cute dresses and hats, but I wanted nothing to do with them. When she picked me up from preschool, I'd hop in the van and immediately whip off my pretty clothes (I know, I know, so wild). I'd strip down to the boxers and tee I wore underneath, just like my brothers, and breathe a sigh of relief.

Growing up in such a big family meant a lot of things. My life was not only fun; it was also never boring. It was hectic, unorganized, and, um, very loud. I am the only person in my family who loves a good routine, loves to be organized, and basically just hates all things chaotic. My mom, on the other hand, thrives on chaos. While I love her to pieces and she is my best friend, we could not be more different. She is an adventure-seeking, go-with-the-flow, fly-by-the-seat-of-your-pants kind of person. Me, I'm a routine-loving, type A, crazy-focused freak. As a kid, it bugged me greatly that every single day in our house was chaotic. It bugged me even more that our dinners were about five times more frenzied than my friends'. I had this picture in my head of the perfect family dinner. You know, where everyone sits down together at a beautifully set table, at a reasonable hour, and eats like civilized people. I blame this perfectly concocted scene on the TV show *7th Heaven*, which I watched religiously (along with *Gilmore Girls*, which I proudly admit I still watch reruns of). For the most part, *7th Heaven* depicted a large family like mine. But they all sat down for dinner at a normal hour, ate a home-cooked meal, and discussed life as if they were actually normal human beings. That's what I wanted, and I wanted it so bad.

My dad worked a full-time job as a bond broker, and after work he would head to the gym to play handball. When my mom was pregnant with me, with three crazy little boys in tow, my parents made a deal that Dad could go play handball after work every day if he'd take care of dinner when he got home. The unspoken part of their deal was that if Dad made dinner, Mom made dessert, which most of the time was ready before dinner.

You see, Dad's usual hour of arrival home wasn't until seven thirty or eight, and that was on a good night. Even on school nights we wouldn't eat until almost nine. (Mom will try to tell you it was earlier, but she's revised the memory a little bit. It was rarely before nine—ask any of my brothers.) Finally, when I was fourteen or so, I said something along the lines of, "Screw it! You guys are so annoying and I'm over it. I'm making my own freaking dinner!" And that right there is how and why I began cooking. At the time, I was cooking for the sole purpose of helping my dad get dinner on the table before nine p.m. What I soon came to realize is that I really had a lot of fun cooking. I was very much a rule-following kid, but in cooking, I was more carefree and creative. I might have used a recipe as a base, but I never followed it to a T. If I didn't have something the recipe called for, I used whatever we had on hand and made it work. I was totally comfortable just doing my own thing, never fearful that something wouldn't turn out. If there's one thing my dad taught me about cooking, it's that pretty much anything can be saved with a giant pile of cheese and a handful of fresh basil.

It wasn't long before I took over all the cooking for the family. I loved it. I loved searching for recipes, going to the store and picking out ingredients, and, probably most important, I loved having control of something. It felt so good to rein in the chaos and take control of dinnertime.

My preteen and teenage years were extremely difficult for me. I struggled a lot with anxiety about school. That, on top of the chaos of my family, was really hard for me. Cooking was my own little escape, and it inspired me in a way I didn't even know I could be inspired. My parents loved the help, too. It was win-win all around. The number one reason I love cooking is the reactions I see on people's faces when they take that first bite of a delicious dish. My favorite thing ever is watching someone's eyes roll back and then open wide into an "oh my gosh, this is heaven" look. Those reactions are what I live for, they're what keep me cooking and running full speed ahead.

Fast-forward a few years. I'm eighteen years old, and living in LA, and working for Barbizon, an acting and modeling agency, as a talent agent. I'm in ready-set-go mode, about to start school at the Fashion Institute of Design & Merchandising, and pumped to begin my life as a fashion stylist, the life I'd been dreaming of since I was little. But after about two months, a case of homesickness kicked in. I freaked out and moved my butt back to Colorado, back to my comfort zone of family and chaos. At the time I was so disappointed in myself, but looking back now, it was without a doubt the best decision I've made in my life. The decision to start my blog, *Half Baked Harvest*, came as soon as I returned home. I was feeling lost, and my mom convinced me to give something completely different a try. Over the years she had seen how happy cooking made me, so she suggested starting a food blog. Since I really had nothing to lose, I went for it and never looked back. That was when I stepped back out of my comfort zone and left it at the door. For good.

That decision is why I am sitting here now, writing this cookbook filled with recipes that I am super excited to share with you. That one decision set me up to create a life I love. You know what's funny, though? The whole reason I even started cooking was because I simply wanted to eat dinner at a normal hour. We all joke now that I eat later than anyone else in the family, and it's true, but only because I love what I do so much that my workaholic self doesn't get around to actually eating until pretty late. I now understand the struggle my parents were faced with all those years ago. Life is busy, and dinner is hard to get on the table at a decent hour! But dinner is something that shouldn't be rushed. It's a time to relax with loved ones at the end of the day when work is done.

Cooking changed me, and my work changed me. I'm not the same timid, fearful, routine-loving person I used to be. Creating recipes for others to share with friends and family has brought me so much happiness! My hope for this cookbook is that it becomes a staple in your kitchen. I want it to be the book that has pasta sauce on the cover and chocolate smeared across the dessert pages, that automatically opens to your most favorite recipe because that's how often you make it. I want this book to be your go-to.

As you will see, these recipes are inspired by the people and places I love most. I talk a lot about my family, as they truly are my favorite people in the world. My parents and each of my siblings have inspired these recipes in their own special way. My philosophy on food—be bright, beautiful, and positively cozy. My philosophy on life—work harder than anyone else.

How to Cook with This Book

>≻≫≻⊱✕⊰≺≪≺<

EVERYONE WHO HAS A FAMILY TO FEED IS LOOKING FOR A NEW WAY TO do it. It's about getting dinner on the table—it always has been for me—and how to keep that exciting and interesting. That's exactly what these recipes are meant to do . . . feed your loved ones, encourage good conversation, and, above all, enjoy something delicious. I tend to take everything up a notch with my recipes. There are a lot of classics that you'll probably recognize, but all with a little twist or surprise that makes them different and helps mealtime feel special. Just a few things before you get started . . .

If you're anything like me, following a recipe to a T is something you struggle with. I get it—I (clearly) like to have fun and be creative when I'm cooking. With these recipes, I want you to feel free to use the ingredients you have on hand. That's how a lot of my recipes came to be in the first place! Or you can even add ingredients that you think will make the dish one that your family will love. The only place where this isn't the case is the baking recipes. Baking is more of an exact science, so using another flour or subbing oil for butter might not yield the same results. Because of this, I recommend that you follow the baking instructions as written.

NOW LET'S TALK MUST-HAVE KITCHEN TOOLS AND TOYS:

SHARP CHEF'S KNIFE AND PARING KNIFE: These are essential for pretty much every recipe here and out there.

STAND MIXER: I use a stand mixer for almost all my baking recipes and a lot of savory recipes as well. It's an essential tool in my kitchen, and, if you love to bake, you should own one! If you don't, you can use a handheld mixer in many instances, or just beat by hand—you'll end up with stronger biceps!

LARGE CAST-IRON SKILLET: Not a day goes by that I don't use my cast-iron skillet. It might be my most used kitchen tool. I employ it for everything from sauces to searing meat to baking up my Nonnie's Dutch Baby (page 29). My favorite brand is Staub.

LARGE DUTCH OVEN: Like my skillet, I use my Dutch oven almost daily. It's great for making stove-to-oven meals like my Roasted Garlic and Tomato–Braised Lamb Shanks (page 184).

RIMMED BAKING SHEETS: Used for baking cookies and roasting veggies, these are also a total must-have. You probably want to have more than one on hand.

HIGH-SPEED BLENDER OR FOOD PROCESSOR: I use both my blender and food processor almost daily to puree soups, make

sauces, or quickly chop veggies. A mini food processor will do the trick (you can work in batches as needed), but I like my full-size one, too.

SLOW COOKER: For anyone with a busy lifestyle, a slow cooker is a must. I use mine weekly throughout the year for recipes like my Healthier Slow-Cooker Butter Chicken (page 133). Most recipes calling for a slow cooker can easily be converted to the stove or oven. If it's a meat-based recipe, sear the meat first and then add the remaining ingredients to the pot. Simmer on Low for 4 hours or more or transfer to a 300°F oven and cook for 3 to 4 hours, or until the meat is tender. Alternatively, you can convert non–slow cooker recipes into slow cooker recipes by searing the meat first on the stove and then transferring it to your cooker. Just add the remaining ingredients and cook on Low for 7 to 8 hours or High for 4 to 6 hours. If cooking a chicken recipe, it is not necessary to sear the chicken first. If cooking a soup recipe, just put all the ingredients in the slow cooker and cook low and slow!

SPIRAL SLICER: This is a great kitchen tool for anyone who cooks with a lot of vegetables or is trying to eat a little healthier. I use mine to spiralize my favorite vegetables, such as squash, zucchini, sweet potatoes, or beets, into healthy noodles that can be used in place of or alongside pasta.

AND NOW THAT YOU'RE FULLY EQUIPPED, WHAT ABOUT INGREDIENTS?

EXTRA-VIRGIN OLIVE OIL: This is the start of so many recipes. Find a good one you like and keep a lot of it on hand!

MILK: You will notice that I use goat's milk in many of my recipes. One, I love it. Two, my family has goats, and I am fortunate enough to be able to have it whenever I want it. In any recipe calling for goat's milk, you can use whole cow's milk in its place. I also use a lot of canned full-fat coconut milk, as it's my favorite healthy way to add creaminess to recipes. Remember, feel free to sub as you like.

CHEESE: No secret here: I *looooove* cheese. I use cheese in many recipes. If you feel a recipe is a little too cheese-heavy for you, feel free to reduce the amount. If a recipe calls for blue cheese (my favorite!) but you're not a fan, try using crumbled goat cheese or shredded cheddar in its place.

BUTTER: As with cheese, I am not afraid of using a little butter. If a recipe calls for unsalted butter and you only have salted, just reduce the salt in the recipe. If a recipe calls for salted butter but you only have unsalted, just add a pinch of salt. You will also notice that I often brown my butter. I find this adds incredible flavor and is the perfect finishing touch to many recipes.

LOW-SODIUM SOY SAUCE: I use only low-sodium soy sauce when cooking. It helps me better control the saltiness of the recipe.

SEMISWEET CHOCOLATE CHIPS: My mom taught me a lot of valuable lessons about how to stock your pantry, and one of those lessons was to never, ever run out of chocolate chips.

OTHER COMMON PANTRY ITEMS: Dry pasta, dry rice (whatever variety you like best—I like white, brown, jasmine, wild, and forbidden), quinoa, instant polenta, Thai red curry paste, fish sauce, red harissa, canned chipotle peppers in adobo, and sun-dried tomatoes. These come up frequently in my recipes and add enough flavor and fun to meals that they're worth investing in.

Breakfast

Fancy Toast, Eight Ways

I'll eat toast anytime, anywhere. Toast is one of my favorite foods, and I have fun getting creative with the toppings. Here are eight of my all-time crave-worthy toast combinations. There's everything from my childhood obsessions—hey, hey cinnamon sugar—to slightly more sophisticated options. Get fancy!

Apple + Honey + Ricotta + Toasted Pumpkin Seed

Spread a piece of warm, toasted bread with ¼ cup of ricotta cheese. Add ½ of an apple, thinly sliced, and top with honeycomb or drizzle with honey. Sprinkle a handful of toasted pumpkin seeds (pepitas) on top and drizzle with warmed almond butter. Top with chopped fresh thyme leaves and flaky sea salt.

Bubble-Up Cheddar and Tomato

Spread a piece of bread with butter and place on a baking sheet. Top with shredded cheddar cheese and then layer on 1 or 2 tomato slices. Place under the broiler and cook for 1 to 2 minutes, or until the cheese is bubbling and melted. Remove the baking sheet from the oven. Top with ½ of an avocado, sliced; drizzle with fresh lemon juice, then sprinkle with flaky sea salt and freshly ground pepper. Finish with 1 fried egg and toasted sesame seeds.

Strawberry + Basil + Goat Cheese

Spread a piece of warm, toasted bread with softened goat cheese and layer on 3 or 4 sliced fresh strawberries. Add torn fresh basil leaves. Drizzle with balsamic vinegar and honey, and sprinkle with flaky sea salt.

Peanut Butter + Honeycomb + Grape

Spread a piece of warm, toasted bread with peanut butter. Add halved red grapes and honeycomb or drizzle with honey. Sprinkle with flaky sea salt.

Tomato + Basil + Burrata

Spread a piece of warm, toasted bread with Basil Pesto (page 99). Break a ball of burrata over the bread. Add halved cherry tomatoes and drizzle with olive oil and balsamic vinegar. Sprinkle with torn fresh basil leaves and finish with flaky sea salt and freshly ground pepper.

Salted Fig + Maple Butter + Tahini

In a small saucepan, bring 2 tablespoons of salted butter and 2 tablespoons of pure maple syrup to a boil over medium heat. Cook for 30 seconds, then remove the pan from the heat. Spread a piece of warm, toasted bread with tahini and top with 2 or 3 sliced fresh or dried figs. Drizzle with the maple butter. Sprinkle with flaky sea salt.

Cinnamon Sugar

Spread a piece of warm, toasted bread with butter and then sprinkle generously with equal amounts of ground cinnamon and sugar mixed together. If desired, gently spread or drizzle with Nutella.

Avocado + Citrus + Microgreens

Top toasted bread with ½ of an avocado, sliced, flaky sea salt, toasted sesame seeds, hemp seeds, blood orange slices, passion fruit (optional), and a handful of microgreens. Drizzle lightly with olive oil.

Sesame Bagels with Avocado, Burrata, and Raspberries

Makes: **2 sandwiches**

You may think of this is an odd combo, but please give it a chance. It is honestly one of my favorite sandwiches of all time. When I was a kid, I insisted my mom make these lunch "bagels" complete with basically whatever was in the fridge, but there was always plenty of cheese, avocado, and eggs. This combination, plus the other stuff here, is the best of the best of the best. Really, I cannot express how incredibly delicious this sandwich is. If you are feeling adventurous, try creating your own sandwich combos using ingredients you have on hand!

2 sesame seed bagels, halved

2 tablespoons extra-virgin olive oil

4 slices deli salami

One or two 4-ounce balls burrata cheese

½ cup fresh raspberries

Honey, for drizzling

1 avocado, pitted, peeled, and sliced

Kosher salt and freshly ground pepper

6 fresh basil leaves, torn

2 Perfectly Poached Eggs (page 47)

1. Preheat the oven to 375°F.

2. Place the bagels on a baking sheet, cut-side up. Rub each with ½ tablespoon of the olive oil. Arrange the salami on the baking sheet around the bagels. Transfer to the oven and bake for 8 to 10 minutes, or until the salami is crisp—watch closely, as it will cook fast toward the end!

3. Remove the baking sheet from the oven and break the burrata over each bottom bagel half. Top with fresh raspberries and drizzle with honey. Add the salami and avocado and season with salt and pepper. Add the basil and top each with an egg.

4. Finish with the top halves of the bagels.

Earl Grey Blueberry Muffins with Cinnamon Streusel

Makes: **15 to 18 muffins**

When my youngest brother, Red, was in kindergarten, I was in seventh grade and would get home from school before he did. On Fridays, I liked to surprise him with fresh-baked treats. I would be sure to get the Betty Crocker wild blueberry muffin mix with the blueberries that came packed in a can. I swore that's what made the muffins so good. These days, though, I do most of my baking from scratch. This version has the slightest hint of Earl Grey tea and is loaded with fresh blueberries that burst while baking, making the berries even sweeter and more delicious. Finish with a generous amount of cinnamon streusel and you'll have the tastiest muffin—maybe even better than Red's after-school snack.

1 cup whole milk

3 Earl Grey tea bags (see Note)

½ cup canola oil

½ cup honey

½ cup packed light brown sugar

½ cup plain Greek yogurt

2 teaspoons pure vanilla extract

1 large egg

2 egg yolks

3 ½ cups all-purpose flour

2 teaspoons baking powder

1 teaspoon kosher salt

2 cups fresh or frozen blueberries (do not thaw if frozen)

4 tablespoons (½ stick) salted butter, cut into cubes

1 teaspoon ground cinnamon

¼ cup walnuts or pecans, chopped

1. Preheat the oven to 375°F. Line 15 to 18 wells of two muffin tins with paper liners.

2. In a small saucepan, bring the milk to a gentle simmer over medium-low heat, then immediately remove the pan from the heat—do not allow the milk to boil. Add the tea bags and steep for about 15 minutes, then discard the tea bags.

3. In a large bowl, combine the canola oil, honey, ¼ cup of the brown sugar, the yogurt, vanilla, egg, and egg yolks and stir until evenly mixed and pale in color. Add the steeped milk and stir to combine. Add 3 cups of the flour, the baking powder, and the salt and stir until just combined. Gently fold the blueberries into the batter, taking care not to overmix (otherwise the batter will turn blue). Divide the batter evenly among the muffins cups, filling them three-quarters of the way full.

4. In a small bowl, combine the remaining ¼ cup brown sugar, ½ cup of flour, the butter, cinnamon, and nuts. Mix together with your hands until a crumbly mixture forms. Sprinkle the streusel topping over the batter, dividing it evenly.

5. Bake for 15 to 20 minutes, or until a toothpick inserted into the center comes out clean. Eat them while they're hot!

NOTE

If you're running short on time, or just don't like the flavor of Earl Grey, you can skip warming the milk and steeping the tea altogether.

Overnight Oats, Two Ways

Serves: 2

I think oatmeal gets such a bad rap. We all know oats are good for us, but that doesn't mean they have to be boring. Enter these two crazy-easy oat recipes. They're perfect to make ahead the night before, then just grab and go in the morning. There are two ways to make them. The first method is to combine the oats in a jar or bowl and allow them to sit in the fridge overnight. The second method is to combine everything in your slow cooker the night before and let it cook low and slow—when you wake up, your kitchen will smell amazing. What I love about this recipe is that you can change up the flavors depending on the seasons. In the fall, I'll top my oats with apples; in the winter, fresh citrus; in the spring, strawberries; and in the summer, stone fruits.

Pecan Banana Bread

1 cup old-fashioned rolled oats

1½ cups milk of your choice (I like canned coconut milk)

2 very ripe bananas, mashed, plus sliced banana for topping

¼ cup plain Greek yogurt

2 tablespoons unsweetened coconut flakes, toasted

2 tablespoons honey, plus more for serving

1 tablespoon chia seeds

2 teaspoons pure vanilla extract

¼ teaspoon flaky sea salt

½ cup pecans, toasted

Fresh or dried figs, halved, for serving

Pomegranate seeds, for serving

1. In a medium bowl, stir together the oats, milk, mashed banana, yogurt, coconut, honey, chia seeds, vanilla, and salt until well combined. Divide the mixture evenly between two bowls or two 8- to 12-ounce glass jars. Cover and refrigerate for at least 6 hours or overnight.

2. In the morning, stir the oats, then top with sliced banana, toasted pecans, and figs. Drizzle with honey and sprinkle with pomegranate seeds.

Warm Cranberry Apple

Butter or nonstick cooking spray, for greasing

1¼ cups steel-cut oats

1½ cups milk of your choice (I like canned coconut milk)

1 cup apple cider

2 apples (I like Honeycrisp), cored and chopped, plus more for serving

½ cup dried cranberries, plus more for serving

2 tablespoons pure maple syrup, plus more, if desired, for serving

2 teaspoons pure vanilla extract

½ teaspoon ground cinnamon, plus more for serving

¼ teaspoon flaky sea salt

Toasted pecans, for serving

Toasted pumpkin seeds (pepitas), for serving

1. Lightly grease your slow cooker with cooking spray or butter. In the slow cooker, combine the oats, milk, cider, apples, cranberries, maple syrup, vanilla, cinnamon, salt, and 1 cup of water and stir to combine. Cover and cook on Low for 6 to 9 hours.

2. In the morning, stir the oats, then serve warm, topped with apple, cranberries, cinnamon, pecans, and pumpkin seeds. Drizzle with additional maple syrup, if desired.

Peanut Butter Crunch French Toast

You think you know French toast, but you have no idea. This is a recipe you have to try; it is like no other. Think about it: a brioche peanut butter sandwich, coated in a bourbon-y egg-and-milk batter, dredged through a mixture of crushed cornflakes and almonds, then pan-fried with butter. But wait, there's more. Top it off with cinnamon whipped cream, maple syrup, fresh berries, and more butter (of course). I'll take a stack . . . please and thank you. While the bourbon is optional, I highly, highly recommend including it. It adds loads of flavor and pairs perfectly with the vanilla in the batter and the peanut butter snuggled inside the French toast. Yum!

Cinnamon Whipped Cream

1 cup heavy cream

1 tablespoon confectioners' sugar or pure maple syrup

¼ teaspoon ground cinnamon

1 teaspoon pure vanilla extract

French Toast

1 loaf brioche, cut into sixteen ½-inch-thick slices

½ cup creamy peanut butter

4 large eggs

1½ cups whole milk

3 tablespoons bourbon (optional)

1 tablespoon pure vanilla extract

½ teaspoon flaky sea salt

3 cups crushed cornflakes

1 cup sliced almonds

Butter, for the pan, plus more for serving

Confectioners' sugar, maple syrup, and/or fresh berries, for serving

1. **MAKE THE WHIPPED CREAM.** In a large bowl using a handheld mixer, whip the cream until it holds soft peaks. Add the sugar, cinnamon, and vanilla and whip until combined.

2. **MAKE THE FRENCH TOAST.** Spread half the brioche slices with peanut butter, using about 1 tablespoon for each, then top them with the remaining slices to make peanut butter sandwiches.

3. In a shallow medium bowl, whisk together the eggs, milk, bourbon (if using), vanilla, and salt until combined. In a separate shallow medium bowl, stir together the cornflakes and almonds.

4. Working with one at a time, dip the sandwiches into the egg mixture, allowing them to soak on each side for 1 to 2 minutes. Remove from the egg mixture, allowing any excess to drip back into the bowl, then dredge in the cornflake-almond mixture, pressing gently to adhere.

5. Heat a large skillet or griddle over medium and coat generously with butter. When the butter has melted, cook the French toast in batches (do not overcrowd the pan) until golden and crisp, 3 to 4 minutes per side. Remove and serve immediately with butter, the cinnamon whipped cream, confectioners' sugar, maple syrup, and/or fresh berries.

NOTE

To prep this ahead of time, assemble the peanut butter sandwiches as directed. In a 9 x 13-inch baking dish, whisk together the eggs, milk, bourbon, vanilla, and salt. Dredge each sandwich in the mixture, being sure to coat both sides. Place each sandwich in the baking dish, mostly submerging them. Cover and refrigerate until ready to cook, up to overnight, flipping once, if possible. When ready to cook, dredge the sandwiches in the cornflake-almond mixture and cook as directed.

Croque Madame Breakfast Pizza

Makes: **One 10- to 12-inch pizza**

I think a breakfast pizza makes so much sense. Call me crazy, but it has all the elements of any killer breakfast: bread, vegetables, maybe a meat, and cheese. Add eggs and you have a complete, well-rounded breakfast! Enter this croque madame pizza. It's just like the classic sandwich, only on pizza dough. The eggs get cracked right on top, then baked. This is an easy dish to make for brunch, whether for guests or just for yourself. And don't forget about that whole breakfast-for-dinner thing, either!

Extra-virgin olive oil, for greasing

1 tablespoon salted butter

1 tablespoon all-purpose flour, plus more for dusting

½ cup milk

1 tablespoon Dijon mustard

Kosher salt and freshly ground black pepper

½ pound pizza dough, store-bought or homemade (page 212)

1 cup shredded Gruyère cheese

½ cup shredded fontina cheese

3 ounces thinly sliced prosciutto or 3 crumbled cooked bacon slices

¼ cup grated Parmesan cheese

1 or 2 large eggs

1 or 2 handfuls of baby spinach or arugula

Flaky sea salt

Crushed red pepper flakes

Chopped fresh chives

1. Preheat the oven to 450°F. Grease a baking sheet with olive oil.

2. In a small saucepan, melt the butter over medium heat. Add the flour and whisk for 1 minute. Slowly add the milk and mustard, whisking continuously. Bring to a simmer and season with kosher salt and black pepper. Cook for 1 to 2 minutes, then remove the pan from the heat.

3. On a lightly floured surface, roll the dough out into a very thin 10- to 12-inch circle. Transfer the dough to the prepared baking sheet. Spread the cream sauce over the dough. Sprinkle evenly with the Gruyère and fontina. Add the prosciutto, leaving space for the eggs. Sprinkle with the Parmesan.

4. Bake for 5 minutes, then remove from the oven and crack the eggs on top. Bake for 8 to 12 minutes more, or until the cheese is melted and gooey and the eggs are just set.

5. Sprinkle the pizza with spinach, then add a pinch or two of flaky sea salt, black pepper, red pepper flakes, and some chives. Serve right away.

Crunchy Oats 'n' Honey Bars

Makes: **12 bars**

I have been making these bars for years, and every time I do, the whole batch is gone within a day. They are so simple, full of healthy ingredients, and a million times better than any store-bought granola bar. Trust me—once you make these, you'll be kicking yourself for all the years you've been eating bland, sugar-loaded, prepackaged granola bars.

3 cups old-fashioned rolled oats

1 cup puffed brown rice cereal

½ cup finely ground cornmeal

½ teaspoon ground cinnamon (optional)

½ teaspoon baking soda

½ teaspoon kosher salt

½ cup plus 1 to 2 teaspoons honey

⅓ cup coconut oil

1 tablespoon coconut sugar or light brown sugar

2 teaspoons pure vanilla extract

Nonstick cooking spray

1. Preheat the oven to 350°F. Line a 9 x 13-inch baking dish with parchment paper.

2. In a medium bowl, combine the oats, cereal, cornmeal, cinnamon (if using), baking soda, and salt.

3. Put ½ cup of the honey and the coconut oil in a microwave-safe bowl. Microwave for 30 seconds to 1 minute, or until melted. Stir in the coconut sugar and vanilla. Whisk to combine.

4. Pour the honey mixture over the oats and toss well, being sure all the oats are coated. Transfer the oat mixture to the prepared baking dish. Spray the bottom of a drinking glass or a glass measuring cup with cooking spray. Press down on the oats with the bottom of the glass to really pack them into the baking dish.

5. Bake for about 15 minutes, until light golden. Remove from the oven and drizzle with the remaining 1 to 2 teaspoons of honey. Bake for 5 to 8 minutes more, until deep golden on top. Remove from the oven and let cool in the dish for 10 to 15 minutes. Cut into bars when firm, but still somewhat soft. Do not wait longer than 15 minutes after the bars have been removed from the oven, or cutting them will be zero fun.

6. Place the cut bars on a wire rack to cool completely. Store in a sealed container or wrapped in plastic in a cool place for up to 1 month.

Nonnie's Dutch Baby

Serves: **2**

Some of my greatest memories are of hanging out with my nonnie in Florida. The two of us would go down to her and Grandpa's house together every June when I was a kid. I remember the first time she made me this Dutch baby; it was the very first year we went. I was young, maybe in fourth grade. I was amazed when it came out of the oven—those giant puffs are impressive! Nonnie added pats of butter and let me pile it high with whipped cream from a can, fresh strawberries, and plenty of Aunt Jemima pancake syrup. I can still taste it! I probably went into a food coma at the pool afterward, but isn't that what being a kid is all about? Now I make Nonnie's Dutch Baby all the time. It's also one of Mom's, and now Asher's, very favorite recipes. To keep it the way Nonnie makes hers, I top this baby with butter, whipped cream (freshly whipped, because now I know a little better), fresh berries, and real maple syrup (ditto).

4 tablespoons (½ stick) salted butter, plus more for serving

4 large eggs

⅔ cup whole milk

⅔ cup all-purpose flour

2 teaspoons pure vanilla extract

½ teaspoon kosher salt

For Serving

Whipped cream

Fresh fruit

Confectioners' sugar

Pure maple syrup

1. Preheat the oven to 450°F with a rack in the center. Set a 10- to 12-inch cast-iron or other oven-safe skillet on the rack and put 2 tablespoons of the butter in the skillet to melt. (Do not leave the pan in the oven longer than 10 minutes.)

2. In a small saucepan, melt the remaining 2 tablespoons of butter. Set aside to cool.

3. In a blender or food processor, combine the eggs, milk, flour, vanilla, salt, and cooled melted butter. Pulse for 30 seconds to 1 minute, or until the batter is smooth, being sure no lumps of flour remain. Remove the hot skillet from the oven and pour in the batter. Return the skillet to the oven and bake for 20 to 25 minutes, or until the pancake is fully puffed and browned on top. Do not open the oven during the first 15 minutes of cooking or your pancake might deflate.

4. Remove the Dutch baby from the oven and serve with butter, whipped cream, fruit, confectioners' sugar, and maple syrup . . . go big or go home.

Buddha Smoothie Bowl

Makes: 2 smoothie bowls with 2 servings of chia pudding leftover

As much as I love an over-the-top sweet breakfast, I love a fruity, super-healthy one just as much. As I always say, it's all about a good balance. This bowl combines two of my favorite easy, light breakfasts. It's one part chia seed pudding, one part berry smoothie, and then topped with every smoothie bowl topping there could ever be. The toppings are the best part!

Chia Pudding

2¼ cups milk of choice
(I like canned coconut milk)

½ cup chia seeds

2 tablespoons honey or
pure maple syrup

2 teaspoons pure
vanilla extract

¼ teaspoon kosher salt

Smoothie

1 cup milk of choice
(I like canned coconut milk)

½ cup fresh or frozen
strawberries, hulled

½ cup fresh or
frozen raspberries

1 ripe fresh or
frozen banana

1 teaspoon pure
vanilla extract

Toppings

Plain Greek yogurt

Nut butter, toasted
coconut, seeds and/or nuts

Granola, store-bought
or homemade (page 33)

Assorted fresh berries
and fruits

Honey

1. **MAKE THE CHIA PUDDING.** In a medium bowl, combine the milk, chia seeds, honey, vanilla, and salt and stir well to combine. Cover and let sit in the fridge for at least 2 hours or preferably overnight.

2. **MAKE THE SMOOTHIE.** Combine the milk, strawberries, raspberries, banana, and vanilla in a blender and blend until completely smooth.

3. To assemble, spoon a little chia pudding into the bottom of your bowl and pour the smoothie to the side of the pudding. Top as desired with yogurt, nut butter, granola, and fruits. Drizzle the whole bowl with honey. Eat!

FRESH OR FROZEN FRUIT?

I prefer using fresh fruit for dishes like salads and desserts or other
baked items, but for smoothies, I love using frozen fruit. The frozen
fruit adds the same body as ice cubes would, but doesn't water
the smoothie down. Genius! If you have tons of fresh fruit on hand,
that obviously works great, too, but if it's the dead of winter, don't
hesitate to go with frozen!

Maple-Roasted Pumpkin Spice Granola

Makes: **About 6 cups**

Granola is one of my favorite foods. I eat it like cereal with milk or yogurt, or sprinkle it over smoothies or a bowl of oats. Occasionally I'll even add it to savory dishes like salads. And, okay, sometimes I just eat it by the fistful. Most of the time when I'm throwing granola together, I use whatever odds and ends I have in my kitchen at that moment, which means that it comes out a little different every time. But this blend of fall superfoods is my favorite. I love using a mix of nuts and seeds to make great textures and flavors. Sesame seeds are my secret weapon here, as they not only add an unexpected element, but delicious flavor as well. The best part about this granola is that you can truly eat spoonful after spoonful and not feel even a little guilty. Serve it with milk or yogurt, fresh fruit, and honey.

2½ cups old-fashioned rolled oats

1 cup cooked quinoa

2 cups mixed raw nuts (I like a combination of almonds, cashews, pecans, and pistachios)

1 cup unsweetened flaked coconut

1 cup raw pumpkin seeds (pepitas)

⅓ cup raw sesame seeds

¼ cup hemp seeds

¾ cup pure maple syrup

¼ cup coconut oil

2 teaspoons pure vanilla extract

2 teaspoons ground cinnamon

½ teaspoon ground ginger

½ teaspoon freshly grated nutmeg

1 teaspoon kosher salt

Nonstick cooking spray

1½ cups dried cranberries

1. Preheat the oven to 325°F. Line a rimmed baking sheet with parchment paper.

2. On the prepared baking sheet, toss together the oats, quinoa, nuts, coconut, pumpkin seeds, sesame seeds, and hemp seeds to combine.

3. In a small saucepan, heat the maple syrup and coconut oil over medium. Stir in the vanilla, cinnamon, ginger, nutmeg, and salt. Pour the mixture over the oat mixture and toss well for 2 to 3 minutes to fully combine. Spread the granola out in an even layer.

4. Bake for 35 to 40 minutes, stirring two or three times throughout cooking, until the oats smell toasted and are golden brown. Remove the granola from the oven and let cool for 5 minutes.

5. After 5 minutes, spray the bottom of a flat 1-cup measuring cup or a flat-bottomed glass with cooking spray. Press the granola into the baking sheet using the bottom of the measuring cup so you have a flat slab of granola. Let the granola sit for 1 hour to cool and harden.

6. Break the granola into clusters. Stir in the dried cranberries. Store in an airtight container at room temperature for up to 1 month.

Salted Brioche Cinnamon Rolls

Makes: **12 to 15 rolls**

I could go on for pages about my love for cinnamon rolls. It began many years ago at our family cabin in Ripley, New York, where we would traditionally spend the week following Christmas. Rip-roaring fires, tons of snow, and plenty of canned, sugary cinnamon rolls—I can't remember a time at the cabin without them! Once we made our move out to Colorado and I came to the realization that processed foods might not be my best choice, I attempted to make my own version of cinnamon rolls. I was surprised at how easy they were and how delicious they turned out. No one could stop eating them!

This eggy brioche dough is the only way to go; it's soft, sweet, and glazed with a vanilla cream cheese frosting (if you're feeling extra festive, add a tablespoon or two of eggnog to the frosting). It took a little while to fine-tune this recipe, but without a doubt this is the best version. It's especially great because the rolls sit overnight, or up to twenty-four hours, which helps them to develop more flavor and also makes them perfect for making ahead. These rolls are always a hit at Christmas!

Dough

¼ cup warm water

1 tablespoon instant yeast

3 tablespoons granulated sugar

½ cup whole milk, warmed

3 large eggs

¾ cup (1½ sticks) tablespoons unsalted butter, melted, plus butter for greasing

1½ teaspoons kosher salt

3½ to 4 cups all-purpose flour, plus more for dusting

Filling

½ cup packed dark brown sugar

2 tablespoons ground cinnamon

½ vanilla bean, split lengthwise and seeds scraped out (optional)

Pinch of sea salt

½ cup (1 stick) unsalted butter, at room temperature, plus more for greasing

1. **MAKE THE DOUGH.** In the bowl of a stand mixer fitted with the dough hook, combine the warm water, yeast, and sugar and mix until incorporated, about 30 seconds. Add the warm milk, eggs, melted butter, and salt and mix on medium speed until combined. Gradually add 3 ½ cups of flour and mix until the dough comes together and pulls away from the sides of the bowl. If the dough feels sticky, add the remaining ½ cup of flour.

2. Turn the dough out onto a lightly floured surface. Knead it into a smooth ball. Grease the mixer bowl lightly with butter and return the dough to the bowl. Cover with plastic wrap and let sit in a warm spot for 1 to 2 hours, or until the dough has doubled in size.

3. **MEANWHILE, MAKE THE FILLING.** In a small bowl, combine the brown sugar, cinnamon, vanilla bean seeds (if using), and salt and mix well.

6 tablespoons (¾ stick) unsalted butter

4 ounces cream cheese, at room temperature

1¼ cups confectioners' sugar

1 teaspoon pure vanilla extract

Milk or water, as needed

Flaky sea salt, for sprinkling

4. Lightly dust your work surface with flour again. Turn out the dough, punch it down, and roll it into a rectangle about 10 x 16 inches. Position the dough with a long side closest to you. Spread the ½ cup of softened butter evenly over the dough. Sprinkle evenly with the filling and lightly push it into the butter. Starting with the side closest to you, pull the edge up and over the filling and carefully roll the dough into a log, keeping it fairly tight. Pinch the edge to seal.

5. Slide dental floss or a thin piece of string (it works so well!) under the log and wrap it across and around the roll. Keeping one end in each hand, tighten the floss so it starts to cut through the roll, making 12 to 15 rolls, each ¾ to 1 inch wide.

6. Place the rolls cut-side up in a generously greased 9 × 13-inch baking dish. Cover with a damp cloth or plastic wrap and let rise in a warm place until doubled in size, about 30 minutes.

7. If time allows, once the rolls have doubled in size, place them in the fridge overnight or for up to 24 hours. When you're ready to bake, let the rolls sit at room temperature for 30 minutes. (This allows the dough to develop more flavor, but if you are short on time, you can skip this step and continue on with the recipe.)

8. Preheat the oven to 350°F.

9. Bake the rolls for 25 to 30 minutes, or until golden brown.

10. MEANWHILE, MAKE THE FROSTING. In a small saucepan, melt the butter over medium heat. Cook for about 5 minutes, until the butter is lightly browned and smells toasted. Immediately remove from the heat. Let cool.

11. In a medium bowl, beat together the cooled browned butter, cream cheese, confectioners' sugar, and vanilla until smooth. If the frosting is too thick for your liking, add a tablespoon of milk or water to thin it.

12. Spread the frosting over the warm rolls. Sprinkle with flaky sea salt and serve.

HOW TO PEEL AND CUT
A FRESH MANGO

Place the mango on a cutting board and stand it upright, finding the tallest point of the mango—this is where the pit is. Take a sharp knife and cut downward along the pit. If you hit the pit, just adjust the angle of your knife and keep slicing downward. Repeat with the other sides, working your way around the pit, then discard the pit. Use a paring knife to peel the skin from the mango flesh, cutting as close to the skin as possible so you don't waste any of the fruit.

Super Breakfast Mango Lassi

Serves: **2 to 4**

This smoothie reflects everything I love to eat. I eat mango almost every day, honey is my sweetener of choice, ginger is my secret health weapon, and Greek yogurt is my favorite protein source. Put it all together into one tropical lassi (just another word for smoothie) and I am a super-happy (and -healthy) girl! Pineapple, berries, and stone fruits can all be used in place of or in addition to the mango. Just keep the measurements the same and sub in a different fruit. FYI, a mango-peach lassi is insanely delicious . . . like, insanely. Use 2 cups of mango and 2 cups of sliced peaches. So good.

I like this best super cold and right on the verge of being able to eat it with a spoon, but not quite thick enough to do so. If you want yours the same way, simply add a large handful of ice cubes. If you prefer a thinner lassi, add two handfuls of ice cubes (or more, until you get the consistency you like). Then drink up!

2 cups plain Greek yogurt

4 cups very ripe fresh or frozen mango, thawed if frozen (from about 3 mangoes)

1 ripe banana

2 tablespoons honey, plus more for drizzling

2 teaspoons grated fresh ginger

⅓ cup old-fashioned rolled oats

Juice of ½ lemon

1 teaspoon pure vanilla extract

Large handful of ice cubes

3 teaspoons chia seeds, plus more for topping

1 to 2 teaspoons bee pollen

A few pinches of ground turmeric

1. In a high-speed blender, combine the yogurt, mango, banana, honey, ginger, oats, lemon juice, vanilla, ice cubes, and 2 teaspoons of the chia seeds. Blend until completely smooth. Stir in the remaining 1 teaspoon of chia seeds. Pour the drink into glasses and top with a drizzle of honey and a sprinkling of chia seeds, bee pollen, and turmeric.

2. Store any leftovers in the fridge for 4 to 5 days. Stir before drinking.

Soufflé Omelet with Spinach, Artichokes, and Brie

Serves: 1

I am seriously picky when it comes to omelets. If I'm being honest, I just prefer a runny egg over a fully cooked one—I'm a little bit of a freak for that drippy yolk. That said, I'm head over heels for this soufflé omelet! Spinach, artichokes, spinach, Brie . . . and honey butter! Yes, yes, yes! Wait, what is a soufflé omelet? Exactly what it sounds like. Instead of mixing the egg whites and yolks together, you whip the egg whites until they are super stiff and cloudlike. Only then do you mix the whites with the yolks. This technique creates the lightest, airiest, and fluffiest omelet you'll ever see. I like to serve this with blueberries on top, which really balances all the flavors.

3 large eggs, separated

¼ cup whole milk or heavy cream

Kosher salt and freshly ground pepper

3 tablespoons unsalted butter

¼ cup marinated artichokes, quartered

Handful of baby spinach

2 ounces Brie cheese, thinly sliced (rind on or off)

½ cup honey

Pinch of flaky sea salt

Fresh blueberries, for serving

1. In a medium bowl, whisk together the eggs yolks, milk, and a pinch each of kosher salt and pepper until combined.

2. In a large bowl using a handheld mixer, beat the egg whites until they hold stiff peaks, about 1 minute. Using a spatula, gently fold the egg whites into the yolk mixture until just combined. It is okay if the mixture is not completely smooth; just be careful not to deflate the whites.

3. In a 10- to 12-inch skillet, melt 1 tablespoon of the butter over medium heat. Add the egg mixture and cook without moving until the top of the egg just begins to set, about 4 minutes. Add the artichokes, spinach, and Brie to one side of the omelet, cover the skillet, and cook for 2 to 3 minutes more, or until the cheese just begins to melt. Carefully fold over the empty side of the omelet to enclose the filling and cook for 1 minute more.

4. Remove the pan from the heat and slide the omelet onto a plate.

5. In a small saucepan, melt the remaining 2 tablespoons of butter with the honey over medium heat. Stir until melted and smooth. Remove the pan from the heat and stir in a pinch of flaky salt.

6. Drizzle the omelet with the honey butter and top with blueberries.

Waffles with Browned Honey Butter and Chamomile Syrup

Makes: **6 to 8 waffles (depending on your waffle maker)**

These have quickly become my go-to waffles any time I need to butter Mom up. She loves all breakfast food, especially sweet dishes. I guess we now know where I get my love of brunching from—thanks, Mom! If you prefer, you can use all-purpose flour instead of whole-wheat; I like the white whole-wheat because it makes the waffles just a smidge healthier! Just don't use regular whole-wheat flour, which will make the waffles too dense.

Chamomile Honey Syrup

¾ cup honey

3 chamomile tea bags

Browned Honey Butter

6 tablespoons (¾ stick) salted butter, at room temperature

¼ cup honey

Waffles

3 large eggs, separated

2 cups buttermilk

6 tablespoons (¾ stick) unsalted butter, melted, plus more for serving

1 tablespoon pure vanilla extract

1 cup white whole-wheat flour or whole-wheat pastry flour

1 cup all-purpose flour

2 teaspoons baking powder

1 teaspoon baking soda

½ teaspoon kosher salt

Handful of mini chocolate chips (optional)

Sliced banana, for serving

1. **MAKE THE CHAMOMILE HONEY SYRUP.** In a small saucepan, combine the honey and ¼ cup of water and bring to a low boil over medium heat. Add the tea bags, cover, and remove the pan from the heat. Let steep for 15 minutes, then discard the tea bags. If not using immediately, pour the mixture into a glass jar and store in a cool place for up 2 months; warm slightly before using.

2. **MAKE THE BROWNED HONEY BUTTER.** In a small saucepan, melt 4 tablespoons of the butter over medium heat. Cook the butter, stirring often, until it browns lightly and smells toasted, about 5 minutes—the butter will foam and then settle back down. Remove the pan from the heat and pour the butter into a small bowl. Stir in the honey. Place in the fridge to chill for 10 to 15 minutes. Remove from the fridge and stir in the remaining 2 tablespoons of butter.

3. **MAKE THE WAFFLES.** Preheat your waffle iron.

4. In a large bowl using a handheld mixer or whisk, whip the egg whites on high until they hold stiff peaks, 3 to 5 minutes. Set aside.

5. In a medium bowl, whisk together the egg yolks, buttermilk, melted butter, and vanilla until combined. Stir in the flours, baking powder, baking soda, and salt until just combined. Add a scoop of the whipped egg whites and stir until combined. Add the remaining whites to the batter and stir until no white streaks remain—don't worry if the batter is a little bit lumpy. Stir in the mini chocolate chips, if desired.

6. Cook the waffles in the waffle iron according to the manufacturer's instructions. Serve with butter, chamomile syrup, and bananas.

Apple Ricotta Pancakes with Bacon Butter

Serves: **4**

This has to be my favorite pancake recipe ever. I found a way to combine my love of sweet breakfast food with everyone's favorite savory breakfast food, bacon. This is the kind of pancake recipe that will make your eyes roll back with complete satisfaction after the first bite. Not much can beat a fluffy ricotta pancake . . . that is, unless you add apples and salty bacon butter. Sweet, savory, and bacon-y: What more could you want for breakfast?

16 ounces ricotta cheese

⅓ cup heavy cream

Zest of ½ lemon

2 large eggs, separated

¾ cup buttermilk

1 cup white whole-wheat flour or all-purpose flour

1 tablespoon honey

½ teaspoon baking soda

½ teaspoon ground cinnamon

Pinch of kosher salt

Butter, for greasing

2 apples (I like Honeycrisp), cored and cut into ¼-inch-thick slices

Bacon Butter (opposite), maple syrup, honeycomb, or honey, for serving

1. Preheat the oven to 200°F.

2. In a large bowl using a handheld mixer, beat half the ricotta and the cream until whipped, about 3 minutes. Stir in the lemon zest. Place in the fridge until ready to use.

3. In a clean large bowl, using a handheld mixer with clean beaters, beat the egg whites until they hold stiff peaks, about 5 minutes.

4. In a separate large bowl, stir together the remaining ricotta, the egg yolks, and the buttermilk. Add the flour, honey, baking soda, cinnamon, and salt to the batter and stir gently until just combined. Stir in a small scoop of the beaten egg whites to lighten the batter, then use a spatula to carefully fold in the remaining egg whites.

5. Heat a large skillet over medium. Coat with butter. When the butter has melted, add 2 or 3 apples slices and cook for 1 minute, until lightly golden. Turn the slices over and overlap them slightly. Pour ¼ cup of the pancake batter over the apples. Cook until bubbles appear on the surface, about 1 minute, then use a spatula to gently flip the pancake. Cook on the second side until golden, 2 minutes. Repeat with the remaining apple slices and batter. Keep the pancakes warm in the oven until ready to eat.

6. To serve, top each pancake with bacon butter, a light drizzle of maple syrup, honeycomb, or a drizzle of honey.

BACON BUTTER

Makes: ½ cup

4 thick-cut bacon slices

6 tablespoons (¾ stick) unsalted butter, at room temperature

1 tablespoon honey

Pinch of flaky sea salt

1. Arrange the bacon in a single layer in a large skillet. Cook over medium heat until the bacon is very crisp, 3 to 4 minutes per side. Transfer to a paper towel–lined plate to drain and cool. Finely chop the bacon into crumbs.

2. In a small bowl, mix together the bacon crumbs, butter, honey, and salt until combined.

3. Store in the fridge for up to 3 days. It's delicious on these pancakes, of course, but also on toast with fruit jam, brushed over grilled chicken, or swirled into creamy polenta.

Herb-Whipped Goat Cheese with Harissa, Poached Eggs, and Toast

Serves: 2 to 4 with extra whipped goat cheese...maybe!

If there was ever a savory breakfast to love, it's this one. When I was about thirteen, I begged my parents to let me go with them to a Kenny Chesney concert at the Cleveland Browns' stadium. It was awesome. But we didn't eat dinner before we left for the concert, so by the time we got home, we were starving. So Dad made us eggs, over easy, with a side of toasted, buttered, and extra-seedy whole-grain bread. That little memory is what inspired this recipe. It's as good for breakfast as it is for dinner.

Whipped Goat Cheese

1 (10.5-ounce) log goat cheese

½ cup plain Greek yogurt

¼ cup chopped fresh herbs (I like a mix of basil, cilantro, and dill)

Kosher salt and freshly ground black pepper

Toast

1 loaf crusty, seedy whole-grain bread, sliced

Extra-virgin olive oil

Flaky sea salt

4 tablespoons (½ stick) salted butter

1 to 2 teaspoons crushed red pepper flakes

½ teaspoon sweet paprika

½ cup green or red harissa, plus more for serving

2 to 8 Perfectly Poached Eggs (opposite)

1 avocado, pitted, peeled, and sliced

Toasted sesame seeds, for garnish (optional)

1. Preheat the broiler to high.

2. MAKE THE GOAT CHEESE. Combine the goat cheese and yogurt in a food processor and pulse until completely smooth and creamy. Add the herbs and a pinch each of salt and black pepper and pulse until just combined. Taste and season with salt and black pepper as needed.

3. MAKE THE TOAST. Place the sliced bread on a baking sheet and rub with olive oil. Sprinkle with salt and place under the broiler for 1 to 2 minutes, or until toasted. Watch closely, as the broiler cooks fast!

4. Meanwhile, in a small saucepan, melt the butter with the red pepper flakes and paprika over medium heat.

5. For each serving, spoon a little of the whipped goat cheese into a shallow bowl or plate. Top the goat cheese with a couple spoonfuls of harissa and 1 or 2 poached eggs. Drizzle the eggs with the spicy butter. Add a few slices of avocado and sprinkle with sesame seeds, if desired. Serve with the toasted bread for dipping, extra butter sauce, and more harissa on the side.

MORE WAYS TO EAT THAT WHIPPED GOAT CHEESE

If I could, I would eat this with pretty much all meals. It's that flipping good. If, by chance, you have any leftovers, this makes for a really great crostini base. Spread the goat cheese on toasted bread and top with fresh strawberries or roasted veggies. You can make it 3 to 4 days in advance and keep it in the fridge.

PERFECTLY POACHED EGGS

Makes: **4 eggs**

4 eggs

1 tablespoon distilled
white vinegar

1. Crack each egg into a small prep bowl.

2. Bring a medium saucepan of water to a simmer over
medium heat. Add the vinegar. Using a wooden spoon, gently
swirl the water in a circular motion to create a whirlpool.
Carefully slide one egg into the water. It will swirl around in
the water and look crazy. Once the egg has stopped moving,
use the spoon to gently lift the egg off the bottom of the pan.
Cook the egg in the simmering water for 3 to 4 minutes,
then carefully remove it with a slotted spoon. Repeat with the
remaining eggs.

Whole-Wheat Chocolate Hazelnut Challah

Makes: **One loaf**

If you follow my blog, or know anything about me, you are probably well aware that I grew up with a mother who could live solely on carbs, butter, and chocolate. (Somehow she's the healthiest, fittest person I know, but we can try to figure that one out later.) Combining her love of fresh-baked bread and chocolate just seemed like the right thing to do. I look at this bread as a healthier way to eat the two together. I know that's kind of a stretch, but cut me a little slack here—this is a whole-wheat bread, after all.

Instead of using just any chocolate, I use Nutella—my little sister Asher would have it no other way. Like most seven-year-olds (and humans of all ages) Asher is Nutella obsessed. I make this bread often, and the three of us girls like to eat it straight out of the oven, alongside a big glass of cold milk. How awesome would this be made into French toast? Ahh, yes, let's do that next!

1 cup warm water

2¼ teaspoons instant yeast

3 tablespoons dark brown sugar

¼ cup extra-virgin olive oil

2 large eggs

1½ teaspoons kosher salt

2 cups white whole-wheat flour or whole-wheat pastry flour

2 cups all-purpose flour, plus more for dusting

Salted butter, for greasing

1 cup Nutella

1 large egg, beaten

Granulated sugar, for dusting

1. In the bowl of a stand mixer fitted with the dough hook, combine the warm water, yeast, brown sugar, olive oil, eggs, and salt and mix on medium speed until combined. With the mixer running, gradually add the whole-wheat and all-purpose flours and mix until the dough comes together and pulls away from the sides of the bowl, about 5 minutes. Continue to knead the dough on medium speed for 2 to 3 minutes more.

2. Turn the dough out onto a floured surface and knead by hand until smooth. Grease the mixer bowl lightly with butter and return the dough to the bowl. Cover with plastic wrap and let rise in a warm place for 1 hour, until almost doubled in size.

3. When the dough has doubled in size, punch it down, cover, and let rise for 30 minutes more.

4. Turn out the dough onto a floured surface and divide it into three equal-size balls. Using your hands, roll each ball into a rope about 12 inches long. Roll out each rope into a 12 x 6-inch rectangle. Spread ⅓ cup of the Nutella over each rectangle. Roll each rectangle up from one long edge to the other to form a rope again, pinching the edge to seal.

(recipe continues)

5. Line a baking sheet with parchment paper and place the dough ropes side by side, seam-side down, on the prepared baking sheet. Pinch the tops of the three ropes together. Braid the ropes: Bring the right rope over the center rope; that rope now becomes the center. Bring the left rope over the new center rope; that rope now becomes the center. Repeat until you reach the end. Pinch the ropes together to seal at the bottom.

6. Brush some of the beaten egg over the loaf. Set the loaf aside to rise in a warm place for 30 minutes, or cover with plastic wrap and place in the fridge to rise overnight. Keep the beaten egg; you will use it again later in the recipe.

7. Preheat the oven to 350°F with a rack in the center.

8. When ready to bake, brush the challah again with beaten egg. Sprinkle the bread with granulated sugar.

9. Bake for 40 to 45 minutes, or until golden. If the crust becomes too brown before the inside is fully cooked, tent the challah with aluminum foil. Let the challah cool slightly on a wire rack for 15 to 20 minutes, if you can wait that long. Slice and serve warm!

Appetizers
&
Snacks

Harvest Cheese Board

Cheese boards are one of my favorite appetizers to create. They are loved by everyone in my family and easily adaptable to each season. This isn't so much a recipe as it is a guide. Think of this as your go-to reference for making a perfect cheese board.

·· ▸ ▸ ❯ The Cheese ❮ ◂ ◂ ··

I like to have three to five main cheeses, five being the absolute max. Any more than that and the cheese will overwhelm the board—and the people eating it. If you're going for the wow factor of a large board, go for two or three wedges of the same type of cheese scattered throughout the board to make it look super full. I've found that for smaller parties, three cheeses seems to be THE number, but for events like Thanksgiving and Christmas, I go for five of my favorites: sharp cheddar or merlot, goat, Mimolette, blue, and burrata.

Semi-Hard Aged Cheese

I always like to use an aged cheese; cheddar, merlot, Gouda, or Havarti work well. I look at these as my more "approachable" cheeses that seem go over best with guests. Be sure to get a cheddar that's aged long enough to have formed crystals. The crystals add a little crunch to the cheese, which is really nice.

Funky Cheese

Ahh, the funky cheese, my favorite! These are most commonly going to be your blue cheeses. You simply cannot have a cheese board without a blue cheese—you just can't! I like to get a blue cheese that's on the milder side, for those people who may be new to it or who are somewhat undecided about their feelings on blues. Ask your cheesemonger for a blue that's slightly mellow; a Danish-style blue typically works. But if you know your guests can handle their blues, then by all means, go for the super-strong stuff!

Firm Cheese

I love using Mimolette, a hard cheese from France. It has an electric-orange color and is sweet with a caramelized nutty flavor and a smooth finish. It. Is. Delish. If you can't find Mimolette, try Prairie Sunset, which is similar, but has a slightly sweet hint of butterscotch flavor. Or be a little bolder and try Red Rock, which is a mix of sharp cheddar and blue. If you prefer something simpler, use aged Gouda, which has more of a sweet, buttery flavor, or opt for the always-loved wedge of Parmesan.

Fresh Cheese

I always go with either fresh goat cheese, feta, or burrata. I like to drizzle the fresh cheese with olive oil, sprinkle it with salt and pepper, and scatter fresh autumn fruits or cherry tomatoes around it. Gimme. Fresh mozzarella works, too, but doesn't feel as worthy to me. Note that burrata only keeps for about 48 hours, so be sure to serve it within two days of buying.

Soft Cheese

I am all about a soft goat cheese or creamy Brie, both of which pair well with sweet *and* savory foods. When I'm working with a log of goat cheese, I like to roll it in chopped mixed fresh herbs. My favorite combo is basil, dill, and oregano. Another popular goat cheese option is Humboldt Fog; I'm also a big fan of truffled goat cheese, which is all kinds of incredible! Ask your cheesemonger about it—trust me.

If you are going the route of a creamy Brie, I love, love, love warming it in the oven just before serving. It makes for a super-cozy autumn board. Just bake and then drizzle with honey, top with fruit, and finish with toasted nuts. Yum!

Spreads

Every cheese board needs something sweet to spread on crackers, such as honey, honeycomb, or fruit jam. Honeycomb is one of my favorites. Not only is honey beautiful in its rawest form, it's also delicious with pretty much any cheese. I believe both a jar of honey and a block of honeycomb have a place on any cheese board.

I also find it nice to include fig preserves, apple chutney, bacon jam, hot jelly, and/or honey mustard for variety.

Nuts and Seeds

Roasted, salted nuts and seeds are a natural add-on to any board because their taste and mouthfeel reflect those of hard and blue cheeses. For the autumn months, I really like using candied roasted walnuts and pecans. I also love roasted pumpkin seeds—just toss 1½ cups of them with 3 tablespoons of olive oil and season with salt and pepper. Then roast them for 15 to 20 minutes in a preheated 350°F oven.

Fresh Fruits

Fresh fruits are a must because they add color, texture, and flavor, and also pair well with all cheeses. The sweetness of the fruit contrasts with the saltiness of the cheese. My favorite fall fruits are apples, fresh figs, pomegranates, and grapes. Dried cranberries make a great addition to this autumnal board as well.

Olives

No matter the season, olives should always be on a cheese board. Their salty, fruity flavor pairs well with most cheeses. I prefer to use plump green olives, but all varieties work.

Cured Meats

Meats are an essential part of any cheese board, as they add a layer of richness. My three favorites are fresh prosciutto, pepperoni, and salami. You cannot go wrong with this combo.

Crackers and Bread

Lastly, you need some carbs on the board to eat alongside all that cheese! Grilled bread, crackers, breadsticks, and popcorn are just a few of my favorites.

··▸▸❯ Putting It Together ❮◂◂··

3 to 5 cheese wedges or blocks

1 cup honey

1 block honeycomb

1 jar fig preserves, bacon jam, pumpkin butter, and/or apple chutney

1 cup sliced apples, sliced persimmons, figs, pomegranates, and/or grapes

4 ounces thinly sliced prosciutto

3 ounces thinly sliced salami

1 cup green olives

1 cup candied walnuts, candied pecans, or roasted pumpkin seeds (pepitas)

Grilled bread and assorted crackers

1. Remove the cheeses from the fridge 1 hour prior to serving. Room temperature is always best for a cheese board. While the cheeses are still cold, slice the hard cheeses into slices and crumble some of the blue cheese.

2. Arrange the cheeses on a large platter or a wooden cheese board. Add the honey, honeycomb, and fruit preserves. Arrange the fresh fruits and meats around the cheeses. Place the olives in a bowl and set it next to the blue cheese. Scatter the nuts and crackers around the board. Serve with bread and crackers.

PB & J Grilled Cheese

Serves: **2**

Here's a food pairing that sounds like it wouldn't work, but totally does. Actually, not only does it work, it's EPIC. This grilled cheese is everything. There are three essentials. Essential 1: Real peanut butter, meaning no sugar added. There is a time and a place for the creamy peanut butter we all ate as kids (most baking recipes), but this is not it. All you need here are ground-up peanuts (with some salt). Essential 2: Sharp cheddar. Nothing fake and no slices wrapped in plastic. Use real cheddar. Essential 3: A glass of ice-cold milk for washing it all down. *Mmmm.*

4 tablespoons (½ stick) salted butter

4 slices crusty whole-wheat or sourdough bread

4 tablespoons blueberry jam, store-bought or homemade (recipe follows)

4 tablespoons natural creamy or crunchy peanut butter

2 slices sharp cheddar cheese

1. Using 3 tablespoons of the butter, coat one side of each bread slice. Spread the non-buttered side of two pieces with jam. Spread the non-buttered side of the other two pieces with peanut butter. Place a slice of cheddar on the peanut butter sides and close up the halves to make sandwiches.

2. Melt the remaining tablespoon of butter in a medium skillet over medium heat. Add the sandwiches and cook for 2 to 3 minutes per side, or until the bread is golden brown and the cheese has melted. Serve immediately.

QUICK BLUEBERRY JAM

Makes: **2 cups**

3 cups fresh blueberries

¼ cup packed light brown sugar

1 tablespoon balsamic vinegar

1 teaspoon fresh lemon juice

Pinch of kosher salt

In a medium saucepan, combine the blueberries, sugar, vinegar, lemon juice, and salt. Cook over high heat, mashing the fruit with a potato masher or fork, until the berries have released their juices. Reduce the heat to medium-high and cook, stirring occasionally, for 15 to 20 minutes, until the mixture has thickened. Let cool and then transfer the jam to a clean glass jar. Store in the refrigerator for up to 1 month.

Shrimp and Mango Summer Rolls

Makes: **12**

I really don't enjoy the process of frying, so I love that summer rolls, unlike egg rolls or spring rolls, aren't fried but are still the perfect finger food. They're light and pretty and oh so yummy! I stuff these with all my favorites—fresh mango, avocado, bell peppers, and shredded cabbage—but you can make up your own mix of veggies. Zucchini would be amazing, as would shredded beets. Just have fun and be creative! One thing you can't mess with, though, is the sweet Thai chili sauce. Trust me—just smother it all over!

Sweet Thai Chili Sauce

⅔ cup store-bought sweet Thai chili sauce

¼ cup low-sodium soy sauce

2 tablespoons fish sauce

2 tablespoons tahini

Zest and juice of 1 lime

1 (1-inch) knob fresh ginger, peeled and grated

1 garlic clove, minced or grated

Summer Rolls

Juice of 1 lime

1 large avocado, pitted, peeled, and thinly sliced

1 yellow or red bell pepper, cut into matchsticks

2 large carrots, cut into matchsticks

1 cup shredded purple cabbage

¼ cup chopped fresh Thai basil or regular basil

¼ cup chopped fresh mint

1 ripe mango, peeled and sliced into matchsticks (see Tip, page 34)

24 cooked small shrimp, tails removed

12 rice paper wrappers (see Tip, opposite)

Freshly ground pepper

Chopped peanuts, for garnish (optional)

1. **MAKE THE SAUCE.** In a small bowl, whisk together the Thai chili sauce, soy sauce, fish sauce, tahini, lime zest, lime juice, ginger, and garlic until smooth and combined.

2. **MAKE THE SUMMER ROLLS.** Squeeze a little lime juice over the sliced avocado, being sure to coat the pieces so they don't brown.

3. Set up an assembly line of the avocado, bell pepper, carrot, cabbage, herbs, mango, and shrimp.

4. Fill a shallow medium bowl with warm water. Working with one rice paper sheet at a time, soak the sheet in the warm water for about 10 seconds, until softened. Transfer to a work surface, narrow edge toward you. On the end of the rice paper closest to you, layer 1 or 2 slices of avocado, basil, mint, mango, 2 cooked shrimp, and a handful of the veggies. Be careful not to overstuff the wrappers. Season with pepper.

5. Fold both short sides into the center of the paper and roll the sheet away from your body as tightly as possible without ripping the wrapper. Place the finished rolls on a serving platter, seam-side down, and cover with a damp dish towel to keep the rolls from drying out.

6. Sprinkle the finished rolls with chopped peanuts, if desired. Serve with the sweet Thai chili sauce alongside for dipping.

WORKING WITH RICE PAPER

Rice paper wrappers can seem scary and delicate, but I promise they're really not that hard to work with. Remember, your summer rolls don't need to be perfect; as long as you end up with something you are able to dip, you'll be good to go! You can find the wrappers in the ethnic foods aisle of most major grocery stores.

NOTE
For easier and faster rolling, you can combine your vegetables and herbs in a bowl, season with black pepper, and then roll them up in the wrappers as directed.

Pan-Fried Feta with Thyme and Greek Marinated Olives

Serves: 6

Here, salty feta is breaded in panko bread crumbs and pan-fried to golden perfection. Nothing beats that crispy fried layer surrounding the entire block of feta. It is to die for. I like to serve this warm, crumbled over toasted naan, and topped with cherry tomatoes and Greek marinated olives. It's the perfect quick-and-easy appetizer for pretty much any occasion, because no one can not love this. It's gone within seconds of being set out! If you're alone while making this, have no shame about taking a fork right to that fried block of cheese. Been there, done that!

Greek Marinated Olives

½ cup extra-virgin olive oil

6 garlic cloves

4 bay leaves

2 sprigs fresh thyme

½ teaspoon dried fennel seeds

Zest of 1 lemon, peeled in strips with a vegetable peeler

2 cups mixed olives (I like kalamata and green olives)

Crushed red pepper flakes

Feta

1 large egg, beaten

⅓ cup panko bread crumbs

1 (10- to 12-ounce) block feta cheese

2 tablespoons extra-virgin olive oil

2 sprigs fresh thyme

Freshly ground black pepper

Crushed red pepper flakes

Grilled naan, heirloom tomatoes, and fresh basil leaves, for serving

1. **MARINATE THE OLIVES.** In a small saucepan, combine the olive oil, garlic, bay leaves, thyme, and fennel. Bring the oil to a simmer over medium-low heat, then reduce the heat to low. Simmer, stirring occasionally, for about 10 minutes, until fragrant. Remove the pan from the heat. Stir in the lemon zest and olives. Season with red pepper flakes. (The olives can be prepared up to 1 week in advance and stored in a glass jar in the fridge.)

2. **MAKE THE FETA.** Pour the beaten egg into a shallow medium bowl. Put the panko in a separate shallow medium bowl. Dip the block of feta in the egg, coating all sides completely, then remove and allow any excess egg to drip off. Place the block of feta in the panko, pressing the crumbs gently to adhere.

3. In a medium skillet, heat the olive oil over medium. When it shimmers, add the feta and cook for 2 to 3 minutes on each side, or until golden. Transfer the feta to a serving platter and garnish with fresh thyme, black pepper, and red pepper flakes. Serve warm, with the marinated olives, naan, and tomatoes alongside.

Provolone and Salami Phyllo Rolls

Makes: **12**

I like to make these rolls every year for the holidays. They've truly become my go-to appetizer. They are so easy and take almost no time to throw together—and you can prep them the day before and just bake before serving. I have yet to meet a person who has not fallen in love with these rolls and then proceeded to ask me for the recipe! Sweet, savory, and buttery pastry with melty cheese . . . gets 'em every time!

12 sheets frozen phyllo dough, thawed (see "Working with Phyllo Dough," below)

4 tablespoons (½ stick) unsalted butter, melted

12 slices fresh provolone cheese, or 3 cups shredded

12 thin slices salami

1 tablespoon chopped fresh thyme

Honey, for drizzling

⅓ cup roasted pistachios, chopped, for garnish

Flaky sea salt, for garnish

1. Preheat the oven to 350°F. Line a baking sheet with parchment paper.

2. Place 1 sheet of phyllo dough on a clean surface and gently fold it in half widthwise. Brush the phyllo with a little melted butter, being sure to cover the entire top half.

3. On the short end of the dough, place a slice of salami, then a slice of provolone (or ¼ cup, if shredded). Roll the phyllo up over the filling, folding in the side edges to seal it, burrito-style. Place the roll seam-side down on the prepared baking sheet and repeat to make 12 rolls total. Brush the tops of each phyllo roll generously with melted butter. Sprinkle with the thyme.

4. Bake for 20 to 25 minutes, or until the rolls are golden brown on top. Remove and drizzle lightly with honey. Sprinkle with chopped pistachios and a little flaky sea salt. Serve warm.

WORKING WITH PHYLLO DOUGH

Once you get the hang of working with phyllo, it's actually pretty easy to use. For best results, thaw the phyllo dough overnight in the fridge, not on the counter, and prep your filling ingredients before unwrapping the thawed phyllo. Try not to stress over torn sheets. Just remember to keep the dough covered with a damp dish towel while you work to ensure it does not dry out.

Cheesy Kale, Artichoke, and Chorizo Dip

Serves: **8**

In my family, it's tradition to serve Mexican-inspired eats on New Year's Eve. My aunt Katie started doing this many years ago, and I do my best to carry it on every year! My dad made the first version of this dip. His original was simply chorizo, cheese, and rice—nothing wrong with that, but I felt there was room for improvement. I added vegetables, some fun cheeses, and a little smoky chipotle flavor. This dip is great because it can be made and baked all in one skillet, meaning fewer dishes to wash! If you don't have an oven-safe pan, just transfer the dip to a baking dish.

2 tablespoons extra-virgin olive oil

1 sweet onion, thinly sliced

Kosher salt and freshly ground pepper

8 ounces fresh (Mexican) chorizo, casing removed

2 garlic cloves

1 or 2 canned chipotle peppers in adobo, minced

1 (12-ounce) jar marinated artichoke hearts, drained and chopped

1 bunch kale, stemmed and leaves coarsely chopped

¼ cup chopped fresh cilantro, plus sprigs for garnish

8 ounces cream cheese, at room temperature

1 cup shredded fontina cheese

Chopped chives, for garnish

Sliced avocado, for serving

Warm tortillas, tortilla chips, naan, pita, or crackers, for serving

1. Preheat the oven to 425°F.

2. In a large oven-safe skillet, heat the olive oil over medium. When it shimmers, add the onion and ¼ teaspoon each of salt and pepper. Cook, stirring continuously and scraping up the browned bits from the bottom of the pan, until the onion is golden brown, about 10 minutes. Transfer the onion to a plate and set aside.

3. In the same skillet, cook the chorizo, stirring, until browned, about 5 minutes. Add the garlic and chipotles and cook for a minute more, or until fragrant. Stir in the artichokes and kale. Let the kale cook down slightly, 3 to 5 minutes. Remove the skillet from the heat and stir in the cilantro, cream cheese, and ¼ cup of the fontina. Cook until the cheeses are melted and combined. Spread the mixture in an even layer in the skillet and top the dip evenly with the remaining ¾ cup of fontina.

4. Bake for 15 to 20 minutes, or until hot and bubbling.

5. Remove from the oven and garnish with chives and cilantro sprigs. Serve with sliced avocado and warmed tortillas.

NOTE

Turning this dip into something heartier is easy. Just add 2 cups of cooked rice or quinoa to the mixture before adding the final layer of cheese. Bake as directed and enjoy it for dinner!

Lemony Fried Brussels Sprouts

Serves: **4**

Brussels sprouts seem to have made a major comeback in recent years. If you're still skeptical, this is the recipe that's going to change your mind. Pan-frying the sprouts in a skillet really helps to caramelize them and bring out their yummy flavors, making them perfectly crisp and delicious. Finish off the recipe with a creamy goat's milk and Parmesan béchamel sauce (you know, for good measure) and a handful of fresh basil. Take that, Brussels sprout haters! My little goat family on the farm means I have easy access to goat's milk, but if goat's milk is not easily available to you, use whole buttermilk or milk.

2 tablespoons extra-virgin olive oil

¾ pound Brussels sprouts, trimmed and halved

4 garlic cloves, minced or grated

Zest of 1 lemon

⅔ cup full-fat goat's milk

2 ounces goat cheese

1 teaspoon Dijon mustard

1 tablespoon fresh lemon juice

Pinch of crushed red pepper flakes

¼ cup chopped fresh basil, plus more for garnish

1 tablespoon chopped fresh mint, plus more for garnish

⅓ cup grated Parmesan cheese

⅓ cup raw almonds, coarsely chopped

Flaky sea salt and freshly ground black pepper

1. Preheat the oven to 400°F.

2. In a 12-inch oven-safe skillet, heat the olive oil over medium. When it shimmers, add the Brussels sprouts and cook, stirring occasionally, until crisp and lightly caramelized, 3 to 4 minutes. Add the garlic and lemon zest and cook until fragrant, about 30 seconds, being sure not to burn them.

3. Transfer the skillet to the oven and roast the Brussels sprouts for about 10 minutes, or until tender.

4. Meanwhile, in a blender or food processor, combine the goat's milk, goat cheese, mustard, and lemon juice and pulse until smooth. Stir in the red pepper flakes.

5. Remove the Brussels sprouts from the oven. Turn the broiler to high. Stir the basil and mint into the Brussels sprouts. Pour the goat's milk mixture on top. Sprinkle with the Parmesan and almonds. Return to the oven and broil for 2 to 3 minutes, or until the cheese has melted, keeping a close eye on it. Remove and season lightly with flaky sea salt and pepper. Garnish with fresh basil and mint.

Five-Ingredient Honey Butter Beer Bread

Makes: **One 9-inch loaf**

If you're afraid to make bread at home, this recipe is for you. You can't mess it up. Okay, if you added *way* too much baking powder, dumped in tablespoons of salt, or maybe accidentally grabbed the confectioners' sugar instead of the flour, yeah, it might not taste so great. But I have a really good feeling that this is your bread. There really aren't words to describe how beloved this bread is in our family. My Nonnie first started making it when Mom was a little girl. Mom made it while I was growing up, and I'm continuing the tradition, though I've made some slight tweaks, like substituting honey for sugar, and adding extra butter!

Butter or nonstick cooking spray, for greasing

3 cups all-purpose flour

1 tablespoon baking powder

¼ cup honey

1 (12-ounce) bottle beer (see Note)

½ cup (1 stick) salted butter, cut into ½-tablespoon slices

1. Preheat the oven to 375°F. Grease a 9 x 5-inch loaf pan with butter or cooking spray.

2. In a medium bowl, combine the flour, baking powder, and honey. Pour in the beer and stir until just combined— it's okay if the dough is lumpy. Spoon the dough into the prepared pan and smooth out the top. Place the slices of butter evenly on top of the dough.

3. Bake for 35 to 40 minutes, or until the bread is lightly golden on top. Let cool for 5 minutes in the pan on a wire rack, then turn the bread out onto a cutting board. Slice and serve.

NOTE

For this bread, I tend to use lighter beers like Heineken, but I've had great success with dark beers as well. Each beer will change the flavor slightly, so use one you love. In the fall, I like to use a pumpkin beer!

Cuban-Style Black Beans with Guacamole and Plantain Chips

Serves: 6 to 8

I am just a little bit excited about these here beans. Cuban-style beans sitting atop a giant pile of homemade guacamole, served with plantain chips for scooping. I can't decide whether these are more of an appetizer or a side dish, but whichever way you serve them, it won't be the last time. You'll be dishing these out for years to come!

¼ cup extra-virgin olive oil

1 sweet onion, diced

1 green bell pepper, diced

4 garlic cloves, minced or grated

1 jalapeño, seeded, if desired, and diced

1 tablespoon ground cumin

1 tablespoon dried oregano

2 (14-ounce) cans black beans, drained and rinsed

1 cup orange juice

2 bay leaves

1 teaspoon kosher salt, plus more as needed

2 tablespoons fresh lime juice

¼ cup fresh cilantro leaves, chopped, plus sprigs for garnish

2 cups guacamole, store-bought or homemade (page 78), for serving

Garlic Plantain Chips (recipe follows), for serving

Lime slices, for serving

1. In a large Dutch oven, heat the olive oil over medium-high. When it shimmers, add the onion and bell pepper. Cook until the onion is lightly caramelized, about 5 minutes. Add the garlic, jalapeño, cumin, and oregano and cook for about 1 minute more, until fragrant. Add the black beans, orange juice, bay leaves, salt, and ½ cup water.

2. Reduce the heat to medium and simmer for 20 to 30 minutes, or until the liquid has reduced and the beans are thick. Stir in the lime juice and cilantro. Taste and season with salt as needed. Serve the beans warm with guacamole and plantain chips, topped with cilantro sprigs and a few lime slices.

GARLIC PLANTAIN CHIPS

Serves: 4

4 yellow plantains, peeled and sliced into ½-inch-thick rounds

2 to 4 garlic cloves, depending on your taste

Canola oil, for frying

Flaky sea salt

1. Put the plantains and garlic in a medium bowl and add water to cover. Let the plantains sit in the garlic water for 15 to 20 minutes. Drain and pat the plantains dry. Discard the garlic.

2. In a medium skillet, heat an inch or so of canola oil over medium. When it is just smoking, add the plantains, in batches if necessary, and fry for 2 to 3 minutes per side, or until just lightly golden. Transfer to a paper towel–lined plate to drain, then transfer to a cutting board and use the back of a wooden spoon to smash them down into round flat disks.

3. Return the plantains to the hot oil and fry for 2 to 3 minutes more on each side, or until they are golden and crispy. Transfer to a fresh paper towel–lined plate and immediately season with salt.

Pumpkin and Cauliflower Gratin
with Fried Sage

Serves: 4 to 6

You may or may not know that I love all things fall . . . squashes, apples, hot chocolate, Halloween, even the word *harvest*—and pumpkins, of course. Generally, I prefer savory pumpkin recipes over sweet ones, so I made this gratin, full of roasted cauliflower and cheese and finished with fried sage (the best). This is the perfect side dish to go along with pretty much any fall meal, and obviously it's great for Thanksgiving, too!

2 tablespoons salted butter

1 sweet onion, thinly sliced

3 tablespoons all-purpose flour

1 cup heavy cream or whole milk

1 cup pure pumpkin puree

¼ to ½ teaspoon cayenne

2½ cups shredded Gruyère cheese

Kosher salt and freshly ground pepper

1 large head cauliflower, cut into florets (about 3 cups)

1 tablespoon extra-virgin olive oil

12 fresh sage leaves

1. Preheat the oven to 425°F.

2. In a large oven-safe skillet, melt the butter over medium heat. Add the onion and cook, stirring occasionally, until soft and caramelized, about 10 minutes. Stir in the flour and cook for 30 seconds more. Slowly add the cream and pumpkin puree. Stir to combine. Increase the heat to high and bring the mixture to a boil. Cook, whisking continuously, for about 1 minute, or until thickened. Remove the pan from the heat and stir the cayenne and 1¼ cups of the Gruyère. Season with salt and pepper.

3. Add the cauliflower to the skillet and toss to combine, being sure the cauliflower is coated in the cheese sauce. Top with the remaining 1¼ cups Gruyère. Cover the skillet, transfer to the oven, and bake for 30 minutes. Uncover and bake for 10 to 15 minutes, or until the cauliflower is tender and lightly golden on top.

4. Meanwhile, in a small skillet, heat the olive oil over medium. When it shimmers, add the sage leaves. Cook for 30 seconds, flip, and cook for 30 seconds more, or until the sage has darkened in color but is not burned. Season with salt.

5. Serve the cauliflower gratin topped with the fried sage.

Grilled Corn and Basil Salad

Serves: 4 to 6

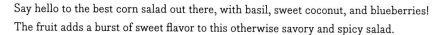

Say hello to the best corn salad out there, with basil, sweet coconut, and blueberries! The fruit adds a burst of sweet flavor to this otherwise savory and spicy salad.

My favorite way to serve it is as a salsa, with a big ol' side of chips for scooping! The salad can be prepared up to a day in advance. Just leave the pureed avocado out and add it right before serving.

6 ears corn, husks and silk removed

1 ripe avocado, pitted

4 tablespoons extra-virgin olive oil

Juice of 2 limes

Kosher salt

2 teaspoons honey

1½ teaspoons chili powder

1 teaspoon smoked paprika

1 jalapeño, seeded and chopped

2 tablespoons chopped fresh chives

Freshly ground pepper

½ cup unsweetened flaked coconut, toasted (see Note)

2 cups fresh basil leaves, torn or chopped

1 cup fresh blueberries

1 (4-ounce) block feta cheese, crumbled

Chips, for serving (optional)

1. Heat a grill or broiler to high.

2. Using a sharp knife, slice the kernels from 3 ears of the corn into a large bowl. Grill or broil the remaining 3 ears of corn until lightly charred all over, then remove and let cool just enough to handle. Slice the cooked corn kernels into the bowl with the raw corn.

3. Scoop the avocado flesh into a food processor or high-speed blender. Add 1 tablespoon of the olive oil, half the lime juice, and a pinch of salt. Puree until completely smooth. Add 2 tablespoons of the avocado puree to the bowl with the corn. Set the remainder aside.

4. To the bowl with the corn, add the remaining 3 tablespoons of olive oil, the remaining lime juice, and the honey, chili powder, paprika, jalapeño, and chives. Toss well to mix evenly. Season with salt and pepper and toss once more. Stir in the coconut, basil, blueberries, and feta. Taste and adjust the seasonings as desired.

5. Spoon the remaining avocado puree over the bottom of a serving bowl and top with the corn salad. Serve the salad as a side or with chips for scooping.

NOTE
You can buy coconut flakes already toasted, but doing it yourself is super easy! Spread the flakes out on a parchment-lined baking sheet and bake in a 350°F oven for 7 to 10 minutes, tossing halfway through, until golden.

Crunchy Roasted Broccoli with Toasted Bread Crumbs

Serves: 4

True story: This is the best roasted broccoli out there. It's quick and easy, and I could truly snack on this all day. Yes, it's that good. The magic comes from fresh lemon zest, added at the end of cooking, along with a handful of shaved Manchego cheese. The lemon zest really brightens up the dish, while the cheese adds a layer of richness. Oh, and of course we can't forget the bread-crumb topping! Known as *pangrattato* in Italian, this crunchy sourdough crumb topping is what all veggies need to be tossed with. It's really important to leave the bread in larger chunks and not break them up too small. A chunky *pangrattato* is what you are going for! If Manchego cheese is not available, use Parmesan or Asiago.

2 large heads broccoli, cut into florets

1 head purple or curly kale, stemmed and leaves torn or coarsely chopped

3 tablespoons extra-virgin olive oil

1 teaspoon kosher salt, plus more to taste

½ teaspoon freshly ground black pepper, plus more to taste

Pinch of crushed red pepper flakes (optional)

Toasted Sourdough Sesame Pangrattato

4 thin slices fresh prosciutto

½ cup raw pecans

2 or 3 thick slices sourdough bread, torn

2 tablespoons salted butter, plus more if needed

2 tablespoons raw sesame seeds

Kosher salt

Zest and juice of 1 lemon

2 to 4 ounces Manchego cheese, shaved

1. Preheat the oven to 375°F.

2. On a rimmed baking sheet, toss together the broccoli, kale, olive oil, salt, and black pepper. If desired, sprinkle the red pepper flakes over the broccoli. Roast for 20 to 25 minutes, tossing halfway through cooking, until the broccoli is lightly charred and the kale is crisp.

3. Meanwhile, make the pangrattato. Line a baking sheet with parchment paper. Lay out the prosciutto slices and place in the oven with the broccoli. Roast for 8 to 10 minutes, or until crisp. Remove and let cool for 5 minutes, then transfer to a food processor and add the pecans. Pulse until fine crumbs form. Add the bread and pulse just until the bread is coarsely chopped, leaving some larger chunks.

4. In a large skillet, melt the butter over medium heat. Cook until the butter is lightly browned and smells toasted, about 2 minutes. Add the bread crumb mixture and stir in the sesame seeds. Toast for about 5 minutes, until the bread crumbs are golden. If they seem as though they need more butter, add another 2 tablespoons. Season with salt. Remove the pangrattato from the skillet.

5. When the broccoli is ready, remove it from the oven and sprinkle with the lemon zest and juice. Serve topped with the pangrattato and shaved Manchego.

Guacamole 101

Each recipe makes about 3 cups

I don't think I could live a full life without guacamole. It is the BEST! I have no shame in admitting that there are plenty of times when a bowl of guacamole is my dinner, with a side of salty homemade tortilla chips—and a spoon for when the chips are gone. This is your ultimate guacamole guide. With these recipes, you can basically rule the world . . . or, okay, maybe just your next fiesta! The most important tip I can give you to make a great guacamole is to use ripe avocados and a generous amount of flaky sea salt—trust me, this is key to a killer guac.

Simple Guacamole

3 large ripe Hass avocados, peeled and halved

Juice of 1 lime

Juice of ½ lemon

½ teaspoon ground cumin

1 large jalapeño, seeded and chopped

⅓ cup chopped fresh cilantro

Flaky sea salt

1. Put the avocado halves in a medium bowl. Squeeze the lime juice and lemon juice over the avocados and toss well to coat. Add the cumin. Grab a fork and lightly mash the avocados. I like to keep my guacamole on the chunky side, but it's up to you.

2. Fold in the jalapeño, cilantro, and a pinch of salt. Taste and season with more salt, if desired.

Summer Guacamole

6 tomatillos, husked and rinsed well

1 recipe Simple Guacamole

2 ears corn, grilled and kernels sliced from the cob

1 tablespoon chopped fresh chives

Flaky sea salt and freshly ground pepper

1. Preheat the broiler to high. Line a baking sheet with parchment paper.

2. Put the tomatillos on the prepared baking sheet and broil for 3 to 5 minutes, turning once or twice, until the tomatillos are mostly charred. Remove from the oven and let cool slightly. Transfer the charred tomatillos to a blender or food processor and pulse until chunky-smooth.

3. Put the guacamole in a medium bowl and fold in the tomatillos, corn, and chives. Taste and season with more salt and some pepper.

Fruity Guacamole

1 recipe Simple Guacamole, prepared without cumin

1 ripe mango, pitted, peeled, and diced (see "How to Peel and Cut a Mango," page 38)

¾ cup pomegranate seeds

¼ cup chopped fresh basil

Flaky sea salt

Put the guacamole in a medium bowl and fold in the mango, pomegranate seeds, and basil. Taste and season with more salt if desired.

Cheesy Guacamole

1 recipe Simple Guacamole

2 tablespoons chopped fresh chives

¼ teaspoon cayenne

4 ounces blue cheese, crumbled

Flaky sea salt and freshly ground pepper

Put the guacamole in a medium bowl and fold in the chives, cayenne, and blue cheese. Taste and season with more salt and some black pepper.

Loaded Guacamole

½ small pineapple, cored and cut into ½-inch-thick rounds

1 recipe Simple Guacamole

1 bacon slice, cooked until crispy and crumbled

½ cup oil-packed sun-dried tomatoes, drained and chopped

¼ cup toasted pumpkin seeds (pepitas)

⅓ cup crumbled feta cheese

Flaky sea salt and freshly ground pepper

1. Heat a grill to high or place a grill pan over high.

2. Brush the pineapple with a little olive oil and sear for 3 to 4 minutes per side, until grill marks appear. Remove and let cool, then chop into small chunks.

3. Put the guacamole in a medium bowl and fold in the grilled pineapple, bacon, sun-dried tomatoes, pumpkin seeds, and feta. Taste and season with salt, if needed (the bacon will make it salty) and some pepper.

Let's Salsa

Each recipe makes about 2 cups

Let's salsa! Or at least, let's talk salsa. From traditional tomato-based salsas to fruity salsas filled with pineapple, I love them all. Thus, I thought it would be fun to share a few of my favorites. Use these as appetizers or snacks, pair them with your favorite tacos, or even serve them atop my Tamale Burrito Bowls (page 143). You really can't go wrong . . . and if all else fails just grab some chips—or a spoon—and dive in.

Tomatillo Salsa

8 tomatillos, husked and rinsed well

½ sweet onion

2 garlic cloves

½ jalapeño, seeded, if desired

Juice of 2 limes

2 canned chipotle peppers in adobo, finely chopped

¼ cup chopped fresh cilantro

Kosher salt

1. Preheat the broiler to high. Line a baking sheet with parchment paper.

2. Put the tomatillos, onion, garlic, and jalapeño on the prepared baking sheet and arrange in a single layer. Broil, turning once or twice, for 3 to 5 minutes, or until the tomatillos are mostly charred all over. Remove from the oven and let cool slightly.

3. Transfer the charred veggies to a blender or food processor. Add 2 tablespoons of water and the lime juice and pulse until mostly smooth. Stir in the chipotles, cilantro, and some salt. Taste and add more salt as needed. Serve immediately, or cover and store in the fridge for up to 3 days.

Pineapple Salsa

1 medium pineapple, diced (see "How to Prep a Pineapple," page 161)

1 cup cherry tomatoes, halved

1 jalapeño, seeded and chopped

¼ cup chopped fresh cilantro

Juice of 1 lime

Kosher salt

Combine the pineapple, tomatoes, jalapeño, cilantro, lime juice, and some salt in a medium bowl. Serve immediately, or cover and store in the fridge for up to 2 days.

Minted Feta and Green Olive Salsa

1½ cups crumbled feta cheese (about 4 ounces)

¼ cup finely chopped green olives

¼ cup extra-virgin olive oil

2 tablespoons chopped fresh mint

Crushed red pepper flakes

Freshly ground black pepper

Combine the feta, olives, olive oil, mint, some red pepper flakes, and a pinch of black pepper in a large bowl. Toss well and let sit for at least 15 minutes to allow the flavors to come together. Serve immediately, or cover and store in the fridge for up to 3 days.

Mango Salsa

2 mangoes, pitted, peeled, and diced (see "How to Peel and Cut a Mango," page 38)

1 ripe but firm avocado, pitted, peeled, and diced

1 ear corn, kernels sliced from the cob

1 red Fresno chile or jalapeño, seeded, if desired, and diced

¼ cup chopped fresh cilantro

¼ cup chopped fresh basil

Juice of 1 lime

½ cup crumbled cotija cheese

Toss together the mangoes, avocado, corn, chile, cilantro, basil, and lime juice in a medium bowl. Stir in the cheese. Serve immediately, or cover and store in the fridge for up to 1 day.

Honeycrisp Apple and Pomegranate Salsa

2 Honeycrisp apples, cored and chopped

Seeds from 1 pomegranate

1 jalapeño, seeded and chopped

¼ cup fresh cilantro leaves, chopped

Juice of 1 lime

Kosher salt

Toss together the apples, pomegranate seeds, jalapeño, cilantro, lime juice, and some salt in a medium bowl. Taste and add more salt as needed. Serve immediately, or cover and store in the fridge for up to 6 hours.

Pasta & Grains

Caprese Quinoa Bake

Serves: 4

Don't get me wrong—I could probably live off pasta bakes, but when I'm feeling the need for a slightly lighter but still completely filling meal, I always turn to quinoa! This is such a great alternative to what could be a heavy meal with pasta. It's also a great option for gluten-free eaters. Plus, you really can't beat the flavors. I mean, baked melty caprese? Done and done.

Extra-virgin olive oil, for greasing and drizzling

3 cups cooked quinoa

1 cup tomato-basil pasta sauce

⅓ cup whole milk

½ cup basil pesto, store-bought or homemade (page 101)

1 cup shredded mozzarella cheese

1 cup cherry tomatoes, halved

Kosher salt and freshly ground pepper

1 or 2 heirloom tomatoes, sliced

Fresh basil leaves or additional pesto, for serving

1. Preheat the oven to 350°F with a rack in the top third. Lightly grease a 9-inch-square baking dish with olive oil.

2. In a large bowl, combine the quinoa, pasta sauce, milk, pesto, half the mozzarella, and half the cherry tomatoes. Season lightly with salt and pepper. Spoon the mixture into the prepared baking dish and top with the remaining mozzarella. Layer on the sliced heirloom tomatoes and the remaining cherry tomatoes. Drizzle the tomatoes lightly with olive oil and sprinkle with salt and pepper.

3. Bake for 10 to 15 minutes, or until heated through, then turn on the broiler and broil for 1 to 2 minutes, or until the cheese is golden and bubbling.

4. Top with fresh basil and/or basil pesto before serving.

No-Guilt Broccoli Fettuccine Alfredo

Serves: **4 to 6**

Listen, it's not like I ever feel any guilt when eating pasta, but there are times, say, on weeknights, when I love knowing that I'm eating a slightly healthier version. Everyone should be able to enjoy a delicious pasta dish any day of the week and feel good about it. Therefore, I decided to create a "no-guilt fettuccine" recipe. I promise, it's not too good to be true.

Combining hummus with a little of the pasta cooking water creates the creamiest, most scrumptious, and truly alfredo-like-tasting sauce ever, and yet there is zero cream. I know, I know. The best part? It's incredibly fast and easy to make. Can you say dinner in thirty minutes, and healthy, too? Well, okay then.

2 small heads broccoli, cut into florets

¼ cup extra-virgin olive oil

½ teaspoon cayenne

½ teaspoon garlic powder

Kosher salt and freshly ground pepper

1 pound fettuccine pasta

1 cup plain hummus

Zest and juice of 1 lemon

2 tablespoons unsalted butter

¾ cup grated Parmesan cheese, plus more for serving

¼ cup chopped fresh basil, plus more for serving

¼ cup chopped fresh parsley, plus more for serving

Pinch of crushed red pepper flakes

1. Preheat the oven to 450°F.

2. On a rimmed baking sheet, toss the broccoli with the olive oil, cayenne, garlic powder, and a big pinch each of salt and black pepper. Roast for 15 to 20 minutes, tossing once, until lightly charred.

3. Meanwhile, bring a large pot of salted water to a boil over high heat. Add the pasta and cook until al dente according to the package directions. Reserve 1 cup of the pasta cooking water, then drain the pasta and immediately return it to the pot. Add the hummus, about ½ cup of the pasta cooking water, the lemon zest, lemon juice, butter, and Parmesan. Toss until a creamy sauce forms. Thin the sauce with more pasta cooking water, a little at a time, as needed. Add the basil, parsley, and red pepper flakes. Taste and season as needed with salt and black pepper.

4. Add the broccoli to the pasta and toss gently. Serve immediately with extra Parmesan and fresh basil and/or parsley on top.

NOTE
Blackened chicken or shrimp would pair well with this pasta.

The Cheese-Maker's Mac and Cheese

Serves: 6 to 8

I think it's pretty obvious that cheese and I just go together, kind of like peanut butter goes with jelly. Well, this is one of my cheesiest recipes of all time. Sometimes mac and cheese can be way too fancy. To me, mac and cheese should be simple and, of course, loaded to the brim with good cheese. I typically use a minimum of four cheeses. I always, always use exceptionally good, really sharp cheddar. As for the others, I like to have a little fun. Say hello to fontina, Havarti, and smoked Gouda—and, most important, their friend, buttery Ritz Cracker–crumb topping. Yes, I did say "buttery Ritz Cracker–crumb topping"—it's the best thing to happen to mac and cheese (other than the cheese). If you can't find a certain cheese or simply don't like one of the cheeses here, use an equal amount of a cheese you do love, or an equal amount of extra-sharp cheddar. You can never go wrong with sharp cheddar.

Nonstick cooking spray, for greasing

7 tablespoons unsalted butter

¼ cup all-purpose flour

3 cups 2% or whole milk

1 pound elbow macaroni

1 garlic clove, minced or grated

1½ cups crushed Ritz Crackers (about 1 sleeve)

4 ounces cream cheese, cut into cubes

1¼ cups shredded sharp white cheddar cheese

1¼ cups shredded fontina cheese

1 cup shredded Havarti cheese

1 cup shredded smoked Gouda cheese

¼ teaspoon cayenne

Kosher salt and freshly ground pepper

Fresh basil leaves, for topping

1. Preheat the oven to 350°F. Spray a 9 x 13-inch baking dish with cooking spray.

2. In a large saucepan, melt 4 tablespoons of the butter over medium heat. Whisk in the flour. Reduce the heat to medium-low and cook for 1 minute, stirring once to avoid burning—it will bubble. Gradually whisk in the milk and 2 cups of water, then stir in the macaroni. Increase the heat to medium-high and bring the mixture to a boil. Stir frequently until the macaroni is just al dente, 8 to 10 minutes.

3. Meanwhile, in a medium skillet, melt the remaining 3 tablespoons of butter over medium-low heat. Add the garlic and cook for 30 seconds, or until fragrant. Add the crushed crackers and toss to coat. Toast the crumbs until browned, stirring frequently to avoid burning, for 3 to 5 minutes. Remove the pan from the heat and set aside.

4. When the macaroni is al dente, remove the pan from the heat and stir in the cream cheese, cheddar, fontina, Havarti, Gouda, and cayenne and season with salt and pepper. Stir until the cheeses have fully melted. Transfer the mixture to the prepared baking dish.

5. Evenly sprinkle the toasted cracker crumbs over the mac and cheese and place the baking dish on a baking sheet. Bake for 15 to 20 minutes, or until the crumbs are golden brown and the sauce is bubbling. Remove from the oven and let sit for 5 minutes (yeah, right). Garnish with fresh basil. Dig in!

Farmhouse Cheddar
and Angel Hair Frittata

Serves: 4

This is one of the best quick dinners in all the land. All you need are eggs, cheese, pasta, and whatever veggies you have on hand. It's my favorite thing to make when my fridge is bursting with produce but I have no specific plans for it. It's my "clean out the fridge" dinner. Obviously, it would be great for brunch, too! If you don't have an oven-safe skillet, just transfer everything to a square or oval baking dish before popping it into the oven.

Kosher salt

⅓ pound angel hair pasta

8 large eggs

1½ cups plain Greek yogurt

2 tablespoons chopped fresh dill

1 teaspoon crushed red pepper flakes

1 cup shredded sharp cheddar cheese

¼ cup extra-virgin olive oil

1 bunch Broccolini, chopped

Freshly ground black pepper

1 roasted red bell pepper, sliced

½ cup oil-packed sun-dried tomatoes, drained and chopped

¼ cup basil pesto, store-bought or homemade (page 101)

1 cup cherry tomatoes, halved

6 ounces prosciutto, torn into pieces

1 avocado, pitted, peeled, and sliced

1. Preheat the oven to 450°F.

2. Bring a large pot of salted water to a boil over high heat. Add the pasta and cook until al dente according to the package directions. Drain and set aside.

3. In a medium bowl, whisk together the eggs, yogurt, dill, and red pepper flakes. Stir in half the cheese.

4. In a large skillet, heat the olive oil over medium. When it shimmers, add the Broccolini and cook for about 5 minutes, until tender. Season with salt and black pepper. Add the pasta, roasted red pepper, sun-dried tomatoes, and pesto and toss to combine. Slowly pour the egg mixture into the skillet, using a spatula to evenly coat the veggies and the pasta. Cook for 1 to 2 minutes, until the eggs begin to set around the edges, then remove the skillet from the heat.

5. Sprinkle the remaining cheese over the top and transfer the skillet to the oven. Bake for 15 to 20 minutes, or until the eggs are just set.

6. Top the frittata with the cherry tomatoes, prosciutto, and avocado. Serve immediately.

Dad's One-Pan Friday Night Pasta

Serves: 6

If there were just one meal I could eat forever and ever, it would be my dad's Friday night pasta. I've made so many delicious recipes, but this remains my favorite dinner of all time. It may have something to do with all the great memories I have surrounding this dish. My dad would make his pasta on Friday nights, and whoever happened to be home would enjoy it, relaxed on the couch or by the fire, watching a good movie. Dad likes to put everything in one baking dish, even the pasta. He covers it with cheese, bell peppers, and pepperoni and bakes it until the edges of the pasta are crisp, almost burnt—but the center of the dish is melty cheese.

1 pound angel hair pasta

½ cup extra-virgin olive oil

1 tablespoon dried basil

2 teaspoons dried oregano

1 teaspoon dried parsley

1 teaspoon dried dill

1 teaspoon crushed red pepper flakes

½ teaspoon freshly ground black pepper

⅓ cup kalamata olives, pitted and halved

⅓ cup oil-packed sun-dried tomatoes, drained and chopped (see Note)

2 tablespoons chopped pickled pepperoncini (optional)

Kosher salt (optional)

16 ounces mozzarella cheese, torn into pieces

1 cup shredded Havarti cheese

3 or 4 red, orange, and/or yellow bell peppers, sliced

10 to 12 slices of pepperoni

½ cup grated Parmesan cheese, plus more for serving

Torn fresh basil leaves, for topping

1. Preheat the oven to 375°F with a rack in the center.

2. Put the dry pasta in a 9 x 13-inch baking dish. Add the olive oil, dried basil, oregano, parsley, dill, red pepper flakes, black pepper, olives, sun-dried tomatoes, and pepperoncini (if using). If your olives are not salty, add a pinch of salt. Use your hands to gently toss to evenly distribute the ingredients.

3. Add 3 cups of water and gently toss once more. Add the mozzarella and Havarti in a single layer. Add the bell peppers and pepperoni. Sprinkle with the Parmesan.

4. Bake for 45 to 50 minutes, or until the pasta has absorbed the water, the cheese has melted, and the peppers are lightly charred. If there is a little grease on top, you can blot it away with a paper towel.

5. Serve the pasta hot with fresh basil and extra Parmesan.

NOTE
I like to use the drained oil from the sun-dried tomatoes in place of the ½ cup of olive oil in this recipe. So much flavor! If you don't quite have enough, supplement with extra-virgin olive oil.

Mrs. Mooney's Penne

Serves: **6 to 8**

I have been eating this pasta dish for a good twelve-plus years and making it myself for the last six. Mrs. Mooney is my mom's best friend (and yes, even as an adult I still call her Mrs. Mooney—it's just who she is to me). She's an incredible cook, and this penne is some of her best work. Her secret is a heck of a lot of olive oil and probably even more garlic—"globs and globs of garlic," as Mrs. Mooney likes to say. She will also tell you that you must use Newman's Own marinara sauce and nothing else. It has to be Newman's. No arguing.

When I'm properly organized, I always make the penne sauce the day before I plan on serving it. Allowing it to slowly cook all day long and then sit overnight helps the sauce develop amazing flavor. You can easily make this vegetarian by omitting the sausage—it will still be delish. My brother Malachi insists on having grilled chicken with his penne, so from time to time I'll serve some grilled chicken alongside the penne.

2 cups extra-virgin olive oil

25 to 30 garlic cloves, finely chopped

1 tablespoon dried oregano

1 tablespoon dried basil

1 tablespoon dried parsley

Pinch of crushed red pepper flakes

2 (12-ounce) jars Newman's Own Marinara

Kosher salt and freshly ground black pepper

¾ pound spicy Italian sausage, casings removed

Parmesan cheese rind (optional)

1 pound penne pasta

Grated Parmesan, fresh herbs, and crusty bread, for serving

1. In a large saucepan, combine the olive oil, garlic, oregano, basil, parsley, and red pepper flakes. Cook over medium-low heat, stirring often, until the garlic is golden and caramelized, 10 to 15 minutes, taking care not to burn it. Carefully add the marinara sauce and season with salt and black pepper. Stir to combine—it will seem as if the ingredients aren't coming together, but don't worry.

2. Using your hands, roll the sausage into tiny grape-size meatballs and place them in the pot. Stir to combine and then add the Parmesan rind (if using). Partially cover the pot, reduce the heat to low, and cook for at least 3 hours or up to all day, stirring every hour or so.

3. When ready to serve, bring a large pot of salted water to a boil over high heat. Add the penne and cook until al dente according to the package directions. Drain and divide the hot pasta among six plates or bowls. Top with a generous amount of the sauce. Garnish with grated Parmesan and fresh herbs. Serve with crusty bread to soak it all up!

Summer Carbonara

Serves: 6

This recipe is my summer twist on carbonara. Carbonara is one the fastest and simplest pasta dinners to make, yet it's so rich and creamy—it's pretty close to perfect. When you add a ball of burrata, it takes the pasta from ordinary to extraordinary, creating a new level of texture and an extra layer of cheesy flavor. Of course, if you prefer to use a little less cheese, the burrata is optional. The addition of sweet corn and roasted tomatoes makes it an easy summer pasta dish!

2 pints heirloom or cherry tomatoes

2 tablespoons extra-virgin olive oil, plus more for serving

½ cup chopped fresh herbs (I use basil, oregano, and dill)

4 garlic cloves, minced or grated

Kosher salt and freshly ground black pepper

1 pound bucatini pasta

4 thick-cut bacon slices, chopped

3 large eggs, beaten

¾ cup freshly grated Parmesan cheese

3 ears corn, grilled, roasted, or boiled and kernels sliced from the cob

Zest and juice of ½ lemon

¼ cup chopped fresh thyme or oregano, plus more for serving

Pinch of crushed red pepper flakes

8 ounces burrata cheese (optional)

1. Preheat the oven to 400°F.

2. In a 9 x 13-inch baking dish, combine the cherry tomatoes, olive oil, ¼ cup of the fresh herbs, half the garlic, and a generous sprinkle of salt and black pepper. Toss well to coat. Roast for 10 to 15 minutes, or until the tomatoes collapse. Remove from the oven and add the remaining ¼ cup of fresh herbs.

3. Meanwhile, bring a large pot of salted water to a boil over high heat. Cook the pasta until al dente according to the package directions.

4. While the pasta cooks, in a large skillet, cook the bacon over medium heat until the fat renders and the bacon is crispy, 2 to 3 minutes. Add the remaining garlic and cook for 30 seconds to 1 minute, or until fragrant.

5. Reserve ¼ cup of the pasta cooking water, then drain the pasta and add it to the skillet with the bacon. Give it a good toss and cook for about 2 minutes, until warmed through.

6. Beat together the eggs and Parmesan in a medium bowl. Remove the pasta from the heat and pour over the egg-cheese mixture, tossing quickly to ensure the eggs do not scramble until the sauce thickens. Thin out the sauce with just a little bit of the reserved pasta water, adding it slowly until the sauce reaches your desired consistency.

7. Add the tomatoes and all the juices from the baking dish, the corn, lemon zest, lemon juice, and thyme or oregano. Gently toss to combine. Season with black pepper, salt, and the red pepper flakes.

8. Divide the pasta among plates and top with a drizzle of olive oil, freshly torn burrata cheese, if desired, and fresh herbs.

HOW TO MAKE A GOOD CARBONARA

So what's the key to good carbonara? It's all in the eggs. You need to use top-quality eggs, and you need to toss those eggs quickly with your pasta to create a good sauce. Most important is a really vigorous toss until the eggs begin to cook and create the creamiest and most delicious sauce. Think of it as a "workout" before the feast!

Dad's Simple Pasta Salad

Serves: 6

What I love most about my dad's pasta salad is that he doesn't make it with mayo and instead keeps it heavy on the vegetables . . . and the cheese (yes, please!). He tosses the hot pasta with cubes of cheddar, creating gooey, melted goodness. The only thing I added to his recipe is nectarine. It's perfect with the savory flavors happening in the salad, and gives a nice unexpected touch of sweetness. This is my go-to recipe for potlucks and picnics, but I also like to make it on weekends to eat as an easy lunch throughout the week.

Kosher salt

1 pound short-cut pasta, such as fusilli

1½ cups basil pesto, homemade or store-bought (recipe follows)

1½ cups cubed sharp cheddar cheese

1 head broccoli, cut into small florets

1 red or orange bell pepper, sliced

½ cup kalamata olives, pitted

½ cup oil-packed sun-dried tomatoes, drained (oil reserved) and sliced

¼ cup pickled pepperoncini, drained and chopped

Juice of 1 lemon

1 ripe but firm nectarine, pitted and thinly sliced

1 cup cherry tomatoes, halved

½ cup fresh basil leaves, torn

12 slices pepperoni, chopped

½ cup pine nuts or sunflower seeds, toasted

Freshly ground pepper

1. Bring a large pot of salted water to a boil over high heat. Cook the pasta until al dente according to the package directions. Drain the pasta and transfer to a large serving bowl.

2. While the pasta is hot, add the pesto, cheddar, and broccoli and toss well to combine. Add the bell pepper, olives, sun-dried tomatoes, pepperoncini, lemon juice, nectarine, cherry tomatoes, basil, pepperoni, and pine nuts, and gently toss to combine. Drizzle the reserved oil from the sun-dried tomatoes over the pasta and season with salt and pepper. Serve warm or cold.

>>>>> BASIL PESTO <<<<<

Makes: 1 cup

2½ cups fresh basil

⅓ cup pine nuts or almonds, toasted

1 garlic clove, grated

⅓ cup grated pecorino or Parmesan cheese

⅓ cup extra-virgin olive oil, plus more if needed

Crushed red pepper flakes

Kosher salt

In a food processor, combine the basil, pine nuts, and garlic. Pulse until finely chopped. Add the cheese and pulse once more. With the motor running, stream in the olive oil until your desired consistency is reached. Season with red pepper flakes and salt as desired. The pesto can be stored in an airtight container in the fridge for up to 1 week.

Cheesy Chiles Rellenos Farro Bake

Serves: 6

My brother Brendan and his girlfriend, Lyndsie, are always giving me new ideas. Lyndsie, who's traveled extensively in Mexico, informed me that I needed to make chiles rellenos. The whole process of frying the chiles sounded like a lot of tedious work. I was kind of over it before I even started. So instead, I created this Chiles Rellenos Farro Bake. It's complete with all the things you love about chiles rellenos, but just a little lighter and easier to make. This is a great breakfast-for-dinner meal. You can also make it in advance and serve it at your next brunch—it keeps in the fridge for up to three days.

Extra-virgin olive oil, for greasing

1 cup uncooked farro

6 poblano chile peppers

2 ears corn, kernels sliced from the cobs

1 cup cooked black beans

¼ cup chopped fresh cilantro, plus more for serving

1 tablespoon chopped fresh oregano

1 cup crumbled cotija or feta cheese

6 large eggs

2 cups whole milk

2 cups shredded Monterey Jack cheese

Simple Guacamole (page 78) or sliced avocado, for serving

Tomatillo Salsa (page 82), for serving

1. Preheat the oven to 375°F. Lightly grease a 9 x 13-inch baking dish with olive oil.

2. In a medium pot, cook the farro until al dente according to the package directions.

3. Meanwhile, turn a burner to high. Carefully char the chiles directly on the burner, turning with tongs until blackened all over. (Alternatively, or if you don't have a gas stovetop, you can char the chiles under the broiler, turning them every few minutes until charred all over.)

4. Transfer the charred chiles to a medium heatproof bowl and cover with a plate. Let the chiles steam for 10 to 15 minutes, or until cool enough to handle. Wearing gloves or using a paper towel, remove and discard the charred skins—it's okay if a few black specks remain on the chiles. Using a paring knife, slice the chiles lengthwise down the center, leaving the stems intact. Gently peel open the chiles, taking care not to tear them.

5. In a medium bowl, toss together the cooked farro, corn, black beans, cilantro, oregano, and cotija. Stuff each chile with the farro mixture, placing them in the prepared baking dish as you work.

6. In a medium bowl, whisk together the eggs, milk, and 1 cup of the Monterey Jack. Pour the egg mixture around the outside of the chiles, shaking gently to be sure everything is evenly distributed. Sprinkle the remaining cup of Monterey Jack over the chiles. Bake until the cheese is lightly golden and the eggs are just set, about 30 minutes. Serve with guacamole, salsa, and fresh cilantro for topping. Enjoy!

GREEN OLIVE PESTO

Makes: 1 cup

1 cup packed fresh basil leaves, finely chopped

½ cup green olives, pitted and finely chopped

¼ cup pine nuts, toasted

½ cup extra-virgin olive oil

Pinch of crushed red pepper flakes

Kosher salt and freshly ground black pepper

1. In a medium bowl, combine the basil, olives, pine nuts, olive oil, and a pinch each of red pepper flakes and black pepper.

2. Taste and adjust the seasonings as needed, depending on how salty the olives are. Store in an airtight container in the fridge for up to 1 week.

Creamy Polenta with Garlic-Butter Kale and Mushrooms

Serves: **4**

This recipe is for one giant bowl of comfort. I like to call it the single girl's dinner: it's Friday night and you have no plans, so you make a pot of polenta, cook up some kale in garlic butter, throw on an egg, and curl up on the couch to watch a chick flick. Perfection. My mom turned me on to polenta a while ago, and I've since developed a deep affection for it. It's easy to cook, super creamy, and actually a relatively healthy grain . . . yes! The Green Olive Pesto is a must, as its flavors are pretty much out of this world. As a bonus, you can use the leftovers on pasta! If you want to make this a heartier meal, I recommend serving it with grilled steak, chicken, or seafood, but it's super tasty all on its own.

Creamy Polenta

3 cups whole milk

2 cups dry polenta

½ cup grated Parmesan cheese

2 tablespoons salted butter

Kosher salt and freshly ground black pepper

Garlic-Butter Kale and Mushrooms

1 tablespoon extra-virgin olive oil

1 small bunch kale, stemmed and leaves coarsely torn

16 ounces cremini mushrooms, sliced

Kosher salt and freshly ground black pepper

6 tablespoons (¾ stick) salted butter

4 garlic cloves, minced or grated

Pinch of crushed red pepper flakes (optional)

4 Perfectly Poached Eggs (page 47)

Kosher salt and freshly ground pepper

Green Olive Pesto (opposite)

1. **MAKE THE POLENTA.** In a medium pot, bring the milk and 3 cups of water to a boil over high heat. Whisk in the polenta and cook for 15 to 20 minutes, until thickened. Stir in the Parmesan and butter until melted and combined, then season with salt and black pepper.

2. **MEANWHILE, MAKE THE KALE AND MUSHROOMS.** In a large skillet, heat the olive oil over medium. When it shimmers, add the kale and mushrooms and season with salt and black pepper. Cover and cook for about 5 minutes, or until the kale has wilted. Add the butter and cook for about 5 minutes more, or until the veggies are soft and beginning to caramelize. Stir in the garlic and red pepper flakes (if using). Cook for another 1 to 2 minutes, or until the garlic is fragrant. Remove the pan from the heat.

3. To serve, divide the polenta among four bowls or plates and top each serving with some of the mushroom-kale mixture and a poached egg. Season the egg with salt and black pepper. Spoon a little of the Green Olive Pesto on top and serve.

Pumpkin and Oregano-Butter Gnocchi

Serves: 4

I know the idea of homemade gnocchi feels intimidating, but it's simpler than you think. Since I love fall and all things cozy, I'm all about a savory pumpkin dish even though gnocci is traditionally made with potato. Nothing pairs better with pumpkin than a little Manchego cheese and browned butter. The gnocchi can be kept in the fridge for up to one day and then boiled as described here.

1½ cups all-purpose flour, plus more for dusting

1 medium russet potato

1 cup pure pumpkin puree

2 large eggs

½ cup grated pecorino cheese

1 teaspoon kosher salt, plus more as needed

½ teaspoon freshly ground pepper

2 tablespoons extra-virgin olive oil

6 tablespoons (¾ stick) salted butter

¼ cup fresh oregano leaves

½ cup shaved Manchego cheese

Fresh or dried figs, for serving (optional)

1. Preheat the oven to 400°F. Dust a baking sheet with flour.

2. Poke the potato all over with a fork. Bake for about 45 minutes, or until fork-tender. Remove from the oven and let cool for 5 minutes.

3. Halve the potato and spoon the flesh into a large bowl, discarding the skin. Add the pumpkin puree and mash together until mostly smooth. Add the eggs, flour, pecorino, salt, and pepper. Stir until just combined. If the dough seems wet, add more flour, 1 tablespoon at a time, until it can be formed into a ball. The dough should be sticky.

4. Scrape the dough out onto a generously floured work surface. Cut the dough into four equal pieces. Working with one piece of dough at a time, roll it into a rope about 1 inch thick. Using a sharp knife, cut the rope into 1-inch pieces. Place the gnocchi on the prepared baking sheet as you go. Repeat this process with the remaining pieces of dough.

5. Bring a large pot of salted water to a boil over high heat. Add the gnocchi and cook until they float to the top, 3 to 4 minutes. Remove using a slotted spoon.

6. In a large skillet, heat the olive oil over medium-high. Add the gnocchi in a single layer, working in batches if necessary, and cook, undisturbed, until golden and crisp, 3 to 4 minutes. Turn the gnocchi and cook about 3 minutes more. Remove the gnocchi from the skillet and set aside.

7. In the same skillet, immediately add the butter and oregano and cook over medium heat until the butter is browned and the oregano is crisp. Remove the skillet from the heat and gently stir the gnocchi into the butter sauce.

8. Serve immediately with the Manchego and fresh figs on top, if desired.

Honey-Ginger Chicken Stir-Fry

Serves: 4

When I was a kid, my dad often made stir-fry for dinner—it was a quick and simple meal that he could easily whip up after work (it was nine p.m., after all, if you recall). More important, the entire family would eat it! Dad's stir-fry was always pretty simple. I'm talking chicken, bell peppers, and soy sauce, served over white rice—nothing wrong with that combination, but after a while, it got a little boring. Once I started to take over more of the cooking, I kicked up the flavors and ingredients. I change up my recipe a lot, but I love this version. If black rice is new to you, don't be afraid. It's a lot like white rice, but has a nuttier flavor and a little more bite. It works really well in this stir-fry with all the veggies, sweet mandarin oranges, and caramelized cashews. One of my favorite things about a stir-fry is that you can adjust the recipe to use what you have on hand. Really no veggie is off-limits, so feel free to be creative.

1½ cups uncooked black rice (see Notes)

¼ cup low-sodium soy sauce

3 tablespoons orange juice

2 tablespoons hoisin sauce

2 tablespoons honey

1 (1-inch) knob fresh ginger, peeled and grated

1 or 2 garlic cloves, minced or grated

4 tablespoons sesame oil

½ cup whole raw cashews

2 heads baby bok choy, trimmed and halved lengthwise

Kosher salt and freshly ground pepper

2 yellow or orange bell peppers, sliced

8 ounces button mushrooms, sliced

2 scallions, thinly sliced, plus more, if desired, for serving

1 pound boneless, skinless chicken breasts or tenders, cut into cubes

¼ cup chopped fresh Thai basil or regular basil, plus more, if desired, for serving

2 carrots, shredded

2 mandarin oranges or clementines (see Notes), peeled and cut into wedges

Toasted sesame seeds, for garnish

Pickled ginger, for garnish (optional)

1. Bring 3 cups of water to a boil in a medium saucepan over high heat. Add the rice, cover, and reduce the heat to low. Simmer for 10 minutes, then turn off the heat. Let the rice sit, covered, for 15 to 20 minutes, then drain as you would pasta.

2. Meanwhile, in a small bowl, whisk together the soy sauce, orange juice, hoisin sauce, honey, ginger, and garlic to taste to make the stir-fry sauce.

3. In a large skillet or wok, heat 1 tablespoon of the sesame oil over medium heat. When it shimmers, add the cashews and 2 tablespoons of the stir-fry sauce. Cook, stirring often, for 3 to 4 minutes, until the cashews are lightly toasted and caramelized. Remove the cashews from the skillet and set aside.

4. Wipe the skillet clean with a paper towel, then add 2 tablespoons of the sesame oil and heat over high. When it shimmers, add the bok choy and sear on one side for 2 to 3 minutes, then flip, season lightly with salt and pepper, and sear for another minute, or until golden. Remove the bok choy from the skillet and set aside on a large plate.

5. Add the bell peppers and mushrooms to the same hot skillet, still over high heat, and season with salt and pepper. Cook the veggies, stirring frequently, for about 5 minutes, or until soft, then add the scallions and cook for 1 minute more. Slide the veggies out onto the plate with the bok choy.

> **◆◆◆◆ NOTES ◆◆◆◆**
>
> *If mandarin oranges or clementines aren't in season, I sub them out for about 1 cup of fresh pineapple or mango chunks. Pomegranate seeds are delish, too!*
>
> *If black rice is unavailable, use white.*

6. Return the skillet to high heat and add 1 tablespoon of the sesame oil. When it shimmers, add the chicken. Cook, stirring, for 5 to 8 minutes, or until cooked through and no longer pink. Pour in the remaining stir-fry sauce, bring to a boil, and cook until the sauce has thickened and coats the chicken, about 5 minutes.

7. Divide the rice and chicken among four bowls and top with the stir-fried veggies, basil, carrots, and orange wedges. Add a handful of the caramelized cashews and a sprinkle of sesame seeds. If desired, serve topped with extra basil, scallions, and pickled ginger.

Spring Pea and Mint Risotto

Serves: **4 to 6**

I love fall, but with our long mountain winters, by the time spring rolls around I for sure call that my favorite season for at least a month. That's about how long spring lasts up here—it's short but sweet. Its arrival brings fresh new produce (strawberries, please!) and warmer, longer days that are so welcome after a snowy Colorado winter. But one of my favorite winter dishes to carry into spring is risotto. I love adding bright spring veggies, like peas, and then finishing the dish with a ball of burrata and a hit of lemon, for an ultra-fresh feel. Making risotto may seem daunting, but really it's not all that difficult. While it does require some undivided attention in front of the stove, it is completely worth it.

2 tablespoons extra-virgin olive oil

2 tablespoons salted butter

½ sweet onion, finely diced

2 garlic cloves, minced or grated

2 cups Arborio rice

½ cup dry white wine

2½ to 3 cups low-sodium chicken broth or vegetable broth, warmed

¾ cup freshly grated Parmesan cheese, plus more for serving

¼ cup chopped fresh mint, plus more for garnish

¼ cup chopped fresh basil

2 cups fresh or frozen peas

Kosher salt and freshly ground pepper

8 ounces burrata cheese

Pea tendrils or watercress, for garnish

Juice of ½ lemon, for topping

1. In a large saucepan, heat the olive oil and butter over medium. When the butter has melted, add the onion and cook until lightly caramelized, about 5 minutes. Add the garlic and cook for about 1 minute, or until fragrant. Add the rice and stir it around to coat in the butter and oil. Cook for 1 to 2 minutes, or until toasted.

2. Slowly pour in the wine and cook, stirring continuously, until the rice has absorbed all the wine. Add ½ cup of the broth and cook, stirring, until the rice has absorbed it. Continue to add broth, ½ cup at a time, until the rice is tender, about 25 minutes, being sure the previous addition has been fully absorbed before adding the next.

3. When the rice is just tender, add the Parmesan, mint, and basil and stir to combine. Stir in the peas and season with salt and pepper. Remove the pan from the heat.

4. Break the ball of burrata over the risotto and garnish with pea tendrils and fresh mint. Finish with the lemon juice. Serve immediately, with extra Parmesan to pass alongside.

Wild Rice and Havarti–Stuffed Acorn Squash

Serves: 4

When I was kid, Mom used to make acorn squash with brown sugar and butter all the time. She is all about a little butter (okay, a lot of butter) with her fall squash, and I can't blame her—it's a delicious pairing. This is one of my favorite dinners to make on cold fall nights. It's cozy and super easy, and those brown butter bread crumbs are a game changer—don't skimp on those. Depending on the size of your acorn squash, you may have leftover wild rice filling. It's delicious on its own and is also a terrific side dish for almost any meal. Oh, and if you weren't already thinking this, yes, it makes a great Thanksgiving side as well!

Squash

2 medium acorn squash, halved through the stem and seeded

2 tablespoons salted butter, melted

2 tablespoons packed light brown sugar

1 teaspoon ground cinnamon

Kosher salt and freshly ground pepper

Wild Rice

1 cup uncooked wild rice

2 tablespoons extra-virgin olive oil

6 cups baby spinach

1 canned chipotle pepper in adobo, chopped

1 tablespoon chopped fresh dill

1 cup roasted pistachios, chopped

1 cup dried cranberries

Kosher salt and freshly ground pepper

Brown Butter Bread Crumbs

2 tablespoons salted butter

1 cup panko bread crumbs

2 tablespoons finely chopped roasted pistachios

1 cup shredded Havarti cheese

Chopped fresh parsley or cilantro, for topping

1. Preheat the oven to 450°F.

2. ROAST THE SQUASH. Brush the cut sides of the squash with the melted butter and sprinkle with the brown sugar and cinnamon. Season with salt and pepper. Place cut-side up in a baking dish and bake for 45 to 50 minutes, or until the flesh is fork-tender. Remove from the oven (leave the oven on) and brush the liquid from the baking dish around the flesh of the squash, coating the squash well and trying to use all the liquid.

3. MEANWHILE, MAKE THE RICE. Bring 2 cups of water to a boil in a medium saucepot over high heat. Add the rice, cover, and reduce the heat to low. Simmer for 35 to 45 minutes, or until all the water has been absorbed and the rice is tender. Add the olive oil and spinach and toss to combine. Cover the pot again and allow the spinach to wilt, about 10 minutes. Remove the pot from the heat and stir in the chipotle, dill, pistachios, and cranberries. Season with salt and pepper.

4. While the squash and rice cook, make the bread crumbs. In a medium skillet, melt the butter over medium heat. Cook until it is browned and smells nutty, about 5 minutes. Remove the skillet from the heat and whisk the butter for about 30 seconds more. Stir in the bread crumbs and pistachios.

5. Stuff the roasted squash halves with wild rice and top with the Havarti. Return to the oven and bake for 10 to 15 minutes, or until the cheese has melted and the squash is crisp. Remove from the oven and top with the bread crumbs and fresh parsley before serving.

Poultry & Pork

Fig and Cider Pork Chops

Serves: 4

Roasted pork chops are a healthy and easy weeknight dinner. In the fall, I like to roast them in cider with fresh figs and serve them on a bed of anything creamy—polenta, grits, and especially Parmesan Mashers (page 184). While I love figs, I have also made this recipe using apple butter and Honeycrisp apples. If that's more your thing, go for it! Both fruits are delicious when paired with the cider, and are very fall inspired!

4 bone-in pork chops, about ¾ inch thick

2 tablespoons extra-virgin olive oil

Kosher salt and freshly ground pepper

18 fresh sage leaves

4 tablespoons (½ stick) salted butter

4 garlic cloves

1 cup apple cider

½ cup fig preserves

1 or 2 canned chipotle peppers in adobo, chopped

1 tablespoon chopped fresh thyme

8 fresh or dried figs, halved

1. Preheat the oven to 450°F.

2. Rub the pork chops all over with the olive oil and season with salt and pepper. Press 3 or 4 sage leaves onto the tops of the pork chops.

3. Heat a large oven-safe skillet over medium-high. When the skillet is hot, but not yet smoking, add the pork chops, working in batches if necessary, and sear until caramelized, 1 to 2 minutes per side. Remove and set aside.

4. In the same skillet, melt the butter over medium-high heat and cook until it has browned, about 1 minute. Add the garlic cloves and cook for 30 seconds to 1 minute, or until lightly golden. Slowly pour in the cider. Add the fig preserves, chipotles (to taste), and thyme. Bring the sauce to a boil and cook for about 2 minutes. Remove the skillet from the heat and slide the pork chops back into the sauce. Scatter the figs around the pan.

5. Transfer the skillet to the oven and roast for 15 to 20 minutes, or until the pork is cooked through and the sauce has thickened slightly.

6. To serve, place the pork chops and figs on a serving platter, then spoon the sauce from the pan on top.

BBQ Chicken Cobb Salad with Avocado Ranch

Serves: **4**

I know this salad is much-loved because it's on repeat in my home all summer long. I often serve it in the winter months as well, just to take my palate on a little escape. It's easy to make and combines flavors that my family and I love. The avocado ranch is quite possibly one of my favorite dressings ever. It's not only great to top this salad, but it also doubles as a yummy dip for chips and crackers. It's everything you love about ranch without the funky ingredients in the bottled stuff. Yes, please!

Avocado Ranch

1 cup buttermilk

1 ripe avocado, pitted and peeled

¼ cup fresh cilantro leaves

1 tablespoon chopped fresh chives

Juice of 1 lime

Kosher salt and freshly ground pepper

Salad

1½ pounds boneless chicken breasts or tenders

⅓ cup barbecue sauce, store-bought or homemade (pages 195)

4 ears corn, grilled and kernels sliced from the cob (see "How to Grill Corn," opposite)

1 tablespoon extra-virgin olive oil

½ cup fresh cilantro leaves, chopped

Chili powder

Kosher salt and freshly ground pepper

2 or 3 heads romaine lettuce, shredded

1 cup cooked black beans

1 cup halved cherry tomatoes

2 ripe avocados, pitted, peeled, and sliced

4 bacon slices, cooked and chopped

3 or 4 hard-boiled eggs, sliced (optional)

1. **MAKE THE DRESSING.** In a high-speed blender or food processor, combine the buttermilk, avocado, cilantro, chives, and lime juice and puree until smooth. Taste and season with salt and pepper. Cover and refrigerate until ready to use. (The avocado ranch can be made up to 1 day in advance.)

2. **MAKE THE SALAD.** Heat a grill to medium-high or a grill pan over medium-high.

3. In a medium bowl, toss the chicken with the barbecue sauce to coat. Grill for about 5 minutes per side, until lightly charred and cooked through.

4. In a medium bowl, stir together the corn, olive oil, cilantro, and a dash of chili powder. Season with salt and pepper.

5. In a large bowl, toss together the lettuce, black beans, and tomatoes. Top with the corn mixture, sliced avocado, and bacon. Finish the salad with the chicken, a drizzle of the dressing, and hard-boiled eggs, if desired. Serve with the remaining dressing alongside.

HOW TO GRILL CORN

Here's my favorite way to grill corn: Heat a charcoal or gas grill to high. Brush the grates with olive oil. Add the corn, husk on, and grill, turning occasionally with tongs, until cooked through and lightly charred, about 10 minutes. Remove from the grill and carefully peel back the husks, removing them completely. Return the husked corn to the grill and continue to cook, turning every 1 to 2 minutes, until the kernels are lightly charred, about 5 minutes. Watch closely to avoid burning. Season as desired.

HOW TO CLEAN LEEKS

Leeks can be very gritty, so it's important to clean them well. Some people recommend soaking them, but this is my preferred method: Cut ¼ inch off the bottom of the leek, removing the roots completely. Next, cut off the top dark green portion of the leek (down to the light green part). You can save the dark greens to make stock, or discard them. Cut the leek in half lengthwise and rinse each half under cold water. Use your fingers to flex the leek and clean between the layers. When all the grit has been washed away, you can use the leek as directed.

Spring Chicken Soup with Ravioli & Poached Eggs

Serves: **4 to 6**

Who doesn't love really good chicken noodle soup? Just about everyone has found comfort in this classic. But this version—well, it's not your grandma's chicken soup. It is one of my go-to soup recipes, though, because it's super quick, healthy, and, when topped with a poached egg, pretty irresistible. Any ravioli will work here, but I prefer one filled with cheese. To amp up the flavor, I like to stir in some homemade chunky basil pesto. If you're short on time, store-bought pesto works great, too. That, plus peas and a side of crostini, makes this the perfect spring soup!

2 tablespoons extra-virgin olive oil

1 sweet onion, finely chopped

1 leek, rinsed well (see "How to Clean Leeks," opposite) and finely chopped

4 rainbow or regular carrots, chopped

Kosher salt and freshly ground black pepper

1 (1-inch) knob fresh ginger, peeled and grated

2 quarts low-sodium chicken broth

2 tablespoons white miso paste

3 boneless, skinless chicken thighs or breasts

8 ounces fresh or frozen cheese ravioli

¼ cup basil pesto, store-bought or homemade (page 101)

1 to 2 cups frozen peas

Zest and juice of 1 lemon

Crushed red pepper flakes (optional)

4 Perfectly Poached Eggs (see page 47)

Fresh arugula and/or microgreens, for garnish

1. In a large Dutch oven or stockpot, heat the olive oil over medium-high. When it shimmers, add the onion and leek. Cook for 5 to 10 minutes, until the onion and leek are soft, fragrant, and beginning to caramelize. Add the carrots. Season with salt and black pepper and cook for 3 to 5 minutes more, or until the carrots begin to brown. Stir in the ginger and cook for about 1 minute more, until fragrant.

2. Slowly add the broth to the pot, then stir in the miso and chicken. Cover and simmer for 25 to 30 minutes, or until the chicken is cooked through and shreds easily. Shred the chicken in the pot.

3. Increase the heat to high and bring the soup to a boil. Stir in the ravioli and cook for 3 to 5 minutes, or until the ravioli are al dente. Stir in the pesto, peas, lemon zest, and lemon juice. Cook for about 5 minutes, until the peas are tender. Taste and season with salt and black pepper to your liking. Add red pepper flakes, if desired.

4. Divide the soup among four bowls. Top each bowl with a poached egg and a handful of greens.

30-Minute Healthier Chicken Parmesan

Serves: 4

Chicken Parmesan is a beloved classic. When I took over cooking for the family, my oldest brother, Creighton, used to request it—he's all about anything that includes meat, cheese, and carbs. One day I decided to throw him a curve ball and sneak in this healthier version. He loved it! He noticed the zucchini noodles, but when mixed with the regular pasta, he ate them anyway and loved every bite. Can you blame him?

1 large egg

½ cup whole-wheat bread crumbs (recipe follows)

¼ cup panko bread crumbs

½ cup freshly grated Parmesan cheese, plus more for serving

2 tablespoons chopped fresh basil, plus more for serving

2 tablespoons chopped fresh parsley

Kosher salt and freshly ground pepper

4 boneless, skinless chicken breasts (about 1 pound total)

1 tablespoon salted butter

1 tablespoon extra-virgin olive oil

½ pound whole-wheat spaghetti

2 medium zucchini, spiralized (see Note, page 199)

2 cups tomato sauce, store-bought or homemade (opposite)

8 ounces fresh buffalo mozzarella or regular mozzarella, coarsely torn

1. Preheat the oven to 400°F.

2. In a shallow medium bowl, beat the egg. In a separate shallow medium bowl, combine the bread crumbs, panko, Parmesan, basil, and parsley. Season with salt and pepper. Working with one piece at a time, dip the chicken in the egg, allowing any excess to drip off, then dredge through the bread crumb mixture, pressing gently to adhere.

3. In a large oven-safe skillet, melt the butter with the olive oil over medium-high heat. When they start to sizzle, add the chicken in a single layer, working in batches, if necessary, and cook for about 3 minutes per side, until the chicken is browned on all sides. Remove the skillet from the heat and arrange all the chicken in it, if it's not there already. Transfer the skillet to the oven and bake for 8 to 10 minutes, or until the chicken is cooked through.

4. Meanwhile, bring a large pot of salted water to a boil over high heat. Add the pasta and cook until al dente according to the package directions. Drain the pasta and return it to the pot. Toss in the spiralized zucchini.

5. Remove the chicken from the oven and spoon the tomato sauce over the top. Sprinkle on the mozzarella and return the skillet to the oven for about 5 minutes more, or until the cheese is melted and bubbling.

6. Serve immediately over the pasta mixture with more fresh basil and Parmesan.

HOMEMADE BREAD CRUMBS

Preheat the oven to 350°F. Place 4 slices of whole-grain bread in a food processor and pulse until finely ground. Add 1 tablespoon of olive oil and a pinch of salt and pulse once more. Spread the crumbs onto a large rimmed baking sheet and bake for 10 to 15 minutes, stirring occasionally, until browned and dry. Transfer to a large bowl. Drizzle with 1 tablespoon of olive oil and season with salt and fresh herbs (I like to use a mix of basil, parsley, and oregano). Toss to combine. Store in an airtight container at room temperature for up to 1 month.

>✳> QUICK TOMATO SAUCE ✳<

Makes: **3 cups**

1 medium heirloom tomato, chopped, or 1 (14-ounce) can diced tomatoes

1 cup heirloom cherry tomatoes, halved

1 garlic clove, minced or grated

1 cup fresh basil leaves, chopped

1 tablespoon balsamic vinegar

Crushed red pepper flakes

¼ cup extra-virgin olive oil

Kosher salt and freshly ground black pepper

In a medium bowl, combine the tomatoes, garlic, basil, vinegar, red pepper flakes, olive oil, and a pinch each of salt and black pepper and toss well. Taste and season as desired with more salt and black pepper.

NOTE
*If you are short on time, you can
ditch the skewers and simply
grill or roast the chicken breast
whole in a preheated 375°F oven
for 30 to 45 minutes,
or until cooked through.*

Moroccan Lemon Chicken Kebabs with Couscous Pilaf

Serves: 4

I don't know why, but it seems that food on a stick is just better. Enter kebabs. I love the smoky and spicy flavors of this marinade, with its hint of sweetness for balance. It's not overpowering in any way, but if you're sensitive to spicy food, don't be afraid to reduce the cayenne to your taste levels. The couscous pilaf is the perfect light and healthy side dish, and the spicy harissa hummus paired with the pureed avocado rounds everything out. I like to serve this with a side of naan for scooping. A perfect, easy weeknight dinner, and full of flavor.

Chicken

2 garlic cloves, minced or grated

1 (1-inch) knob fresh ginger, peeled and grated

2 tablespoons chopped fresh cilantro

1 tablespoon smoked paprika

2 teaspoons ground cumin

½ to 1 teaspoon cayenne

½ teaspoon chipotle chili powder

1 teaspoon kosher salt

½ teaspoon freshly ground pepper

¼ cup extra-virgin olive oil

Zest and juice of 1 lemon

1½ pounds boneless, skinless chicken breasts or tenders, cut into 1-inch pieces

Couscous Pilaf

2½ cups low-sodium chicken broth

1½ cups couscous

2 tablespoons extra-virgin olive oil

½ cup chopped dried apricots

½ cup chopped toasted almonds

¼ cup chopped fresh mint

Kosher salt and freshly ground pepper

Harissa Hummus

8 ounces plain hummus

2 tablespoons harissa

For Serving

1 avocado, pitted, peeled, and pureed or mashed

⅓ cup kalamata olives

2 Persian cucumbers, sliced

A few handfuls of arugula

Lemon wedges

Fresh naan

1. **MAKE THE CHICKEN.** In a large zip-top bag, combine the garlic, ginger, cilantro, paprika, cumin, cayenne, chili powder, salt, pepper, olive oil, lemon zest, and lemon juice. Add the chicken and toss to combine. Seal and marinate in the fridge for at least 1 hour or up to 12 hours.

2. **MEANWHILE, MAKE THE COUSCOUS.** In a medium saucepan, bring the broth to a boil over high heat. Remove the pot from the heat and add the couscous. Cover and let sit for 5 minutes, then uncover and fluff with a fork. Stir in the olive oil, apricots, almonds, and mint. Season with salt and pepper.

3. Heat a grill to medium-high or a grill pan over medium-high.

4. Thread the chicken pieces onto skewers, discarding the marinade. Grill the kebabs until lightly charred and cooked through, turning occasionally, 10 to 12 minutes total. Transfer to a plate.

5. **MAKE THE HUMMUS.** In a medium bowl, stir together the hummus and harissa until smooth.

6. To serve, smear a little of the harissa hummus into a bowl or onto a plate. Do the same with the avocado puree. Top with the couscous pilaf and a couple of chicken kebabs. Add the olives, cucumbers, and arugula. Garnish with lemon wedges and serve with naan alongside.

Garlic-and-Herb Mascarpone Roasted Chicken

Serves: **4 to 6**

My mom always preferred baking, but there were a few special dishes she would make for dinner back when I was a kid: pot roast, chicken Florentine, lasagne, potato chip chicken (page 140), chicken noodle casserole, and roasted chicken. Her roasted chicken was simple, but it was complete comfort food, especially on a Sunday night in the fall. So cozy. She always, always served it with rice pilaf. Hers came from a box, but it was delicious. This recipe was 100 percent inspired by my mom's love of a simple roasted chicken and rice. To me, it symbolizes fall, comfort food, and family. This whole meal gets made in just one pan. You'll start by butterflying your chicken, but don't be afraid—it's not as scary as you think and my directions will guide you right through. (Or you can just ask your butcher to do it for you.) As the chicken roasts, its juices drip down into the rice, creating an incredibly flavorful pilaf. You really cannot beat this recipe. It's easy, no fuss, and just as perfect for a small dinner party as it is for a Sunday night family dinner!

Rice Pilaf

2 tablespoons salted butter

2 tablespoons extra-virgin olive oil

1½ cups wild rice

3 medium russet potatoes, chopped

Kosher salt and freshly ground pepper

2½ cups low-sodium chicken broth, plus more if needed

2 tablespoons chopped fresh parsley

Chicken

4 ounces mascarpone cheese, at room temperature

8 tablespoons (1 stick) butter, at room temperature

3 garlic cloves, minced or grated

2 tablespoons chopped fresh oregano

1 tablespoon chopped fresh thyme

Zest of 1 lemon

Kosher salt and freshly ground pepper

1 (4- to 5-pound) whole chicken

Extra-virgin olive oil

Fresh thyme and oregano sprigs

1. Preheat the oven to 425°F.

2. **MAKE THE PILAF.** In a 3- to 5-quart covered casserole or Dutch oven, melt the butter with the olive oil over high heat. Add the wild rice and toast, stirring often, for 1 to 2 minutes. Toss in the potatoes and cook for 2 minutes more. Season with salt and pepper. Pour in the broth and use a wooden spoon to scrape up any browned bits from the bottom of the pan. Stir in the parsley. Remove the pan from the heat while you prepare the chicken.

3. **MAKE THE CHICKEN.** In a small bowl, stir together the mascarpone, 4 tablespoons of the butter, the garlic, oregano, thyme, lemon zest, and salt and pepper to taste. Mix well, being sure the butter is smooth and the herbs are evenly distributed throughout.

4. Remove the giblets from the chicken. Pat the chicken dry and place on a cutting board, breast-side down, so the chicken's back is facing you. Using a pair of sharp kitchen scissors, cut closely along either side of the backbone, then remove the bone and discard it. Turn the chicken over so the breast is now facing up and press down firmly to flatten.

5. Slide your fingers underneath the skin of the chicken and carefully stuff in the mascarpone mixture, pushing it as far in as you can without ripping the skin and spreading it evenly.

6. Place the chicken directly on top of the rice. Rub the skin with olive oil and season generously with salt and pepper. Throw in a few sprigs of fresh thyme and oregano. Dot the remaining 4 tablespoons of butter over the chicken.

7. Transfer the pan to the oven and roast for 35 to 45 minutes, or until the liquid has been absorbed and the rice is cooked. If needed, add ½ cup more broth to keep the rice from drying out.

8. Let the chicken rest for 5 minutes, then slice and serve over the rice pilaf.

HOW TO PRESS A PANINI

If you have a panini press, you can cook the sandwich there instead of in the pans. If you have a waffle iron, that works great, too! Alternatively, you can cook the sandwich without the second hot pan on top, but I really love compressing the bread down a bit.

Cheesy Oregano Chicken and Broccoli Pesto Panini

Serves: 4

Chicken, broccoli, and pesto, glazed in melted cheddar, and sandwiched between bread that's crusty on the outside and soft on the inside. Sounds pretty good, right? That is this panini. You can also turn these sandwiches into melts by leaving the top half of the sandwich off and adding an extra handful of fontina or cheddar. Or make them vegetarian by subbing chickpeas for the chicken!

2 boneless, skinless chicken breasts, cooked and shredded (1½ to 2 cups)

1 tablespoon chopped fresh oregano

1 small head broccoli, cut into florets and coarsely chopped

⅓ cup plain Greek yogurt

½ cup shredded fontina cheese

½ cup shredded sharp cheddar cheese

Kosher salt and freshly ground pepper

1 cup basil pesto, store-bought or homemade (page 101)

4 ciabatta rolls, halved, or 1 loaf ciabatta, cut into 8 pieces

1 cup fresh arugula

Extra-virgin olive oil

1. In a medium bowl, combine the shredded chicken, oregano, broccoli, yogurt, fontina, and cheddar. Season with a pinch each of salt and pepper and stir to combine.

2. Heat a medium cast-iron skillet or grill pan over high. Heat a second small skillet over high.

3. Evenly spread ¼ cup of the pesto inside each ciabatta roll, top and bottom. Divide the chicken mixture evenly among the rolls, then add ¼ cup of the arugula to each.

4. Rub the outside of each sandwich all over with olive oil. Working with one at a time, put a sandwich in the hot medium pan. Carefully take the small hot pan and press it gently down onto the sandwich, compressing it (see "How to Press a Panini," opposite). Cook for 4 to 5 minutes, or until the cheese has melted and the bread is golden. Reheat the pans after cooking each panini if needed to keep them screamin' hot.

5. Serve immediately while all hot and gooey!

Beer Can Chicken

Serves: **4 to 6**

This is what I call a Gerard Family–style meal. It's not classy in any way, and that's my family. Some people might be slightly embarrassed by that, but I've chosen to embrace it. We are who we are, and I love my family and all our hillbilly ways. If you have yet to experience a beer can chicken, I'm excited to introduce you to it. Unlike a roasted chicken, this one feels more rotisserie-style and way less fancy. The whole bird is roasted upright on a beer can. The beer adds great flavor while keeping the chicken moist and incredibly juicy. I also included my favorite blackened seasoning rub and sometimes serve it with fresh pineapple slices to play up the smoky flavors.

1 (4- to 5-pound) whole chicken

1 tablespoon light brown sugar

2 tablespoons smoked paprika

1 teaspoon cayenne

1 teaspoon garlic powder

1 teaspoon dried thyme

1 teaspoon chili powder

1 teaspoon kosher salt

1 teaspoon freshly ground pepper

Zest of 1 lime

3 tablespoons salted butter, at room temperature

1 (12-ounce) can beer of your choice

2 tablespoons extra-virgin olive oil

1. Preheat the oven to 425°F with a rack in the lower third.

2. Remove the giblets from the chicken and discard them. Pat the outside of the chicken dry.

3. In a small bowl, combine the brown sugar, paprika, cayenne, garlic powder, thyme, chili powder, salt, pepper, and lime zest. In a separate small bowl, combine the butter with one-third of the seasoning mixture.

4. Lay the chicken on a clean surface. Slide your fingers between the meat and the skin of the chicken and then carefully spread the butter under the skin, pushing it as far back as you can without ripping the skin and spreading it evenly.

5. Crack open the beer and pour one-third into the bottom of a 10- to 12-inch round baking dish with low sides. Set the can in the baking dish and slide the chicken right onto the can; it should stand up on its own. Rub the outside of the chicken all over with the olive oil, then rub on the remaining seasoning mixture.

6. Roast for 1 hour, or until the chicken reaches 165°F on a meat thermometer.

7. Cover the chicken with aluminum foil and let it sit for 10 minutes. Then, using tongs, carefully remove the chicken from the can (discard the can and leftover beer), slice, and serve.

NOTE
If you don't drink beer, roast the chicken in a roasting pan with a rack. Pour a little chicken broth into the pan to keep the chicken moist. It won't be beer can chicken, but it'll taste delicious.

Healthier Slow-Cooker Butter Chicken

Butter chicken is a favorite Indian takeout meal, but not many people make it at home. I am going to try to change that. When I started cooking, I had a lot of fun experimenting with flavors from around the world, and this dish became one of my favorites. You just throw everything into the slow cooker and let it cook all day long. The house smells amazing, and, come dinnertime, all you need to do is a make a big batch of steamed rice and warm up some fresh naan. Done and DONE. This is a great recipe to make throughout autumn, as the spices are very warm and the entire meal feels super cozy.

1 (14-ounce) can full-fat coconut milk, plus more as needed

¾ cup plain Greek yogurt

1 (6-ounce) can tomato paste

1 to 2 teaspoons red curry paste

½ sweet onion, finely minced

4 garlic cloves, minced or grated

1 (1-inch) knob fresh ginger, peeled and grated

2 tablespoons garam masala

1 teaspoon paprika

½ to 1 teaspoon ground turmeric

½ to 1 teaspoon cayenne

¼ teaspoon kosher salt

1 pound boneless, skinless chicken breasts, cut into bite-size pieces

2 tablespoons salted butter

2 tablespoons fresh lemon juice

Freshly ground black pepper

For Serving

Cooked white rice

Naan

Fresh cilantro

Mango chutney

Chopped toasted almonds

Crushed red pepper flakes

1. In your slow cooker, stir together the coconut milk, yogurt, tomato paste, curry paste, onion, garlic, ginger, garam masala, paprika, turmeric, cayenne, and salt until smooth. Add the chicken and stir to coat. Add the butter. Cover and cook on High for 4 hours or on Low for 6 to 8 hours. I like to stir mine once or twice during cooking, but it's not essential. Stir in the lemon juice. Taste and season with salt and black pepper as needed.

2. Serve over rice with naan alongside. Top with fresh cilantro, chutney, chopped almonds, and red pepper flakes as desired.

NOTE

If you're vegetarian but love these flavors, replace the chicken with 2 (15-ounce) cans of chickpeas, drained and rinsed. Cook on Low for 5 to 6 hours.

Gyros with Roasted Garlic Tzatziki and Feta Fries

Serves: **4 to 6**

Here's the deal: when I do up a gyro, I do it up right. I'm talking marinated meat, tzatziki, fries, and all the fresh toppings. Basically, my pita is always overflowing, but really, when it comes to a gyro, there's no other way to do it. I like to make these with chicken, but both lamb and steak work really well, too.

Chicken

½ cup plain full-fat Greek yogurt

¼ cup extra-virgin olive oil

¼ cup fresh lemon juice

5 garlic cloves, finely minced or grated

1 tablespoon smoked paprika

1 tablespoon chopped fresh oregano

Kosher salt and freshly ground pepper

1½ pounds boneless, skinless chicken breast

Feta Fries

¼ cup extra-virgin olive oil

2 garlic cloves, minced or grated

3 tablespoons chopped fresh oregano

½ to 1 teaspoon cayenne

Kosher salt and freshly ground pepper

4 medium russet potatoes, cut into ¼-inch-thick matchsticks

½ cup crumbled feta cheese

For Serving

4 to 6 fresh pitas, warmed

Roasted Garlic Tzatziki (page 136)

Pickled red onions

Sliced radishes

1. **MAKE THE CHICKEN.** In a 9 x 13-inch baking dish, combine the yogurt, olive oil, lemon juice, garlic, paprika, oregano, and a pinch each of salt and pepper. Add the chicken and toss to coat. Cover and marinate in the fridge for at least 2 hours or up to 12 hours.

2. Preheat the oven to 425°F. Remove the chicken from the fridge and let it sit at room temperature while the oven preheats.

3. Transfer the chicken to the oven and roast for 20 to 25 minutes, or until cooked through. Remove from the oven and let cool for 5 minutes. Shred the chicken with two forks or thinly slice it.

4. **MEANWHILE, MAKE THE FRIES.** In a small bowl, whisk together the olive oil, garlic, oregano, cayenne, and salt and pepper to taste. Place the potato matchsticks in a large bowl and pour half the garlic mixture over them. Gently toss to coat. Divide the fries between two baking sheets, arranging them in a single layer. Bake with the chicken for 15 to 20 minutes, then flip, reduce the oven temperature to 400°F, and bake for 15 to 20 minutes more. Remove from the oven and toss with the remaining garlic mix and the feta.

5. Stuff the chicken inside the warm pitas and serve with the fries, tzatziki, pickled red onions, and radishes.

(recipe continues)

ROASTED GARLIC TZATZIKI

Makes: **1½ cups**

1 small head garlic, unpeeled

3 tablespoons extra-virgin olive oil

1½ cups plain full-fat Greek yogurt

Juice of 1 lemon

1 small Persian cucumber or zucchini, diced or shredded

1½ tablespoons chopped fresh dill

1 tablespoon chopped fresh mint

Kosher salt and freshly ground pepper

1. Preheat the oven to 425°F.

2. Chop off the top portion of the garlic head to reveal the cloves. Peel any excess papery skin off the garlic, making sure to keep the bulb together. Place the bulb on a piece of aluminum foil large enough to encase the whole bulb and pour about 1 teaspoon of the olive oil on top. Cover with the foil to make a pouch and place in the oven directly on a rack. Roast for about 45 minutes, or until the garlic is golden brown and soft. Remove the pouch from the oven, open, and let the garlic cool for 5 minutes. Squeeze the cloves out of their papery skins into a bowl and mash well with a fork.

3. Spoon half the mashed roasted garlic—or more or less depending on your preference—into a bowl. Add the remaining olive oil, the yogurt, lemon juice, cucumber, dill, and mint and stir well to combine. Taste and season with salt and pepper as needed. Store, covered, in the fridge for up to 3 days.

Easy Coq au Vin with Brown Butter Egg Noodles

Serves: **4 to 6**

Coq au Vin sounds so fancy, doesn't it? Well, this recipe is anything but. I suppose this French dish of chicken braised with wine and mushrooms could be considered fancy, but it's easy to make! Think slow-cooked flavors without standing over your stove all day long. I love to serve this meal when I have people coming over, or during the holidays when my entire family is in town. It can be prepared in advance and warmed up just before serving. This is so cozy with buttery egg noodles and a hunk of fresh bread.

4 thick-cut bacon slices, chopped

4 tablespoons extra-virgin olive oil

1 sweet onion, diced

4 garlic cloves, minced or grated

1 small russet potato, peeled, if desired, and cut into ½-inch pieces

2 medium carrots, cut into ½-inch pieces

2 tablespoons tomato paste

1½ pounds boneless, skinless chicken tenders or small chicken breasts

Kosher salt and freshly ground pepper

2 cups sliced cremini mushrooms

2 cups red wine, plus more as needed

2 cups low-sodium chicken broth

2 bay leaves

4 sprigs fresh thyme

Brown Butter Egg Noodles

Kosher salt

1 pound egg noodles

½ cup (1 stick) salted butter

8 fresh sage leaves

2 garlic cloves, minced or grated

Freshly ground black pepper

¼ cup chopped fresh parsley, for serving

1. In a large Dutch oven, cook the bacon over medium-high heat until the fat renders and the bacon is crisp, about 5 minutes. Add 2 tablespoons of olive oil, the onion, garlic, potato, and carrots. Cook, stirring often, until softened and lightly caramelized, about 5 minutes. Stir in the tomato paste. Push the veggies to the edges of the pan and add the remaining 2 tablespoons of olive oil in the center if the pan is dry. Season the chicken with salt and pepper. Add the chicken and sear on all sides until browned, 4 to 8 minutes per side depending on its thickness. Stir in the mushrooms and cook for another 1 to 2 minutes, until they are softened.

2. Slowly pour in the wine and broth. Add the bay leaves and thyme and season with salt and pepper. Gently stir to combine. Increase the heat to high and bring the mixture to a boil. Reduce the heat to medium and simmer for about 10 minutes, or until the sauce has reduced by about one-third.

3. MEANWHILE, MAKE THE NOODLES. Bring a large pot of salted water to a boil over high heat. Add the noodles and cook until al dente according to the package directions. Drain and set aside.

4. In the same pot, combine the butter and sage over medium heat until just browned. The butter will melt, foam, and froth, then begin to brown along the bottom. Whisk the browned bits off the bottom of the pan. Remove the pot from the heat and stir in the garlic. Add the cooked noodles, tossing well to coat. Taste and season with salt and pepper, if needed.

5. To serve, remove and discard the bay leaves and thyme from the chicken. Divide the noodles among four to six plates and spoon the chicken on top. Sprinkle with fresh parsley.

Potato Chip Chicken

Serves: **6**

If there is any meal in our family that everyone loves, this is the one! I would even go so far as to declare Potato Chip Chicken with rice the Gerard Family signature dish. When my mom was dating my dad, his mother, my Mimi, used to make Potato Chip Chicken. Mom was still in high school when she asked Mimi for the recipe (my parents met when my mom was sixteen). She then made the dish for my dad as a much-appreciated alternative to cafeteria food while he was in college. It was easy, and it was always a hit! Unsurprisingly, this recipe has carried on strong. Seven kids, friends, girlfriends, extended family, and thirty-two-plus years of marriage later, Potato Chip Chicken is still a mainstay. My secret to crushing the potato chips? I like to open the bag just a little bit and carefully stomp on the chips until they are finely crushed . . . it's a great pre-dinner workout!

½ cup (1 stick) salted butter, melted

2 cups finely crushed potato chips

1 cup finely crushed cornflakes

2 pounds boneless, skinless chicken tenders

½ teaspoon seasoned salt

Freshly ground pepper

1. Preheat the oven to 375°F.

2. Put the melted butter in a shallow medium bowl. Put the potato chip and cornflake crumbs in a separate shallow medium bowl and stir to combine.

3. Working with one piece at a time, dip the chicken in the butter, allowing the excess to drip off, then dredge through the potato chip–cornflake crumbs, pressing gently to adhere. Place the coated chicken on a baking sheet as you work. Season with the seasoned salt and pepper.

4. Bake for 25 to 30 minutes, or until the crumbs are golden and the chicken is cooked through. Serve warm.

Braised Pork Tamale Burrito Bowls

Serves: **4**

Have you ever tried to make tamales at home? If so, you know it's not the easiest task. One Christmas a few years ago, I very ambitiously thought it would be a good idea to attempt to make fresh tamales for my family. Christmas at my house means at least twenty people, so it wasn't a small task. Suffice it to say, I have not made real-deal tamales since. But now I've got this recipe, which is SO good and SO easy—the hardest part is cutting the pork. These bowls are great topped with just a little cheese, sliced avocado, and cilantro, but when time allows, I'll also make a quick pineapple salsa . . . because everything is better with a little salsa! If pork isn't your meat of choice, chicken breasts or chicken thighs will work just as well.

Braised Pork

2 pounds pork shoulder, cut into 3-inch cubes

2 tablespoons chili powder

1 teaspoon ground cumin

½ teaspoon kosher salt

½ teaspoon freshly ground pepper

1 tablespoon extra-virgin olive oil

1 poblano chile pepper, seeded and sliced

1 red bell pepper, sliced

2 cups red enchilada sauce, store-bought or homemade (page 204)

2 garlic cloves, minced or grated

1 or 2 canned chipotle peppers in adobo sauce, chopped

2 bay leaves

Creamy Polenta

2 cups whole milk, plus more if needed

1 cup instant polenta

2 tablespoons salted butter, plus more if needed

Kosher salt and freshly ground pepper

For Serving

1 cup cooked black beans

1 cup grilled or roasted corn kernels

1 avocado, pitted, peeled, and sliced

Shredded cheddar or crumbled cojita cheese (I use both!)

Fresh cilantro

Pineapple Salsa (page 82)

1. **MAKE THE BRAISED PORK.** In a medium bowl, combine the pork, chili powder, cumin, salt, and pepper and toss to coat.

2. In a large Dutch oven, heat the olive oil over medium-high. When it shimmers, add the poblano and bell pepper and cook until charred, about 5 minutes. Remove the peppers from the pot.

3. Place the same pot over high heat. Working in batches if necessary, add the pork and sear all over, about 5 minutes total. Reduce the heat to low and pour in the enchilada sauce. Add the garlic, chipotles (to taste), bay leaves, and charred peppers. Bring the mixture to a boil, then reduce the heat to low, cover, and simmer for 1 ½ to 2 hours, until the pork is falling apart. Remove and discard the bay leaves. Shred the meat with two forks and toss with the sauce in the pot.

4. **MAKE THE POLENTA.** In a medium saucepan, bring 2 cups of water and the milk to a boil over medium-high heat. Slowly whisk in the polenta, stirring continuously, until the polenta is soft and thick, about 5 minutes. Stir in the butter and season with salt and pepper. If the polenta seems a little thick, you can add a tablespoon more of butter or milk; if it is on the thin side, simmer for a few minutes more.

5. To serve, divide the polenta among four bowls and top each with black beans, corn, and sliced avocado. Add the shredded pork and top with cheese, cilantro, and salsa.

Hula Pork Sliders

Makes: **12 sliders**

These sliders are pretty much all things tropical and delicious: sweet-and-sour slow-cooked pork, topped with melted Swiss cheese and caramelized pineapple rings. Epic, and kind of addicting—you'll be making this recipe over and over. These sliders are great as a party menu item, or equally amazing for a fun Hawaiian-inspired dinner. If you have leftover Hula Pork, be creative with it. Think cheesy rice bowl with Pineapple Salsa (page 82), tacos, quesadillas, Hawaiian mac and cheese, pizza . . . the options are endless!

2¼ cups pineapple juice

1 (1-inch) knob fresh ginger, peeled and grated

2 garlic cloves, minced or grated

⅓ cup packed light brown sugar

⅔ cup low-sodium soy sauce

⅔ cup ketchup

2 to 3 tablespoons sriracha sauce

2½ pounds pork shoulder or butt, cut into 2 pieces

2 tablespoons coconut oil

6 large pineapple rings, halved (see "How to Prep a Pineapple," page 161)

12 Hawaiian slider buns

12 slices Swiss cheese

1½ cups Grilled Corn and Basil Salad (page 74) or shredded lettuce or cabbage

Melted butter (optional)

Poppy seeds (optional)

1. Preheat the oven to 325°F.

2. In a large bowl, whisk together the pineapple juice, ginger, garlic, brown sugar, soy sauce, ketchup, and sriracha.

3. Place the pork in a Dutch oven and pour over half the sauce. Cover and transfer to the oven. Roast for 3 to 4 hours, or until the pork is falling off the bone and shreds easily—check the pork once or twice throughout cooking to be sure the sauce is not reducing too much. If it is, add the remaining sauce as needed to keep the pork moist. The pork should be submerged in liquid at least halfway. Shred the pork and add some of the remaining pineapple sauce to the pot, if desired.

4. Heat the broiler to high with a rack in the top third.

5. In a large skillet, melt the coconut oil over medium heat. Add the pineapple slices and cook for 3 to 4 minutes per side, or until caramelized.

6. Arrange the bottom halves of the slider buns on a baking sheet and add a scoop of pork to each. Top each with a slice of Swiss cheese. Place under the broiler for 1 to 2 minutes, or until the cheese has melted.

7. Top each slider with a slice of caramelized pineapple and a scoop of corn salad. If desired, brush the top of each bun with melted butter and sprinkle with poppy seeds.

Cuban Mojo Pulled Pork Tacos

Serves: 6

Tacos always excite me, but these are extraordinary. The pork marinade is classic for a Cuban-style roasted pork (heavy on the garlic and oregano!). The mojo sauce is a little different in that I add fresh mango. It's tangy with a kick, and extra saucy, which in my house is always good. The tacos get finished off with fried onions (uh-huh), a fried egg (totally serious), and avocado (obviously). Oh, and there's chipotle mayo involved, too (duh).

Pork

½ cup extra-virgin olive oil

10 garlic cloves, finely chopped or grated

½ cup fresh oregano

½ cup fresh cilantro

3 to 4 pounds pork shoulder or butt

Mojo Sauce

1 ripe mango, pitted, peeled, and chopped (see "How to Peel and Cut a Mango," page 38)

⅓ cup honey

½ cup orange juice

¼ cup fresh lime juice

1 jalapeño, seeded, if desired, and chopped

¼ cup fresh cilantro, coarsely chopped

Kosher salt

For Serving

10 to 12 corn or flour tortillas, warmed

Shredded cheddar cheese

Shredded lettuce

Sliced avocado

Sriracha mayo (see Note, page 171)

4 to 6 fried eggs (optional)

1 cup fried onions, store-bought or homemade (page 148, optional)

1. MAKE THE PORK. In a blender or food processor, combine the olive oil, garlic, oregano, and cilantro and pulse until finely chopped and combined, about 30 seconds. Put the pork in a large zip-top bag and pour in the marinade. Seal the bag and marinate the pork for at least 1 to 2 hours at room temperature or overnight in the fridge. Remove the pork from the fridge 30 minutes prior to roasting.

2. Preheat the oven to 350°F.

3. Place the pork in a Dutch oven, discarding the marinade. Add 1 ½ cups of water. Cover and transfer to the oven. Roast for 3 to 4 hours, or until the pork is falling off the bone and shreds easily. If at any point throughout the cooking process the liquid in the pot gets lower than 1 inch, add about ½ cup of water.

4. MEANWHILE, MAKE THE MOJO SAUCE. In a blender or food processor, combine the mango, honey, orange juice, lime juice, jalapeño, cilantro, and salt to taste and pulse until smooth. Taste and add more salt as needed.

5. Shred the pork in the pot, discarding any fatty pieces. Add the mojo sauce and toss to coat.

6. To serve, spoon the pork onto warmed tortillas and top with cheddar, lettuce, avocado, and a drizzle of sriracha mayo. Add a fried egg and fried onions, if desired.

(recipe continues)

Serves: **4**

2 cups buttermilk

2 large white onions, halved and thinly sliced

2 cups all-purpose flour

Pinch of cayenne

Pinch of freshly ground pepper

Kosher salt

Vegetable oil, for frying

1. In a large bowl, pour the buttermilk over the sliced onions. Using your hands, submerge the onions in the buttermilk and toss to coat.

2. In a separate large bowl, stir together the flour, cayenne, pepper, and some salt.

3. Fill a large pot with oil to a depth of 3 inches. Heat the oil over high to 375°F, or until a pinch of flour sizzles when added.

4. Working in batches, remove a handful of onions from the buttermilk and place them in the flour mixture. Turn to coat, then remove and shake off any excess. Carefully drop the breaded onions into the hot oil. Use a spoon to fiddle with them a bit just to break up the layers. Fry for 1 to 2 minutes, until golden brown—watch closely, as they cook quickly! Using a slotted spoon, transfer to a paper towel–lined plate to drain. Repeat with the remaining onion slices.

5. Fried onions are best served right away, but can be reheated in a 300°F oven for about 5 minutes—keep a careful eye on them to be sure they don't burn.

Healthy Chipotle Turkey Sweet Potato Skins

Serves: **4**

Just about everyone loves a good crispy potato skin filled with melted, gooey cheese. I mean, what's not to love? As much as I adore the traditional skins, I wanted to re-create them in a new and healthier way. Enter these sweet potato skins. They're truly delicious in every way possible: sweet, spicy, oh so cheesy, and packed with vegetables and lean protein. The spice gives them a hit of amazing flavor that no one expects, but everyone loves! I like to reserve the sweet potato flesh for making soup, sweet potato casserole, or homemade gnocchi.

4 medium sweet potatoes

3 tablespoons extra-virgin olive oil

¾ pound ground turkey

2 garlic cloves, minced or grated

1 or 2 canned chipotle peppers in adobo, minced, plus 1 tablespoon adobo sauce from the can

2 teaspoons chili powder

1 teaspoon dried oregano

1 teaspoon ground cumin

½ teaspoon kosher salt, plus more as needed

2 cups baby spinach

Juice of 1 lime

¼ cup chopped fresh cilantro, plus more for serving

Freshly ground pepper

1½ cups shredded sharp white cheddar cheese

Sliced avocado, for serving

Plain Greek yogurt, for serving

1. Preheat the oven to 425°F.

2. Prick the sweet potatoes all over with a fork. Place directly on the oven rack and bake for 50 to 60 minutes, or until fork-tender.

3. Meanwhile, in a large skillet, heat 2 tablespoons of the olive oil over high. When it shimmers, add the turkey and cook, breaking it up with a wooden spoon, until browned all over. Add the garlic, chipotles (to taste), adobo sauce, chili powder, oregano, cumin, and salt. Cook for about 5 minutes, until fragrant. Add the spinach and cook until wilted, 2 to 3 minutes. Remove the skillet from the heat and stir in the lime juice and cilantro.

4. Remove the sweet potatoes from the oven and carefully (they're hot!) halve them lengthwise. Let cool for 5 minutes. Scoop out the flesh, leaving just enough around the edges so the skins don't collapse. Discard the flesh or save it for another use. Place the skins in a 9 x 13-inch baking dish, flesh-side up. Brush with the remaining tablespoon of olive oil and season with salt and pepper. Transfer to the oven and bake for 5 to 10 minutes, or until crisp.

5. Remove from the oven, stuff with the turkey mixture, and top evenly with the cheese. Return to the oven and bake for about 10 minutes more, or until the cheese has melted and the skins are hot and crispy.

6. Serve hot, with cilantro, avocado, and yogurt.

Seafood

Root Vegetable and Sage Pesto Baked Salmon

Serves: 4

I have a confession: dishes are my worst nightmare. I do a lot of cooking, and when I cook, I always make a giant mess. I'm talking flour on the floor, dishes piled high, and anything from cheese to cherries to chocolate smeared on my face. When I'm not cooking for the blog, I still need to eat dinner. On these "computer" days, I don't want to make a mess, but I do want to eat something simple and healthy. This one-pan salmon is the dinner I go for on these kind of nights. What I love about this recipe (other than the fact that cleanup is as easy as possible) is how versatile it is. In the summer, you can use fresh zucchini, bell peppers, and corn; in the fall and winter, root vegetables; and in the spring, asparagus, peas, and artichokes. The sage pesto is an awesome switch-up from the classic basil version, and I love how it pairs with the heartier root vegetables, but feel free to use basil in the warmer seasons. If you don't love fish, use chicken breasts and bake for 25 to 30 minutes.

3 small beets, halved

2 carrots, chopped

1 small to medium sweet potato, diced

12 baby potatoes, halved if larger

12 Brussels sprouts, halved

2 tablespoons extra-virgin olive oil

Kosher salt and freshly ground black pepper

Sage Pesto

1 cup fresh sage leaves

1 cup baby kale

⅓ cup toasted pistachios

⅓ cup grated Parmesan cheese

½ cup extra-virgin olive oil

Kosher salt

Crushed red pepper flakes

4 (5- to 6-ounce) salmon fillets

¼ cup grated Manchego cheese

Fresh lemon juice (optional)

1. Preheat the oven to 425°F.

2. On a rimmed baking sheet, toss the beets, carrots, sweet potatoes, baby potatoes, and Brussels sprouts with the olive oil. Season with salt and black pepper. Roast for about 20 minutes, or until the veggies are slightly tender.

3. MEANWHILE, MAKE THE PESTO. In a food processor, combine the sage, kale, and pistachios and pulse until finely chopped. Add the Parmesan and pulse again. With the motor running, drizzle in the olive oil. Season with salt and red pepper flakes.

4. Remove the veggies from the oven and push them to one side of the pan. Put the salmon on the other side. Rub a few tablespoons of the sage pesto over each fillet.

5. Return the pan to the oven and roast for 10 to 20 minutes more, until the salmon reaches your desired doneness and the veggies are soft. Remove the pan from the oven and top each fillet with some of the Manchego to melt.

6. If desired, squeeze a drop of lemon juice over the salmon. Serve with the roasted veggies and extra sage pesto alongside.

Drunken Late-Summer Corn and Clam Chowder

Serves: **4 to 6**

Late summer is all about using up fresh garden produce: golden ears of sweet corn, perfectly ripe tomatoes, just-plucked basil. This soup does just that. The wine adds a rich flavor and pairs well with the clams. It's a combo you can't beat, and when finished with a handful of basil and garlic-herb toast for dipping, well, it's the perfect way to send off summer and welcome the cooler days of fall. For added flavor, try grilling or broiling your corn before adding it to the soup.

4 thick-cut bacon slices, chopped

2 tablespoons salted butter

1 sweet onion, finely chopped

2 garlic cloves, minced or grated

2 sprigs fresh thyme

3 Yukon Gold potatoes, peeled and diced

1 cup white wine

2½ cups low-sodium chicken broth

¼ to ½ teaspoon cayenne

1 bay leaf

2 cups whole milk

16 to 20 littleneck clams, thoroughly washed and scrubbed clean

4 cups corn kernels

¼ cup fresh basil, chopped, plus more for serving

Shredded sharp white cheddar, for serving (optional)

Toasted French or sourdough bread, for serving (optional)

1. In a large Dutch oven or stockpot, cook the bacon over medium heat until it is crisp and the fat has rendered, about 5 minutes. Transfer to a paper towel–lined plate to drain. Set aside. Discard all but 1 tablespoon of the bacon fat from the pot and return the pot to medium heat.

2. Add the butter and onion to the pot and cook for 5 to 8 minutes, or until the onion is caramelized. Add the garlic and cook for about 30 seconds more, or until fragrant. Stir in the thyme sprigs and potatoes. Slowly add the wine and broth, then add the cayenne and bay leaf. Cover and simmer 15 to 20 minutes, or until the potatoes are fork-tender.

3. Stir in the milk and bring the chowder to a gentle boil. Add the clams and boil for 8 to 10 minutes, or until they open. Discard any clams that have not opened after 12 minutes. Using tongs or a slotted spoon, transfer the clams to a plate. Discard the bay leaf and thyme sprigs. Stir the corn and bacon into the chowder. Reduce the heat to low and cover to keep warm.

4. When the clams are cool enough to handle, remove them from their shells. Coarsely chop the clam meat and stir it back into the chowder. Stir in the basil and cook until warmed through.

5. To serve, divide the chowder among four to six bowls. Top with more fresh basil and cheddar, if desired. Serve with bread for dipping, if desired.

NOTE

Using raw lobster tails in place of, or in addition to, the clams is delicious. I either use 4 lobster tails to replace all the clams, or 2 lobster tails and about 10 clams.

Chipotle Tuna and Avocado Salad Pita

Serves: 2

This is one of the best quick, go-to healthy meals I have up my sleeve. You can throw it together in ten minutes or less, using mostly pantry ingredients. I like to use mashed avocado in place of mayo in my tuna salad, and then kick things up a notch with a chipotle pepper! If you're feeling the need for a little cheese in your life, I'd be super excited if you turned this into a tuna melt . . . 'cause adding cheese is never, ever a bad idea. And yes, I do it often.

1 ripe avocado, pitted

2 canned chipotle peppers in adobo, finely chopped

¼ cup oil-packed sun-dried tomatoes, drained and coarsely chopped

Juice of ½ lemon

2 (5-ounce) cans oil-packed tuna, drained

2 tablespoons chopped fresh basil

1 tablespoon chopped fresh oregano

Freshly ground pepper

2 pitas, warmed

2 butter lettuce leaves

Handful of fresh arugula

Handful of fresh microgreens

1. Scoop half the avocado into a bowl and lightly mash with a fork. Add the chipotles, sun-dried tomatoes, and lemon juice and mix until combined. Stir in the tuna, basil, and oregano. Season with pepper.

2. Layer the butter lettuce onto the pitas and stuff with the tuna salad. Slice the remaining avocado half and add to the sandwiches. Add the arugula and microgreens and serve.

Jerk Mahimahi and Pineapple Salad with Ginger-Chile Vinaigrette

Serves: 4

It's quite possible that I could live solely on pineapple and mango . . . and, okay, burrata, too. Whenever I'm in need of a little tropical flair, I make this salad. I have a pretty good imagination, so it lets me picture myself on a Caribbean island with a tropical, fruity drink in hand. Sounds kind of silly, but when you live in a place as cold as I do and there are only thirty nights out of the entire year that the temperature doesn't drop below freezing, you need to use your imagination . . . and you also need a really great space heater. This jerk mahimahi is amazing. And when crusted with coconut, the spice gets an awesome layer of sweetness. The ginger-chile vinaigrette balances it all out.

Fish

1 pound skin-on mahimahi, cut into 4 pieces

¼ cup jerk seasoning, store-bought or homemade (recipe follows)

4 tablespoons extra-virgin olive oil

⅔ cup unsweetened shredded or flaked coconut

Salad

4 cups baby spinach

1 cup watercress

2 cups cubed fresh pineapple (see "How to Prep a Pineapple," opposite)

1 cup halved cherry tomatoes

¼ cup fresh basil, coarsely chopped

¼ cup fresh cilantro, coarsely chopped

1 avocado, pitted, peeled, and sliced

⅓ cup unsweetened shredded or flaked coconut

1 cup fresh blueberries

Chile-Ginger Vinaigrette

¼ cup extra-virgin olive oil

2 tablespoons fresh orange juice

1 tablespoon cider vinegar

1 (1-inch) knob fresh ginger, peeled and grated

1 red Fresno chile, seeded and finely chopped

Kosher salt and freshly ground pepper

Fresh limes and pickled ginger, for serving

1. **MAKE THE FISH.** Sprinkle the flesh side of the mahimahi with the jerk seasoning. Rub with 2 tablespoons of the olive oil to coat. Press the coconut onto the fish to adhere.

2. In a large skillet, heat the remaining 2 tablespoons of olive oil over medium. When it shimmers, add the fish, skin-side down, and sear for 2 to 3 minutes, then flip and cook for 3 to 4 minutes more, or until flaky and opaque.

3. **MAKE THE SALAD.** In a large bowl, toss together the spinach, watercress, pineapple, tomatoes, basil, and cilantro.

4. Remove the skin from the fish and break the fish apart over the salad. Add the avocado. Sprinkle the salad with the coconut and blueberries.

5. **MAKE THE VINAIGRETTE.** In a bowl, whisk together the olive oil, orange juice, vinegar, ginger, chile, and a pinch each of salt and pepper. Taste and add more salt and pepper as needed.

6. Drizzle the vinaigrette over the salad and serve with fresh limes and pickled ginger.

HOMEMADE JERK SEASONING

Makes: ½ cup

1 tablespoon garlic powder

2 to 3 teaspoons cayenne

2 teaspoons dried thyme

2 teaspoons kosher salt

1 teaspoon ground all-spice

½ teaspoon freshly ground black pepper

½ teaspoon crushed red pepper flakes

½ teaspoon ground cinnamon

Put all the ingredients in a glass jar and shake to combine. Store at room temperature for up to 6 months.

HOW TO PREP A PINEAPPLE

I eat a lot of pineapple, so over the years I have become a pro at prepping them. Cut off the top and bottom and stand the pineapple upright. Slice the skin off the pineapple in a downward motion, working around the pineapple and cutting as close to the flesh as possible. For rings, lay the pineapple flat and slice. For chunks, halve it vertically, then cut each half into quarters. Cut out the tough core. Chop!

Quick Kickin' Cajun Shrimp and Rice

Serves: **4**

Mrs. Mooney isn't just famous for her penne (page 97); she also makes a mean gumbo. Even those who don't think they like Cajun food like Mrs. Mooney's gumbo. Her version takes some time to put together, and it's really best if you let it sit overnight before serving. It's a great meal to make on a Saturday and eat on a Sunday. Sometimes I'm not that organized—I just need a good Cajun meal, and I need it fast! Enter this quick kickin' Cajun shrimp and rice. I often make this on busy weeknights and serve it with my favorite beer bread (page 69) alongside. It's heavy on the flavor and light on the time commitment.

1½ cups jasmine or basmati rice

1 tablespoon Cajun seasoning

1 tablespoon Creole seasoning

1 teaspoon dried thyme

1 teaspoon smoked paprika

¼ teaspoon kosher salt, plus more as needed

¼ teaspoon freshly ground pepper, plus more as needed

2 andouille sausage links, sliced

2 tablespoons salted butter

1 pound shrimp, peeled and deveined

¼ cup all-purpose flour

¼ cup canola oil

1 green bell pepper, chopped

1 cup cubed fresh pineapple (see "How to Prep a Pineapple," page 161)

2 garlic cloves, minced or grated

1 (12-ounce) bottle beer (use whatever you like to drink)

2 tablespoons sweet Thai chili sauce

1 tablespoon Louisiana-style hot sauce

1 tablespoon Worcestershire sauce

Handful of fresh parsley, chopped, plus more for serving

Lemon wedges, for serving

1. Bring 3 cups of water to a boil in a medium pot over high heat. Stir in the rice, then cover and reduce the heat to low. Cook for 10 minutes, then turn off the heat and let the rice sit, covered, for 20 minutes more (no peeking!). Remove the lid and fluff the rice with a fork.

2. Meanwhile, in a small bowl, combine the Cajun seasoning, Creole seasoning, thyme, paprika, salt, and pepper.

3. Heat a large Dutch oven over high. When the pan is just smoking, add the sausage and brown all over, about 5 minutes. Remove the sausage and set aside in a medium bowl.

4. In the same pot, melt the butter over medium-high heat. Add the shrimp and sprinkle with half the seasoning mix. Toss quickly to coat and sear on both sides, about 2 minutes per side, or until pink and opaque. Remove the shrimp from the pot and add to the bowl with the sausage.

5. Reduce the heat to medium. Add the flour and canola oil to the pot and whisk to combine. Cook for about 5 minutes, or until the roux is lightly golden in color. Add the bell pepper, pineapple, garlic, and remaining seasoning mix. Cook, stirring occasionally, for about 5 minutes more. Slowly pour in the beer. Add the Thai chili sauce, hot sauce, and Worcestershire. Bring the mixture to a boil, then reduce the heat to low and simmer for 10 minutes. Stir the shrimp and sausage into the sauce and heat until warmed through. Remove the pot from the heat and stir in the parsley.

6. Divide the rice among four plates, top with the shrimp and sausage, and spoon over the sauce. Garnish with lemon wedges and more parsley.

Beer and Harissa–Steamed Mussels with Parmesan Fries

Serves: 2 to 4

I could eat mussels every day. They're quick and easy, but so mouthwateringly good. I like to serve these in late summer and into fall when mussels are at their best. They are really fun for small gatherings with friends, because unlike chicken or steak, you really can't mess up mussels. You just need to be sure there is plenty of butter (never too much butter), booze (for both cooking and drinking), and carbs (to soak up all the yummy sauce), and you're good to go. Mussels may be meant as more of an appetizer than a full-on meal, but come on, we all know we're going to fill up on them anyway . . . especially when there are Parmesan fries involved. Yep, best kind of dinner there is!

Parmesan Fries

4 russet potatoes, cut into ¼-inch-wide matchsticks

¼ cup extra-virgin olive oil

2 tablespoons chopped fresh basil, plus more for serving

1 tablespoon flaky sea salt

½ cup grated Parmesan cheese

Mussels

2 tablespoons coconut oil

2 tablespoons salted butter

½ sweet onion, finely chopped

2 garlic cloves, minced or grated

2 to 4 tablespoons harissa

1 teaspoon smoked paprika

Kosher salt and freshly ground pepper

12 ounces beer or white wine (use whatever you like to drink)

½ cup canned full-fat coconut milk

2½ pounds mussels, debearded and scrubbed clean

1 cup cherry tomatoes

1 (14-ounce) can chickpeas, drained and rinsed

¼ cup chopped fresh cilantro, plus more for serving

¼ cup chopped fresh basil, plus more for serving

1. Preheat the oven to 425°F.

2. START THE FRIES. Arrange the potatoes on a rimmed baking sheet in a single layer, using a second baking sheet if needed, and drizzle with the olive oil. Add the basil and flaky salt and gently toss to coat. Spread the fries in a single layer again. Transfer to the oven and bake for 15 to 20 minutes, then reduce the oven temperature to 400°F, flip, and bake for 15 to 20 minutes more.

3. MEANWHILE, MAKE THE MUSSELS. In a large Dutch oven, melt the coconut oil and butter over medium heat. When the mixture shimmers, add the onion and cook until lightly caramelized and soft, about 5 minutes. Add the garlic and cook for about 30 seconds more, until fragrant. Stir in the harissa, paprika, and a pinch each of kosher salt and pepper. Slowly pour in the beer and coconut milk.

4. Increase the heat to high and bring the mixture to a boil. Add the mussels and tomatoes. Cover the pot and cook, shaking the pot occasionally, for 4 to 5 minutes, until the mussels have all opened. Discard any mussels that haven't opened after 10 minutes. Stir in the chickpeas, cilantro, and basil.

5. Remove the fries from the oven and toss with more fresh basil and the Parmesan.

6. Garnish the mussels with cilantro and/or basil and serve warm with the Parmesan fries alongside.

Blackened Mahimahi Tacos

Serves: **4**

When I was a kid, my family would eat beef tacos twice a week. No, really—twice a week. Mom and I ate them with a hard shell and cheddar cheese, while most of the boys had their tacos in a soft flour tortilla (Dad wasn't into tacos at all). Occasionally, there was lettuce on the table, too, but no one really touched that. As I got older and became more aware of the foods my family and I were eating, our weekly tacos started to change. First, I began using ground turkey in place of beef. Then I started making my own seasoning mix. And then I got really adventurous and started making my own taco shells. When my older brother Brendan suggested that I try making fish tacos, I was wary—but I gave it try and have never looked back.

1 tablespoon light brown sugar

1 tablespoon paprika

½ teaspoon cayenne

½ teaspoon garlic powder

½ teaspoon dried thyme

1 teaspoon kosher salt

1 teaspoon freshly ground pepper

1½ pounds mahimahi

Extra-virgin olive oil

1 (8-ounce) package cream cheese, at room temperature

8 corn or flour tortillas, warmed

Mango Salsa
(page 83; see Note)

Chopped fresh cilantro, for serving

Lime wedges, for serving

1. Heat a grill to high or a grill pan over high.

2. In a small bowl, combine the brown sugar, paprika, cayenne, garlic powder, thyme, salt, and pepper. Season the fish generously with the spice mix and then rub with olive oil to coat.

3. Grill the fish for about 4 minutes per side, or until cooked through. Remove and let cool for 1 to 2 minutes. Using a fork, flake the fish into pieces.

4. To assemble the tacos, spread some of the cream cheese on a warmed tortilla. Add some flaked fish and top with salsa. Garnish with fresh cilantro and serve with lime wedges alongside.

NOTE

If you have leftover mango salsa, it's great on a variety of dishes. You can spoon it over grilled meats and seafood, use it in salads, or serve it as an appetizer with tortilla chips for scooping. It's also surprisingly delicious when served over a block of feta cheese that's been drizzled in olive oil, or even as a topping for baked Brie.

Pan-Fried Sesame-Crusted Tilapia

Serves: 4

Light, white tilapia tends to be a bit boring, but think of it as a canvas to take on a variety of flavors. Trust me, there is nothing boring about this Asian-inspired tilapia. The fish is glazed in a sweet-and-spicy sauce, served over soba noodles, and topped with crunchy fried wontons for a little fun and texture. Honestly, you really can't go wrong with flavors like these. And don't think those fried wontons are optional . . . because balance is the key to life!

⅓ cup low-sodium soy sauce

¼ cup honey

2 tablespoons fresh lemon juice

1 tablespoon sriracha sauce

1 (1-inch) knob fresh ginger, peeled and grated

1 garlic clove, minced or grated

12 ounces soba noodles

½ cup fresh basil, coarsely chopped

¼ to ½ cup grated Parmesan cheese

4 (4- to 6-ounce) tilapia fillets

Kosher salt and freshly ground black pepper

¼ cup mixed black and white sesame seeds

3 tablespoons sesame oil

1 bunch asparagus spears, tough ends trimmed

½ teaspoon crushed red pepper flakes

For Serving

Sliced avocado

Sliced cucumber

Pickled ginger

Wonton Crisps (recipe follows)

1. In a small bowl, whisk together the soy sauce, honey, lemon juice, sriracha, ginger, and garlic to make a dressing.

2. Bring a large pot of water to a boil over high heat. When the water is boiling, add the soba noodles and cook until tender according to the package directions. Drain and immediately rinse under cold water to stop the cooking. Put the noodles in a large bowl and toss with half the dressing, the basil, and the Parmesan to taste.

3. Season the tilapia on both sides with salt and black pepper. Sprinkle one side with the sesame seeds. In a large skillet, heat 2 tablespoons of sesame oil over medium-high. When it shimmers, add the tilapia, sesame-side down. Cook for 1 to 2 minutes per side, or until golden and cooked through. Remove the fillets from the pan.

4. In the same pan, heat the remaining tablespoon of sesame oil. Add the asparagus. Season with salt and black pepper. Cook, stirring once or twice, until lightly charred and tender, about 5 minutes. Remove the pan from the heat and season the asparagus with the red pepper flakes.

5. Divide the soba noodles among four bowls and top with the tilapia. Add the asparagus, sliced avocado, cucumber, and pickled ginger. Top with fried wontons. Serve with any remaining dressing alongside.

WONTON CRISPS
Serves: 4

Canola or vegetable oil, for frying

20 to 40 wonton wrappers

Kosher salt

Lime zest

Fill a large skillet with about 1 inch of oil and heat over medium. When it shimmers, add the wonton wrappers a handful at a time. Fry until golden, about 1 minute. Remove with a slotted spoon and drain on a paper towel–lined plate. Season immediately with salt and lime zest. Repeat with the remaining wrappers.

Lobster BLT

Serves: **4**

BLTs are classic. You really can't mess them up. The addition of buttery lobster to this sandwich is possibly one of the best ideas ever. Lobster and bacon just go together—like two peas in a pod. Add fresh tomatoes, butter lettuce, fontina cheese, and sweet chili butter, and you've got one tasty sandwich. BLT or seafood purists may look down on me for adding cheese, but I'm not concerned. If they only tried this, they would be convinced it's okay, and it's necessary.

6 tablespoons (¾ stick) salted butter

1 to 2 tablespoons sweet Thai chili sauce

1 tablespoon extra-virgin olive oil

2 to 4 lobster tails, meat removed and patted dry

8 slices sourdough bread

1 cup shredded fontina cheese

⅓ cup sriracha mayo (see Note)

4 butter lettuce leaves

2 heirloom tomatoes, sliced

1 avocado, pitted, peeled, and sliced

8 bacon slices, cooked

1. Preheat the broiler to high with a rack in the top third.

2. In a small bowl, mash together the butter and Thai chili sauce until well combined.

3. In a medium skillet, heat the olive oil and 2 tablespoons of the chili butter over medium. When the butter has melted, add the lobster tails and cook until bright red and cooked through, about 3 minutes per side. Remove the skillet from heat.

4. Smear both sides of the sourdough bread with the remaining chili butter and place on a baking sheet. Place under the broiler for 1 minute. Remove and set aside 4 of the slices. Divide the cheese evenly among the remaining 4 slices of bread on the baking sheet and place back under the broiler to melt, 30 seconds to 1 minute—watch closely, as the broiler cooks fast. Remove from the oven.

5. Spread a little mayo on the inside of the cheese-less slices of bread. Layer on the lettuce, tomato, avocado, and bacon. Add the lobster tails, and place the bread with the melted cheese on top, cheese-side down.

NOTE
The recipe calls for sriracha mayo, which is easy to throw together: just mix 1 to 2 tablespoons of sriracha sauce into ¼ cup of mayo. You can also use plain mayo in a pinch. I actually don't love mayo, so I make a sriracha-tahini sauce, too, just subbing tahini for the mayo and slowly adding water until the consistency is right.

Garlic Lemon Butter Shrimp

Serves: **4**

There are not enough words to describe just how good this plate of food is. If you've ever traveled to Hawaii, you may know about the very famous shrimp trucks that sell garlic lemon butter shrimp daily on the shores of Oahu. Sadly, I've never actually visited these trucks, only read about them, looked at photos of them, and researched all about their shrimp and just how they make it. Still, I feel pretty confident in my recipe. It's essential that you serve this shrimp with a big side of rice for soaking up any sauce, plus plenty of fresh pineapple wedges. In Hawaii, they serve the shrimp shell on, tail on. The idea is that you suck the butter sauce off the shells and then remove the shell and eat the shrimp. If all you really want to do is just eat the shrimp with zero interruptions (I get that), simply peel the shrimp before marinating, but leave the tail on for easy eating.

1 pound shell-on, tail-on raw shrimp

¼ cup extra-virgin olive oil

Juice of 1 lemon

6 garlic cloves, minced or grated

1 tablespoon chopped fresh parsley

½ teaspoon cayenne

Coconut Rice

1 (14-ounce) can full-fat or lite coconut milk

1 cup basmati rice

¼ cup unsweetened shredded or flaked coconut

Hawaiian sea salt (alaea) or kosher salt

Kosher salt and freshly ground pepper

6 tablespoons (¾ cup) salted butter

1 tablespoon chopped fresh parsley, plus more for serving

Zest and juice of ½ lemon

Pineapple wedges and lemon wedges, for serving

1. In a large zip-top bag, combine the shrimp, olive oil, lemon juice, garlic, parsley, and cayenne. Toss well to coat. Marinate in the fridge for at least 30 minutes or up to 24 hours.

2. In a medium pot, bring the coconut milk and 1 ½ cups water to a boil over high heat. Add the rice, shredded coconut, and Hawaiian salt. Stir to combine, then cover and reduce the heat to low. Cook for 10 minutes, then turn off the heat and let the rice sit, covered, for 20 minutes more (no peeking!). Remove the lid and fluff the rice with a fork.

3. Heat a large skillet over medium. When the skillet is just smoking, use a slotted spoon to scoop the shrimp and garlic out of the marinade and into the skillet. Season with kosher salt and pepper. Discard the remaining marinade. Cook the shrimp until pink, 2 to 3 minutes per side. Add the butter and a pinch each of kosher salt and pepper. Cook until the garlic begins to caramelize and turns light golden brown, another 1 to 2 minutes—be careful not to burn it. Remove the skillet from the heat and stir in the parsley, lemon zest, and lemon juice

4. Divide the rice among plates and top with the shrimp. Drizzle the warm garlic butter over the shrimp. Serve with pineapple and lemon wedges. Garnish with parsley.

ABOUT FISH SAUCE

My love for fish sauce is REAL. It's my secret weapon when a little flavor is needed. You'll notice I use this sauce a lot in my Thai-inspired recipes. Actually, I use it in a lot of my recipes, period. When it's cooked or mixed into sauces, the stink does go away, and it adds a salty flavor you can't get from any other condiment. If fish sauce isn't already a staple in your pantry, I highly recommend making it one.

Seafood Bánh Mì

Serves: 4

While I do love the classic bánh mì, this seafood version is pretty incredible. I took the bones of the traditional Vietnamese sandwich—meat, cilantro, cucumber, pickled carrots, radish—and turned it into my own little sweet-and-spicy creation, complete with caramelized fish, Thai basil chimichurri, a fried egg, and sliced avocado.

Thai Basil Chimichurri

1 cup chopped fresh Thai basil or regular basil

¼ cup chopped fresh cilantro

⅓ cup extra-virgin olive oil

¼ cup red wine vinegar

1 garlic clove, minced or grated

1 red Fresno chile, seeded and chopped

1 teaspoon kosher salt

Fish

½ cup honey

Juice of 1 lime

1 red Fresno chile, seeded and chopped

2 tablespoons fish sauce

Freshly ground pepper

3 tablespoons sesame oil

1 pound white fish, such as mahimahi or tilapia, skin removed

2 to 3 tablespoons Thai red curry paste

6 tablespoons (¾ stick) salted butter, at room temperature

1 French baguette, toasted and cut into quarters

1 cup shredded fresh or pickled carrots

1 cucumber, thinly sliced

1 avocado, pitted, peeled, and sliced

4 fried eggs

Toasted sesame seeds, basil leaves, and sliced red Fresno chiles, for garnish

1. MAKE THE CHIMICHURRI. Combine the basil, cilantro, olive oil, vinegar, garlic, chile, and salt in a small bowl and let sit for at least 10 minutes or overnight in the fridge. Taste and add salt as needed.

2. MAKE THE FISH. In a small bowl, whisk together the honey, lime, chile, fish sauce, and pepper until combined.

3. In a large skillet, heat 1 tablespoon of the sesame oil over medium-high. Rub the fish with the remaining 2 tablespoons of sesame oil and 1 tablespoon of the curry paste. When the oil shimmers, add the fish and sear for about 3 minutes per side, until golden. Reduce the heat to low and add the honey mixture. Cook until the sauce has reduced by one-third and begins to glaze the fish, about 5 minutes. Remove the skillet from the heat.

4. In a small bowl, mash together the remaining 1 to 2 tablespoons of curry paste (to taste) and the butter.

5. To assemble, spread the curry butter on the bottom half of each baguette piece and add the fish. Top with some of the chimichurri, carrots, cucumber, avocado, and a fried egg. Sprinkle the avocado and egg with sesame seeds. Garnish with basil and jalapeños. Serve with extra chimichurri alongside.

Cedar Plank Salmon with Lemon Butter

Serves: 4

If I had my way, grilling on a cedar plank would be my sole way of cooking fish. Obviously, that lovely stuff called snow and rain make that impossible, but I always do it when I can. Using a cedar plank gives your fish great flavor, and it makes cooking and cleanup super easy, too. If you just can't wait for those summer months (I know I can't!), you can make this on a grill pan.

White wine or water, for soaking

1 tablespoon smoked paprika

2 teaspoons ground cumin

½ teaspoon ground cinnamon

½ to 1 teaspoon cayenne

Kosher salt and freshly ground pepper

1 whole salmon fillet (about 2 pounds), skin removed

Extra-virgin olive oil

1 tablespoon honey

6 ripe apricots, nectarines, or peaches, halved and pitted

6 tablespoons (¾ stick) salted butter, at room temperature

Zest of ½ lemon

Minted Feta and Green Olive Salsa (page 82)

1. Soak a large cedar plank in white wine or water for at least 30 minutes before grilling, though 2 to 4 hours is ideal.

2. Heat a grill to medium.

3. In a small bowl, combine the paprika, cumin, cinnamon, cayenne, and salt and pepper to taste.

4. Lay the salmon fillet on top of the cedar plank, being sure none of it is hanging off the edges. Sprinkle the salmon with the seasoning mixture and then rub with olive oil. Drizzle with the honey. Place the cedar plank directly on the grill and cover. Grill for 12 to 15 minutes, until the salmon is uniformly pink in the center (check by inserting the tip of a small knife). Using a large spatula, transfer the cedar plank to a flat surface and let the salmon rest for 5 minutes.

5. Meanwhile, toss the apricots with 1 teaspoon of olive oil. Add them directly to the grill grates and cook for about 3 minutes per side, or until they begin to caramelize and grill marks appear.

6. In a small bowl, stir together the butter and lemon zest.

7. Serve the salmon warm, with the lemon butter, Minted Feta Salsa, and grilled apricots alongside.

NOTE
You can also make this salmon on a baking sheet under the broiler. Cook for 6 to 8 minutes, or until the salmon is opaque and flakes easily with a fork.

Triple-the-Fish Seafood Hot Pot with Herb Toast

Serves: 4

Decisions are my worst nightmare. I hate making them; I truly avoid them at all costs. Especially big ones—I tend to sit on them for days and days until I'm finally forced to commit one way or the other. Well, this recipe was born out of pure indecisiveness. I could not decide whether I wanted clams, shrimp, lobster, or mahimahi, so I just threw them all into one big pot with some butter . . . okay, a lot of butter . . . and called it a day. Turns out, that was actually a pretty great call, because this recipe has turned into one of my favorites. It's fast-cooking, very simple, and really tasty! The clams and shrimp are a must, but the mahimahi can be subbed for salmon or lobster tails. It really just depends on what you are feeling, what you have available, or maybe what your budget allows. Some kind of toast is pretty essential here, but serving this with fries would be equally amazing.

Herb Toast

6 tablespoons (¾ stick) salted butter, at room temperature

1 tablespoon chopped fresh parsley

1 tablespoon chopped fresh basil

1 tablespoon chopped fresh cilantro

6 to 8 (1-inch-thick) baguette slices

Fish

4 tablespoons (½ stick) salted butter

¼ cup coconut oil

8 clams, scrubbed

8 shell-on jumbo shrimp

1 pound mahimahi or salmon, cut into 2-inch pieces, or lobster tails

6 garlic cloves, minced or grated

1 stalk lemongrass, tender white inner core only, minced

2 tablespoons fish sauce

¼ cup sweet Thai chili sauce

Juice of 1 lime

¼ cup chopped fresh basil

¼ cup chopped fresh cilantro

1. **MAKE THE TOAST.** Preheat the oven to 350°F.

2. In a small bowl, mix together the butter and herbs. Arrange the bread on a baking sheet. Spread the butter evenly over each slice. Bake for 10 to 15 minutes, or until the bread is toasted and golden brown.

3. **MEANWHILE, MAKE THE FISH.** In a large skillet, melt the butter and coconut oil over medium heat. Add the clams, shrimp, and mahimahi and cook, stirring occasionally, until the shrimp are opaque and the clams have opened, 8 to 10 minutes. Discard any clams that have not opened after 10 minutes. Add the garlic and lemongrass and toss to combine. Cook for about 1 minute, or until the garlic is fragrant. Stir in the fish sauce and Thai chili sauce and cook until warmed through. Remove the skillet from the heat and add the lime juice, basil, and cilantro.

4. Serve warm, with the toast alongside for mopping up the sauce.

Cheesy French Scallops

Serves: 4

Cheesy. French. Scallops. How can you go wrong when words like these are involved? Really, you can't. This recipe is decadent; there's no denying that. The croissants add a real wow factor, and the creamy white wine sauce is what all scallops should be sitting in. I highly recommend serving this to anyone you are trying to impress (I'm talking future mothers-in-law, bosses, boyfriends, etc.). The moment they sink their teeth into these melt-in-your-mouth scallops, you'll become their very favorite person. Well, that might be a tad dramatic, but give it a try. I like to serve this with my Crunchy Roasted Broccoli (page 77).

¼ cup all-purpose flour

8 large fresh sea scallops

Kosher salt and freshly ground black pepper

4 tablespoons (½ stick) salted butter

½ sweet onion, finely diced

2 garlic cloves, minced or grated

⅔ cup white wine

½ cup heavy cream

1 bay leaf

2 or 3 sprigs fresh thyme, plus more leaves, if desired, for garnish

½ teaspoon crushed red pepper flakes

2 large croissants, halved horizontally

1½ cups shredded Gruyère cheese

1. Preheat the broiler to high with a rack in the top third.

2. Place the flour in a small bowl. Season the scallops with salt and black pepper on both sides, then dredge in the flour.

3. In a large skillet, melt 2 tablespoons of the butter over medium heat. Add the scallops and sear on both sides until golden and just tender, 1 to 2 minutes per side. Remove from the skillet and set aside.

4. In the same skillet, melt the remaining 2 tablespoons of butter over medium-high heat. Add the onion and cook until softened and lightly caramelized, about 5 minutes. Add the garlic and cook for about 30 seconds, until fragrant. Slowly pour in the wine, then stir in the cream. Add the bay leaf, thyme, and red pepper flakes. Increase the heat to high, bring the sauce to a simmer, and cook for about 5 minutes, or until slightly reduced. Remove the skillet from the heat and discard the bay leaf and thyme. Season the sauce with salt and black pepper.

5. Layer the croissants on the bottom of a clean medium skillet or in the bottom of 4 ramekins, then add the scallops (2 per ramekin if using). Spoon the sauce over the scallops and top with the Gruyère.

6. Place the skillet or ramekins under the broiler and broil until the cheese is melted and golden, 2 to 3 minutes. Garnish with fresh thyme, if desired.

Beef & Lamb

Roasted Garlic and Tomato–Braised Lamb Shanks with Parmesan Mashers

Serves: 4

These shanks, while they may seem fancy, are an easy, simple meal. The key is to not rush the cooking time. The shanks need some lovin' from the oven to become tender and delicious. With a little red wine and a whole head of roasted garlic, they can do no wrong, especially when paired with my all-time favorite Parmesan mashers. Oh my gosh, these mashers! If I could eat just one side dish for the rest of my life, it might just be these mashed potatoes. They are exceptional, and there's not a better side these lamb shanks could be paired with. Sometimes I swap the Parmesan for crumbled Gorgonzola, which pairs nicely with the lamb.

Lamb

4 (1-pound) lamb shanks

Kosher salt and freshly ground pepper

2 tablespoons extra-virgin olive oil

1 sweet onion, finely chopped

2 carrots, cut into 1-inch pieces

2 tablespoons tomato paste

2 cups red wine (use whatever you like to drink)

1 cup low-sodium beef broth

1 (28-ounce) can whole peeled San Marzano tomatoes (I like DeLallo)

4 sprigs fresh thyme, plus more leaves for garnish (optional)

2 bay leaves

1 head garlic

2 tablespoons chopped fresh parsley, plus more for garnish

Parmesan Mashers

1½ pounds Yukon Gold potatoes (6 medium), peeled and cut into 1-inch cubes

4 garlic cloves, smashed

Kosher salt

6 tablespoons (¾ stick) unsalted butter, at room temperature

½ cup heavy cream or whole milk, plus more if needed

½ cup grated Parmesan cheese

Freshly ground pepper

1. MAKE THE LAMB. Preheat the oven to 350°F.

2. Heat a large oven-safe pot with a lid over high. Season the lamb shanks all over with salt and pepper. Sear the lamb until browned, 4 to 5 minutes per side. Remove and set aside on a plate.

3. Reduce the heat to medium and add the olive oil. When it shimmers, add the onion and cook, stirring occasionally, for 5 to 7 minutes, until the onion is translucent. Add the carrots and cook for about 5 minutes, until the edges begin to caramelize. Stir in the tomato paste and cook for another minute or so. Slowly pour in the wine, scraping up the browned bits from the bottom of the pan as you pour. Add the broth, then the tomatoes, crushing them by hand as you add them carefully into the sauce. Stir to combine. Add the lamb shanks, thyme sprigs, and bay leaves. Season the sauce lightly with salt and pepper.

4. Chop off the top portion of the garlic head to reveal the cloves. Peel off any excess papery skin from the bulb, being sure to keep the head of garlic together. Place the garlic in the sauce, but do not submerge it; it should be peeking up out of the sauce. Cover the pot and transfer to the oven. Braise the lamb for 1 hour, then remove the lid and cook for about 30 minutes more, or until the shanks are tender and cooked to your liking. Remove the lamb from the oven and set aside.

(recipe continues)

5. MEANWHILE, MAKE THE MASHERS. Put the potatoes and garlic in a large pot and add cold water to cover. Salt the water and bring to a boil over high heat. Cook until the potatoes are tender, 25 to 30 minutes.

6. In a small saucepan, melt the butter over medium-high heat. Cook until browned, about 5 minutes. Remove the pan from the heat and set aside.

7. Drain the potatoes, then return them to the pot. Add the browned butter and mash the potatoes over low heat. Add the cream and 1 teaspoon of salt as you mash, then stir in the Parmesan. (Alternatively, transfer to the bowl of a stand mixer fitted with the paddle attachment and mash the potatoes for 1 to 2 minutes, until smooth.) Taste and season with more salt and pepper.

8. FINISH THE SAUCE. Remove the roasted garlic head from the lamb sauce and let it cool slightly. Squeeze the cloves into a bowl. Using a fork, finely mash the garlic to create a paste. Stir as much of the roasted garlic paste back into the sauce as you like (I like to use half). Stir in the parsley. Taste the sauce and season with salt and pepper, if needed.

9. To serve, divide the mashed potatoes among four plates. Top each mound of potatoes with a lamb shank. Drizzle the tomato sauce over the shanks and garnish with parsley or thyme.

Korean Beef, Sweet Potato, and Quinoa Bibimbap

Serves: **4**

Bibimbap is one of the most well-known dishes in Korean cuisine. This recipe is my own little healthified, Mexican-Korean fusion version. The Korean chili paste used in bibimbap, called *gochujang*, is quite possibly one of my favorite condiments out there—and that's coming from someone who's not a huge condiment person in general. (Ketchup is a good friend and hot sauce and I get together on a regular basis, but mayo is my worst nightmare and everything else I can take or leave.) I like to swap the white rice for quinoa, add a whole bunch of miso-roasted sweet potatoes, and drizzle the entire bowl with a spicy roasted tomatillo sauce. Whoa, kind of a mouthful, right? I know, I know, but it's a truly delicious mouthful. And despite the longer ingredients list, I think you'll be surprised to find that this is actually a fast and simple dinner to make. Oh, and the leftovers? They make an epic lunch the next day.

Korean Beef

¾ cup low-sodium soy sauce

½ cup rice vinegar

½ cup packed light brown sugar

1 tablespoon gochujang (Korean chili paste; see Note, page 189) or sriracha sauce

1 (1-inch) knob fresh ginger, peeled and grated

2 garlic cloves, minced or grated

2 tablespoons sesame oil

1½ pounds skirt steak

Sweet Potatoes

2 medium sweet potatoes (about 1½ pounds), cut into small cubes

2 tablespoons extra-virgin olive oil

1 to 2 tablespoons white miso paste

Kosher salt and freshly ground pepper

1. **MARINATE THE BEEF.** In a large zip-top bag, combine the soy sauce, vinegar, brown sugar, gochujang, ginger, garlic, and sesame oil. Add the steak, seal the bag, and toss well to coat. Marinate in the fridge for at least 1 hour or up to overnight.

2. **MAKE THE SWEET POTATOES.** Preheat the oven to 425°F.

3. On a rimmed baking sheet, toss the sweet potatoes with the olive oil, miso, and salt and pepper to taste. Arrange in a single layer and bake for 15 to 20 minutes, or until lightly charred and tender.

4. **COOK THE BEEF.** Heat a grill to medium-high or a grill pan over medium-high. When the grill is just smoking, add the steak and cook until your desired doneness is reached, 4 to 5 minutes per side for medium-rare. As the steak cooks, spoon over some of the marinade for extra flavor. Remove the steak from the grill, let rest for at least 10 minutes, then thinly slice into strips.

5. While the steak is resting, pour the remaining marinade into a small saucepan and bring to a boil over high heat. Reduce the heat to low and simmer for about 5 minutes, or until slightly thickened.

(recipe and ingredients continue)

Bibimbap

½ bunch kale, stemmed
and leaves coarsely torn

Juice of ½ lime

Kosher salt

3 cups cooked quinoa

2 carrots, shredded

4 radishes, thinly sliced

1 avocado, sliced

4 fried eggs

Toasted sesame seeds

Microgreens

Spicy Tomatillo Sauce
(recipe follows)

6. MEANWHILE, MAKE THE BIBIMBAP. Put the kale in a large bowl and add the lime juice and a large pinch of salt. Massage with your hands for 1 to 2 minutes, or until the kale has broken down a bit.

7. Divide the quinoa among four bowls and top evenly with the sliced steak and sweet potatoes. Arrange the carrots, radishes, kale, and avocado around the bowl. Add the fried eggs and sprinkle with sesame seeds and microgreens. Serve with the tomatillo sauce drizzled over the top.

SPICY TOMATILLO SAUCE

Serves: 6

6 tomatillos, husked and rinsed well

2 tablespoons gochujang (Korean chili paste; see Note) or sriracha sauce

2 tablespoons low-sodium soy sauce

2 tablespoons rice vinegar

Juice of 1 lime

1. Preheat the broiler to high. Line a baking sheet with parchment paper.

2. Put the tomatillos on the prepared baking sheet and place under the broiler. Broil, turning once or twice, for 3 to 5 minutes, or until the tomatillos are mostly charred. Remove from the oven and let cool slightly.

3. Transfer the charred tomatillos to a blender or food processor and add the gochujang, soy sauce, vinegar, and lime juice. Pulse until smooth. Store in a glass jar in the fridge for up to 1 week.

NOTE

You can find gochujang in the ethnic foods aisle of your grocery store or purchase it online. I always buy Mother-in-Law's brand, which has "good for you" ingredients—nothing weird or scary-sounding, just simple, real-food ingredients.

Steak Fajita and Sweet Potato Fry Salad

Serves: 4

I like my salads big, bright, and loaded with texture. I learned all this from my dad—his wacky salads inspired so many of the loaded salads you'll find throughout this book. Most weeknights when I was growing up, my dad would have salad for dinner, probably because he wasn't interested in the "kid food" he made us. The only consistent things about his salads were the pile of lettuce and half a bottle of blue cheese or ranch dressing (actually, one of my theories is that Dad ate salad every night so he could enjoy all that dressing). He always killed it with the toppings, adding a little of whatever everyone else was eating, or a mix-and-match of leftovers from the fridge. My all-time favorite salad topper of his is french fries. For the longest time, I just thought that was a normal thing to do—I mean, they are a million and one times better than croutons. This Mexican-inspired version of Dad's salad is loaded with bell peppers, avocado, grilled steak, and sweet potato fries and finished with a cilantro vinaigrette. Delish.

Steak

¼ cup extra-virgin olive oil, plus more for cooking

1 teaspoon chili powder

1 teaspoon smoked paprika

½ teaspoon ground cumin

1 teaspoon honey

Zest and juice of 2 limes

Kosher salt and freshly ground pepper

1½ pounds flank steak, cut into 2 or 3 pieces

Fries

2 medium sweet potatoes, cut into ¼-inch-wide strips

1 tablespoon extra-virgin olive oil

Kosher salt and freshly ground pepper

1 red bell pepper, sliced

1 yellow bell pepper, sliced

1 poblano chile pepper, seeded and sliced

Kosher salt and freshly ground pepper

2 heads romaine lettuce, chopped

(ingredients continue, opposite)

1. **MARINATE THE STEAK.** In a large zip-top bag, combine the olive oil, chili powder, paprika, cumin, honey, lime zest and juice, and a large pinch each of salt and pepper. Add the steak and rub in the marinade. Seal the bag and place it in the fridge for at least 1 hour or up to 12 hours to marinate.

2. **MAKE THE FRIES.** Preheat the oven to 425°F.

3. Place the sweet potatoes on a rimmed baking sheet (or two, if needed), making sure to not overcrowd the pan. Drizzle with the olive oil and season with salt and pepper. Gently toss to coat.

4. Bake for 15 minutes, then reduce the oven temperature to 400°F, flip, and bake for 15 minutes more, until crispy.

5. **MEANWHILE, COOK THE STEAK.** In a large cast-iron skillet or grill pan, heat 1 tablespoon of olive oil over medium-high. When it shimmers, add the steak and sear for 3 to 4 minutes, then flip and cook for 4 to 5 minutes more for medium-rare. Remove the steak from the skillet and let it rest on a cutting board for 5 to 10 minutes.

1 mango, pitted, peeled, and sliced (see "How to Peel and Cut a Fresh Mango," page 38)

1 jalapeño, seeded and chopped

⅓ cup fresh cilantro leaves, coarsely chopped

1 or 2 avocados, pitted, peeled, and sliced

½ cup shredded cheddar cheese or crumbled queso fresco

Cilantro-Lime Vinaigrette

¼ cup extra-virgin olive oil

¼ cup fresh lime juice

2 tablespoons chopped fresh cilantro

1 tablespoon honey

½ teaspoon chili powder

Kosher salt and freshly ground pepper

6. Add the peppers and a pinch each of salt and black pepper to the same skillet. Cook for 4 to 5 minutes, until softened, then remove from the heat.

7. MAKE THE SALAD. In a large bowl, toss together the lettuce, mango, jalapeño, and cilantro. Add the avocado (to taste), cooked peppers, and sweet potato fries. Slice the steak across the grain and add it to the salad. Sprinkle with the cheese.

8. MAKE THE VINAIGRETTE. Whisk together the olive oil, lime juice, cilantro, honey, chili powder, and a pinch each of salt and pepper. Taste and add more salt and pepper as needed.

9. Serve the salad with the vinaigrette alongside.

Slow-Cooker Tuscan Beef and White Bean Ragù

Serves: 6

It's no secret that I love a really good cozy meal, whether it's the dead of winter or full-on summer. Gimme a blanket, a roaring wood-burning fireplace, and a bowl filled to the brim with this ragù. How do I love this ragù? Let me count the ways. 1) It's made in the slow cooker, which means easy peasy, lemon squeezy. 2) Short ribs. 3) The rich red wine sauce the short ribs are slowly cooked in—yum and yes, please. 4) The fact that I don't feel guilty about eating this dish . . . hello, very green and healthy kale and protein-filled white beans. 5) All day long it smells like a Tuscan *nonna* has been cooking up a storm in my kitchen. Are you sold yet?

2 (28-ounce) cans whole peeled San Marzano tomatoes (I like DeLallo)

½ sweet onion, finely chopped

4 garlic cloves, minced or grated

½ cup oil-packed sun-dried tomatoes, drained and chopped

2 tablespoons tomato paste

¾ cup red wine

2 teaspoons dried basil

2 teaspoons dried oregano

2 sprigs fresh thyme

1 teaspoon kosher salt, plus more as needed

½ teaspoon freshly ground pepper, plus more for garnish

3 to 4 pounds beef short ribs

1 bunch Tuscan kale, stemmed and leaves coarsely chopped

1 (14-ounce) can white beans, drained and rinsed

1 pound pappardelle or other egg pasta

2 tablespoons salted butter

Handful of fresh basil, chopped, plus more for serving

1 cup basil pesto, store-bought or homemade (page 101)

8 ounces buffalo mozzarella or regular mozzarella, torn into pieces

1. Using your hands, crush the whole tomatoes into a 6- to 8-quart slow cooker. Add the onion, garlic, sun-dried tomatoes, tomato paste, wine, dried basil, oregano, thyme, salt, and pepper. Give everything a good stir. Add the short ribs.

2. Cover the slow cooker and cook on Low for 6 to 8 hours or High for 4 to 5 hours. When the short ribs are falling off the bone, remove them from the sauce and let cool slightly, then shred the meat, discarding the bones.

3. Stir the kale and white beans into the sauce. Crank the heat up to High, cover, and cook for 20 to 30 minutes more. Stir in the shredded meat.

4. Meanwhile, bring a large pot of salted water to a boil over high heat. Add the pasta and cook until al dente according to the package directions. Drain, then return to the pot and toss with the butter and basil.

5. To serve, divide the pasta among six plates or bowls. Top with the ragù and spoon over some pesto. Add a little mozzarella. Garnish with more basil and a sprinkle of pepper.

BBQ Short Ribs

Serves: **4**

When I'm cooking beef, short ribs are my preferred cut. As long as you let them slow cook, they always turn out delicious. I have made many different flavored short ribs—Thai, Korean, Italian, saucy, well-seasoned—but these BBQ short ribs are hands-down the favorite among my family. I think it may have something to do with the classic, feel-good flavors of barbecue, and the tender, juicy meat. The seasoning mix on these ribs is one I have been using for many years. It's the seasoning mix that Mrs. Mooney (yup, Mrs. Mooney from pages 97 and 163) wrote down on a piece of paper years ago, which still sits in my desk drawer, even as I write this. Of course, it's now so stained with barbecue sauce and God knows what else that I can barely read it, but thankfully I have the mix memorized, which tells you just how much I make it! I serve these ribs with a side of rice and grilled corn.

4 to 5 pounds beef short ribs

2 tablespoons honey

1 tablespoon smoked paprika

2 teaspoons chipotle chili powder

1 teaspoon garlic powder

½ teaspoon ground cinnamon

½ teaspoon crushed red pepper flakes

½ teaspoon kosher salt

½ teaspoon freshly ground black pepper

1 (12-ounce) bottle beer (use whatever you like to drink)

3 cups barbecue sauce, store-bought or homemade (recipe follows)

1. Preheat the oven to 325°F.

2. In a large Dutch oven, combine the short ribs, honey, paprika, chili powder, garlic powder, cinnamon, red pepper flakes, salt, and black pepper. Toss well to coat the ribs evenly. Pour in the beer and cover the pot. Transfer to the oven and braise for 2½ to 3 hours, or until the meat shreds easily. Check once or twice while the ribs are cooking to be sure there is enough liquid—add water as needed to keep the ribs submerged about one-third of the way.

3. To serve, leave the ribs on the bone and baste with barbecue sauce, or remove the bones, shred the meat, and toss it with the sauce.

THE SKINNY ON SHORT RIBS

Short ribs can be pricy, so if you're feeling the flavors happening here, but are not into the short ribs, swap in chicken or pork in their place. If you use boneless chicken breasts, I recommend grilling or roasting them in a 375°F oven. If you go the pork route, I would use either pork ribs or a pork butt, but they will need a much longer cooking time, 6 to 8 hours.

MY FAVORITE BBQ SAUCE
Makes: 3 cups

1¼ cups ketchup

1 cup packed dark brown sugar

¼ cup molasses

¼ cup pineapple juice

1 tablespoon Worcestershire sauce

1 tablespoon Dijon mustard, or 2 teaspoons mustard powder

2 teaspoons smoked paprika

½ teaspoon garlic powder

¼ to ½ teaspoon cayenne

1½ teaspoons kosher salt

1 teaspoon freshly ground pepper

Combine all the ingredients in a large bowl with ¼ cup of water and whisk until well combined. Store in a glass jar in the fridge for up to 1 month.

The Down Under Aussie Burger

Serves: **6**

The only way I would eat burgers as a kid was if they were stuffed with blue cheese or loaded with two slices of sharp cheddar. But this burger is different than others, and in the most insane way. In fact, maybe it should be called the insanity burger. It's inspired by the classic burgers of Australia. Over there, they call these "burgers with the lot." Let me break it down for you from bottom to top: toasted bun, spicy special sauce, lettuce, tomato, BBQ beef patty, sharp cheddar cheese, beet pesto, grilled pineapple, fried egg, toasted bun. So . . . these burgers have "a lot" going on and "a lot" of layers of flavor. Don't let this intimidate you. If you're wondering how you'll fit this whopper of a burger into your mouth, I understand your concern, but it happens somehow. It is messy, but one heck of a beautiful, yummy mess.

Spicy Special Sauce

¼ cup ketchup

¼ cup tahini

1 tablespoon sambal oelek

Burgers

2 pounds 80% lean ground beef

¼ cup barbecue sauce, store-bought or homemade (page 195)

1 garlic clove, minced or grated

1 medium-large roasted or canned red beet, chopped

½ cup basil pesto, store-bought or homemade (page 101)

2 tablespoons salted butter

Kosher salt and freshly ground pepper

6 slices sharp white cheddar

½ ripe pineapple, cut into ½-inch rings (see "How to Prep a Pineapple," page 161)

6 burger buns

6 butter or romaine lettuce leaves

2 heirloom tomatoes, sliced

6 fried eggs

1. MAKE THE SPECIAL SAUCE. In a small bowl, whisk together the ketchup, tahini, and sambal oelek. If needed, thin the sauce with water.

2. MAKE THE BURGERS. In a medium bowl, using your hands, combine the beef, barbecue sauce, and garlic until well mixed. Form the mixture into six equal patties and place on a plate. Cover the burgers and place in the fridge for at least 20 minutes or until ready to cook.

3. Meanwhile, in a food processor or blender, pulse the cooked beet and pesto until smooth, adding water 1 tablespoon at a time as needed to thin.

4. In a large skillet, melt 1 tablespoon of the butter over high heat. Working in batches, add the burger patties and season with salt and pepper. Cook for 2 to 3 minutes, flip, add a slice of cheese, and cook for 2 to 3 minutes more for medium-rare.

5. When all the burgers have been cooked, in the same skillet, melt the remaining 1 tablespoon of butter. Add the pineapple slices and cook until caramelized, 2 to 3 minutes per side.

6. To assemble, spread the bottom of each bun with special sauce. Add a lettuce leaf and tomato slices. Top with a burger. Spread with beet pesto and add a slice of pineapple and a fried egg. Season the egg with salt and pepper. Finish with the top bun. Open wide and enjoy!

Fresh Summer Bolognese

Serves: **4 to 6**

For me, cooking in the summer means using the freshest produce I can find and spending no more than an hour in the kitchen. This Bolognese is one of my favorite quick-and-easy summer dinner recipes, and it has won the heart of every person I've ever served it to. To keep it light, I like to use half pasta and half zucchini noodles. The real secret here is topping the sauce with fresh summer cherry tomatoes and all the basil you can get your hands on!

Kosher salt

½ pound dried spaghetti

1 pound lean ground beef or ground chicken

2 garlic cloves, minced or grated

1 (14-ounce) can crushed San Marzano tomatoes (I like DeLallo)

½ cup white wine

⅓ cup sun-dried tomato pesto, store-bought or homemade (recipe follows)

1 roasted red pepper, chopped

Kosher salt and freshly ground black pepper

½ to 1 teaspoon crushed red pepper flakes

1 cup fresh basil, chopped, plus more for serving

½ cup freshly grated Parmesan cheese

2 zucchini, spiralized (see Note)

2 tablespoons extra-virgin olive oil

Zest of 1 lemon

8 ounces burrata or fresh mozzarella cheese

2 cups halved cherry tomatoes

½ cup kalamata olives, pitted

1. Bring a large pot of salted water to a boil over high heat. Add the pasta and cook until al dente according to the package directions. Drain and return to the pot.

2. Meanwhile, heat a large skillet over medium. When the skillet is just smoking, add the ground beef and brown all over, breaking it up as it cooks. Add the garlic and cook for about 1 minute, or until fragrant. Add the tomatoes, wine, pesto, roasted red pepper, and ½ cup of water. Increase the heat to high and bring the sauce to a simmer. Cook for about 10 minutes, or until the sauce has thickened slightly. Season with salt, black pepper, and red pepper flakes to taste. Remove the sauce from the heat and stir in the basil and Parmesan.

3. Toss the hot pasta with the spiralized zucchini, olive oil, and lemon zest.

4. Divide the pasta among four to six bowls and top with the sauce. Break the burrata over the pasta. Add a handful of cherry tomatoes and olives to each. Garnish with basil.

 ## SUN-DRIED TOMATO PESTO

Makes: **About 1½ cups**

1 (8.5-ounce) jar sun-dried tomatoes packed in olive oil

1 cup fresh basil leaves

Juice of 1 lemon

½ cup Parmesan cheese

Kosher salt and freshly ground pepper

In a food processor, combine the sun-dried tomatoes and the oil left in the jar. Add the basil, lemon juice, and Parmesan. Season with salt and pepper to taste. Pulse until the tomatoes are finely chopped. Taste and season with salt and pepper as needed. Transfer the pesto to a jar. Store in the fridge for up to 2 weeks.

NOTE
If you do not have a spiralizer,
you can use a mandoline or a
julienne peeler to cut the zucchini
into ribbons, or thinly slice it
into matchsticks.

Soy-Marinated Flank Steak with Sesame-Herb Roasted Potatoes

Serves: **4**

In my family, the boys (six) outnumber the girls (three). My brothers are guy's guys—they like their meat and potatoes. Well, this recipe contains both, and they like it! Most of us are all grown up and living on our own now, but I make this whenever we do a family dinner. Typically, flank steak is not their favorite cut of meat—they're actually kind of snobby and would prefer beef tenderloin, and, if not that, then a New York strip or rib-eye. But in recent years I have changed their thinking, and this was the recipe that did the convincing. It's all about the soy-and-coffee marinade. It adds a truly amazing flavor to the steak that even the pickiest of eaters love. I prefer to grill my steak, but in a pinch broiling works, too.

Steak

½ cup extra-virgin olive oil

8 garlic cloves, smashed

1 cup low-sodium soy sauce

2 tablespoons freshly ground coffee

2 tablespoons chopped fresh oregano

Zest and juice of 1 lime

2 pounds flank or skirt steak

Sesame-Herb Roasted Potatoes

4 russet potatoes, cut into 1-inch cubes

2 tablespoons sesame oil

2 tablespoons raw sesame seeds

Kosher salt and freshly ground pepper

2 tablespoons chopped fresh oregano

Thai Basil Chimichurri (page 175), for serving

1. **MARINATE THE STEAK.** In a small saucepan, heat the olive oil over medium. When it shimmers, add the garlic and cook until fragrant and lightly caramelized, 8 to 10 minutes. Remove the pan from the heat and stir in the soy sauce, ground coffee, oregano, lemon zest and juice. Let cool for 10 minutes.

2. Put the steak in a large zip-top bag, add the marinade, and toss to coat well. Marinate in the fridge for at least 4 hours or up to overnight. Remove the steak from the fridge 30 minutes prior to grilling.

3. **MAKE THE POTATOES.** Preheat the oven to 425°F.

4. On a rimmed baking sheet, toss the potatoes with the sesame oil, sesame seeds, and salt and pepper to taste. Arrange in a single layer and bake for 15 to 20 minutes, then flip and bake for 15 to 20 minutes more. During the last 5 minutes of cooking, add the oregano and toss well. You want the potatoes to be tender, but crisp on the outside.

5. **MEANWHILE, GRILL THE STEAK.** Heat a grill to high or a grill pan over high. When the grill is just smoking, remove the steak from the marinade and add it to the grill. Pour over some of the marinade and discard the rest. Grill the steak for 3 to 4 minutes per side for medium-rare. Transfer to a cutting board and let rest for 10 minutes.

6. Slice the steak across the grain. Serve with a generous amount of chimichurri and the roasted potatoes alongside.

ABOUT THAT SOY SAUCE

I always prefer using a low-sodium soy sauce to help me better control the salt levels in my recipes. Regular soy sauce is very salty and can ruin dishes if used in large amounts.

Al Pastor–Style Beef Enchiladas

Serves: 6

Believe it or not, I was the ripe old age of nineteen the first time I had an enchilada. Meaning, I went nineteen years without the bliss that is attained when eating a Mexican enchilada. Well, now I'm making up for lost time. Al pastor tacos are pork or beef tacos that have been stewed in a sweet-and-spicy pineapple sauce. I took that concept and turned it into enchiladas. They are, hands-down, my favorite enchiladas. I attribute this fact to the sweet-spicy-savory combo that is beef, pineapple, and cheese.

Extra-virgin olive oil, for greasing

2 garlic cloves

2 tablespoons chili powder

2 teaspoons paprika

2 canned chipotle peppers in adobo

1 cup pineapple juice

¼ cup distilled white vinegar

2 cups fresh pineapple chunks (see "How to Prep a Pineapple," page 161)

1 pound lean ground beef

½ sweet onion, thinly sliced

1 jalapeño, seeded and diced

¼ cup chopped fresh cilantro, plus more for serving

1½ cups shredded sharp cheddar cheese

1½ cups shredded Monterey Jack cheese

1 to 2 cups red enchilada sauce, store-bought or homemade (recipe follows)

12 corn tortillas, warmed

Sliced avocado, for serving

1. Preheat the oven to 350°F. Lightly grease a 9 x 13-inch baking dish with olive oil.

2. In a blender or food processor, combine the garlic, chili powder, paprika, chipotles, pineapple juice, vinegar, and 1 cup of the pineapple chunks. Pulse for 1 to 2 minutes, until completely smooth.

3. In a large skillet, combine the ground beef and onion and cook over medium-high heat, breaking up the beef with a wooden spoon, until browned, 8 to 10 minutes. Reduce the heat to low and add half the pineapple sauce, the remaining 1 cup of pineapple chunks, and the jalapeño. Simmer for 8 to 10 minutes, or until the sauce has reduced and coats the beef. Remove the skillet from the heat and stir in the cilantro and half the shredded cheeses.

4. Pour half the red enchilada sauce into the bottom of the prepared baking dish. Working with one at a time, lay a tortilla flat on your work surface. Spoon ⅓ cup of the pineapple-beef mixture onto the tortilla and roll it up. Place seam-side down in the baking dish. Repeat with the remaining tortillas and filling. Pour over the remaining pineapple sauce and as much of the remaining red enchilada sauce as desired. Sprinkle with the remaining shredded cheeses.

5. Bake for 20 to 25 minutes, or until the cheeses are melted and gooey. Top with fresh cilantro and serve immediately.

(recipe continues)

NOTE

For a vegetarian version, use 1½ to 2 cups of cooked lentils or black beans, adding them to the skillet at the same time you add the last half of the pineapple chunks, and jalapeño.

EASY RED ENCHILADA SAUCE

Makes: **2 cups**

2 tablespoons extra-virgin olive oil or canola oil

2 tablespoons all-purpose flour

2 tablespoons tomato paste

2 tablespoons chili powder

2 canned chipotle peppers in adobo, finely chopped

1 teaspoon ground cumin

½ teaspoon garlic powder

⅛ teaspoon cayenne

¾ teaspoon kosher salt

2 cups low-sodium chicken broth or vegetable broth

1. In a medium saucepan, whisk together the oil and flour over medium heat. Cook for 1 to 2 minutes, or until the mixture is light golden. Stir in the tomato paste, chili powder, chipotles, cumin, garlic powder, cayenne, and salt. Cook for another minute or so, until thick. Slowly pour in the broth and whisk until smooth.

2. Reduce the heat to low and simmer for 10 to 15 minutes, until slightly thickened. Remove the pan from the heat and let cool completely. Store in a glass jar in the fridge for up to 1 month.

Steak Shawarma Bowls

Serves: **4**

Shawarma is the best of Middle Eastern street food. If you are unfamiliar with it, it is thinly sliced cuts of meat (poultry, beef, or lamb) served in or on a pita with a savory yogurt sauce. If you were to get this on the streets of Turkey it would look pretty similar to a Greek gyro, but the meat is seasoned differently and the toppings vary from chef to chef. I like to grill the meat, though slow-roasting is traditional. If you'd like to try it, roast the steak at 325°F for 4 to 6 hours, or until it shreds easily. Fries are an obvious must here. The sweet potato version is not traditional, but are sweet potato fries ever not a good idea? Lastly, never skimp on the feta—and that's life advice.

Steak

1 tablespoon honey

2 teaspoons paprika

2 teaspoons ground cumin

1 teaspoon dried oregano

1 teaspoon kosher salt

½ teaspoon freshly ground black pepper

Juice of 2 lemons

6 garlic cloves, minced or grated

Pinch of crushed red pepper flakes

½ cup extra-virgin olive oil

2 pounds flank steak

Sweet Potato Fries

2 sweet potatoes, cut into matchsticks

2 tablespoons extra-virgin olive oil

Kosher salt and freshly ground black pepper

For Serving

2 cups cooked quinoa

1 to 2 cups baby kale, coarsely chopped or shredded

1 cup halved cherry tomatoes

2 Persian cucumbers, sliced

½ cup kalamata olives, pitted

1 avocado, pitted, peeled, and sliced

8 ounces feta cheese, crumbled

Greek yogurt or tzatziki, store-bought or homemade (page 136)

Hummus (optional; I like roasted red pepper–flavor here)

1. **MARINATE THE STEAK.** In a large zip-top bag, combine the honey, paprika, cumin, oregano, salt, black pepper, lemon juice, garlic, red pepper flakes, and olive oil. Add the steak, seal the bag, and toss to coat well. Marinate in the fridge for at least 1 hour or up to 12 hours.

2. **MAKE THE FRIES.** Preheat the oven to 425°F.

3. On a rimmed baking sheet, toss the sweet potatoes with the olive oil and salt and black pepper to taste. Arrange in a single layer and bake for 15 to 20 minutes, then flip and bake for 15 to 20 minutes more, until tender but still crisp on the outside.

4. **COOK THE STEAK.** Heat a grill to high or a grill pan over high. When the grill is just smoking, add the steak. Pour over some of the marinade and discard the rest. Grill for 3 to 4 minutes per side for medium-rare. Transfer the steak to a cutting board and let it rest for 10 minutes. Slice the steak across the grain.

5. To assemble, add the quinoa, kale, tomatoes, cucumbers, olives, avocado, feta, and steak to bowls, dividing them evenly. Finish with a smear of yogurt and a dollop of hummus (if using).

Miso Beef and Ramen Noodle Peanut Stir-Fry

Serves: 4

I have so many memories of being snuggled up by the fireplace with Mom in our Rocky River, Ohio, house slurping bowls of ramen together after school. Yeah, my mom ate Top Ramen because she was the "cool" mom, and because back then we never looked at what was in the ingredients list. I'd say I feel bad about how much of it we ate, but I don't. Eventually we discovered it wasn't all that amazing for us. A lot has changed since then, but I still have a love for all things ramen. Enter this homemade stir-fry version. Peanutty, colorful, and super quick, this dish could easily become a new, better weeknight staple for a new (healthier) generation!

Stir-Fry Sauce

½ cup low-sodium soy sauce

2 tablespoons honey

1 tablespoon white miso paste

1 (1-inch) knob fresh ginger, peeled and grated

1 tablespoon sambal oelek

Juice of 1 lime

1 teaspoon freshly ground pepper

½ teaspoon ground cinnamon

Stir-Fry

10 ounces ramen noodles (see Note)

2 tablespoons peanut oil or vegetable oil

1 head broccoli, chopped into florets

1 red bell pepper, seeded and sliced

1 orange bell pepper, seeded and sliced

8 ounces button mushrooms, sliced

2 carrots, shredded

1 pound flank steak, thinly sliced across the grain

½ cup roasted peanuts, coarsely chopped

¼ cup chopped fresh cilantro

4 scallions, chopped, for garnish

4 soft-boiled eggs, for serving (optional)

1. MAKE THE STIR-FRY SAUCE. In a medium bowl, whisk together the soy sauce, honey, miso, ginger, sambal oelek, lime juice, pepper, and cinnamon until smooth.

2. MAKE THE STIR-FRY. Bring a large pot of water to a boil over high heat. Add two-thirds of the ramen noodles and cook for about 2 minutes, or until just tender. Drain and set aside.

3. In a large wok or skillet, heat 1 tablespoon of the peanut oil over high heat. When it shimmers, add the broccoli, bell peppers, and mushrooms and cook until just tender and bright. Add a few tablespoons of the stir-fry sauce and cook, stirring occasionally, until the sauce coats the veggies. Add the carrots and toss. Carefully transfer to a plate.

4. Add the remaining tablespoon of peanut oil to the wok. When it shimmers, add the steak and sear until caramelized on one side, about 3 minutes, then toss and cook on the other side for 2 minutes more. Add a few tablespoons of the stir-fry sauce and cook, stirring, until the sauce coats the steak.

5. Crush the remaining raw ramen noodles and add them to the wok along with the peanuts. Toss with the steak and cook for another minute. Return the veggies to the wok and add the cooked ramen noodles. Add the remaining stir-fry sauce and toss everything together. Cook for 2 to 3 minutes, or until the sauce has thickened slightly and coats the noodles. Remove the wok from the heat and stir in the cilantro.

6. Divide the stir-fry among four bowls. Garnish with the scallions. Add a soft-boiled egg to each bowl, if desired.

Sunday Meatballs

Serves: **4 to 6**

My brother Creighton is the most meat-loving human I know. Without a doubt, one of his favorite meals on earth is our nonnie's meat loaf. I kid you not, he talks about this meat loaf ALL THE TIME. Fortunately, I know exactly why it's so dang good. When Nonnie first told me, I was like, "Wait, what?" She takes two pieces of white bread (it has to be white bread), runs the slices under water, wrings the water out, and mixes the damp bread into her meat. At first this sounded so bizarre to me, but thinking about later, it all started to make sense. Moist bread = moist meat loaf = success! I applied this idea to my meatball recipe (swapping the water for milk) and in turn created the yummiest meatballs ever. Thank you to Creighton and Nonnie for helping me create some of the best meatballs ever!

Extra-virgin olive oil

2 slices white bread

½ cup whole milk or water, as needed

1 pound ground beef (see Note)

1 large egg

¼ cup red wine

1 (28-ounce) can whole peeled San Marzano tomatoes (I like DeLallo), crushed with your hands

¼ cup oil-packed sun-dried tomatoes, drained and chopped

½ sweet onion, finely chopped

2 garlic cloves, minced or grated

4 pickled jalapeño slices (optional)

2 teaspoons dried basil

2 teaspoons dried parsley

1 teaspoon dried oregano, plus more for serving (optional)

½ teaspoon dried thyme

½ teaspoon crushed red pepper flakes

Kosher salt and freshly ground black pepper

8 ounces mozzarella cheese, sliced

½ cup cubed provolone cheese

Cooked pasta, for serving

Fresh basil and/or oregano, chopped, for serving

1. Preheat the oven to 450°F. Grease a 9 x 13-inch baking dish with olive oil.

2. Place the bread in a small bowl. Pour over enough milk to moisten the bread and let it soak for 5 to 10 minutes. Gently squeeze out the excess milk, then crumble the dampened bread into a medium bowl.

3. Add the ground beef and egg and mix well with your hands. Grease your hands with a bit of olive oil and roll the meat mixture into ten to twelve 2-tablespoon-size balls. Place the meatballs in the prepared baking dish and bake for about 15 minutes, until the meatballs are crisp on the outside but not yet cooked through on the inside.

4. Meanwhile, in a medium bowl, combine the wine, crushed tomatoes, sun-dried tomatoes, onion, garlic, jalapeño (if using), dried basil, parsley, oregano, thyme, red pepper flakes, and a pinch each of salt and black pepper.

5. Pour the sauce over the meatballs. Cover the pan with aluminum foil and bake for about 25 minutes more, until the meatballs are cooked through. Remove the foil and sprinkle evenly with the cheeses. Return to the oven, uncovered, and bake until the cheeses are melted and golden, about 10 minutes. Serve over your favorite fresh pasta, topped with fresh basil and/or oregano!

Spicy Italian Sausage and Arugula Pizza

Serves: **2 to 3**

I make pizza once a week, and no two pizzas are ever the same. I have made some crazy combos, but this pizza is one you can never go wrong with. My dad made a ton of pizzas when we were growing up, and while I loved them at the time, his cardboardlike store-bought pizza crust has nothing on my easy homemade dough. That may sound harsh, but Dad agrees that nothing beats a fresh crust.

Extra-virgin olive oil

½ pound spicy Italian sausage, casings removed

All-purpose flour, for dusting

½ pound pizza dough, store-bought or homemade (recipe follows), at room temperature

½ cup marinara sauce

1 cup coarsely torn fresh basil, plus more for serving

1 roasted red pepper, sliced

½ cup oil-packed sun-dried tomatoes, drained and chopped

1 pound buffalo mozzarella or smoked mozzarella, torn into pieces

2 handfuls of fresh arugula

½ cup shaved Parmesan cheese

Truffle oil, for drizzling (optional)

Crushed red pepper flakes

1. Preheat the oven to 450°F. Grease a baking sheet with olive oil.

2. In a large skillet, cook the sausage over medium heat, until browned, about 8 minutes. Remove the skillet from the heat.

3. On a lightly floured surface, roll out the dough until it reaches ¼-inch thickness. Transfer to the prepared baking sheet. Spread the marinara sauce over the dough, leaving a 1-inch border, then sprinkle with the basil. Add the sausage, roasted red pepper, and sun-dried tomatoes. Layer the mozzarella on top. Bake for 10 to 15 minutes, or until the cheese is melted and gooey.

4. Sprinkle the pizza with more basil, the arugula, and the Parmesan. Drizzle lightly with truffle oil, if desired, then add a pinch or two of red pepper flakes. Slice and serve.

 PIZZA DOUGH

Makes: **½ pound**

½ cup warm water

1½ teaspoons instant yeast

1 teaspoon honey

1 cup bread flour, plus more for kneading

¼ teaspoon kosher salt

1 tablespoon extra-virgin olive oil

1. In a stand mixer fitted with the dough hook attachment, combine the water, yeast, and honey. Add the flour and salt. Knead with the dough hook for 3 minutes, or until smooth, adding flour as needed until the dough pulls away from the sides of the bowl.

2. Rub a large bowl with olive oil, and transfer the dough to the bowl. Turn to coat dough.

3. Cover the bowl with plastic wrap and let rise in a warm spot for 1 to 2 hours, or until doubled in size. Punch it down, cover it again, and place the bowl in the fridge overnight or up to 3 days, or in the freezer for up to 3 months.

4. Remove the dough from the fridge 3 to 4 hours before baking or from the freezer the night before.

(Mostly)
Meatless Meals

Candied Beet Salad with Pumpkin Seeds, Blue Cheese, and Cranberries

Serves: 6

I only started cooking with beets a year or two ago. For the longest time I wasn't really sure how I felt about them. I had in my head that beets were just not a food that I liked. Well, that all changed the day I saw the most beautiful photograph of red and yellow beets. The second I saw how pretty they could be, I knew I had to give beets a try. I mean, how could I miss out on photographing one of the world's prettiest vegetables? This salad is just the start of my obsession: sweet roasted beets tossed with crunchy, salty seeds, bold blue cheese, and tangy dried cranberries. It's beyond perfect, and so pretty! If you're not a fan of blue cheese, use goat cheese instead.

6 small to medium mixed red and yellow beets, quartered (see "You Got the Beet," opposite)

3 tablespoons extra-virgin olive oil

Kosher salt

½ cup raw pumpkin seeds (pepitas)

½ teaspoon smoked paprika

2 tablespoons butter

¼ cup pure maple syrup

Zest and juice of 1 orange

¼ teaspoon ground cinnamon

¼ teaspoon cayenne

4 cups baby arugula

4 cups watercress

4 ounces crumbled blue cheese

Seeds from 1 pomegranate

½ cup dried cranberries

Balsamic Fig Vinaigrette

⅓ cup extra-virgin olive oil

¼ cup balsamic vinegar

Juice of 1 lemon

1 tablespoon fig preserves

Kosher salt and freshly ground pepper

1. Preheat the oven to 400°F. On a rimmed baking sheet, toss the beets with 2 tablespoons of the olive oil and a good pinch of salt. Spread out the beets in an even layer. Roast for 30 to 35 minutes, or until tender.

2. Meanwhile, in a medium skillet, heat the remaining tablespoon of olive oil over medium. When it shimmers, add the pumpkin seeds and paprika. Toast the seeds for 3 to 5 minutes, until golden and fragrant. Remove from the heat and add a pinch of salt. Set the mixture aside on a plate to cool.

3. In a small saucepan, combine the butter, maple syrup, orange zest and juice, cinnamon, and cayenne. Bring to a boil and cook for 2 minutes, then remove the pan from the heat.

4. When the beets are tender, remove them from the oven, pour over the maple-butter sauce, and toss to coat. Roast for about 10 minutes more, until the beets are beginning to caramelize—watch closely, because the sugar can burn fast. Let cool slightly.

5. In a large bowl, combine the arugula and watercress. Add the roasted beets and pumpkin seeds. Sprinkle with the blue cheese, pomegranate seeds, and cranberries.

6. In a small bowl, whisk together the olive oil, vinegar, lemon juice, fig preserves, and a pinch each of salt and pepper. Taste and adjust seasoning as needed.

7. Serve the salad with the vinaigrette alongside.

YOU GOT THE BEET

I prefer to leave the skins on my beets. I find peeling them to be a
giant, messy pain, and I love the texture the skins have. If you'd like
to peel your beets, though, I recommend doing so after roasting but
before tossing them with the maple-butter sauce. To avoid turning your
hands red, use a paper towel to peel the skins, wear disposable gloves,
or peel them under running water. If they do turn red and you can't get
the color off your hands, try scrubbing with kosher salt.

Thai Butternut Squash and Peanut Soup

Serves: 4

This soup is Thai-inspired, with lime, ginger, and peanut swirled through it. The butternut squash keeps the soup sweet and creamy, while the roasted peanuts add crunch. A heaping pile of coconut rice on top is a must—what's soup without starchy goodness to accompany it? Thai rice noodles would be equally delicious in place of the coconut rice. Oh, and the slices of fresh ripe mango? Just trust me on this.

Coconut Rice

1 cup canned full-fat coconut milk

1 cup uncooked jasmine or black rice

½ teaspoon kosher salt

3 tablespoons unsweetened flaked coconut

Soup

1 tablespoon extra-virgin olive oil

2 garlic cloves, minced or grated

1 (1-inch) knob fresh ginger, peeled and grated

1 stalk lemongrass, tender white inner core only, minced

2 scallions, chopped

3½ cups low-sodium chicken broth or vegetable broth

3 cups cubed butternut squash

⅓ cup creamy peanut butter

2 to 3 tablespoons Thai red curry paste

1 tablespoon fish sauce

1 (14-ounce) can full-fat coconut milk

Juice of 1 lime

2 cups baby kale

4 ounces shiitake mushrooms

¼ cup chopped fresh cilantro

¼ cup chopped fresh basil

1 ripe mango, pitted, peeled, and sliced or chopped (see "How to Peel and Cut a Fresh Mango," page 38), for garnish

⅓ cup chopped roasted peanuts, for garnish

Fresh mint, Thai basil, and/or sliced Fresno chiles, for garnish

1. **MAKE THE COCONUT RICE.** Combine the coconut milk and 1 cup of water in a medium pot over medium heat. Bring to a boil, then add the rice, salt, and coconut flakes. Stir to combine, then cover and reduce the heat to low. Cook for 30 to 40 minutes, until the liquid has been absorbed. Remove the lid and fluff the rice with a fork.

2. **MEANWHILE, MAKE THE SOUP.** In a large stockpot, heat the olive oil over medium. When it shimmers, add the garlic, ginger, lemongrass, and scallions. Cook for about 1 minute, until fragrant, being sure the garlic doesn't burn. Slowly add the broth and the squash. Bring the soup to a boil, then cover and simmer for 15 to 20 minutes, or until the squash is fork-tender. Remove from the heat and let the soup cool slightly.

3. Carefully transfer the soup to a blender or food processor, working in batches, if necessary, and blend until completely smooth. Return the soup to the pot over medium heat. Add the peanut butter, curry paste, fish sauce, coconut milk, and lime juice and stir to combine. When the soup is smooth and creamy, add the kale and mushrooms and cook until the mushrooms are hydrated and tender, 8 to 10 minutes.

4. Remove the pot from the heat and stir in the cilantro and basil. Divide the soup among four bowls and add a scoop of coconut rice to each. Garnish with mango, then add chopped peanuts, fresh mint, Thai basil, and/or a few slices of chile.

Harissa Veggie Burgers

Serves: **6**

One summer, I spent many days and nights babysitting my little cousin Khaden. Whenever I was at his house for lunch or dinner, we ate frozen veggie burgers. Fast-forward a few years and one blog later to when I started making my own version of a veggie burger. The day I tested my first one was also the day I vowed to never eat a dry, flavorless, frozen veggie patty again. I've since made a bunch of veggie burger versions. There have been extra-cheesy and buffalo-flavored variations, some topped with crunchy sweet potatoes, and even one with zucchini. These harissa veggie burgers are perfection, and totally unique. Hello, tahini peanut sauce, spicy quinoa patties, veggie slaw, and a fried egg (obviously).

Burgers

1 cup cooked quinoa

1 (14-ounce) can cannellini beans, drained, rinsed, and mashed until smooth

1 cup sunflower seeds, toasted

½ cup panko bread crumbs

1 large or 2 small carrots, grated

1 large egg

1½ tablespoons harissa

2 ounces goat cheese

½ teaspoon smoked paprika

½ teaspoon kosher salt

½ teaspoon freshly ground pepper

3 tablespoons extra-virgin olive oil

Tahini Peanut Sauce

2 tablespoons tahini

2 tablespoons creamy peanut butter

1 teaspoon pure maple syrup

1 tablespoon fresh lemon juice

1 teaspoon low-sodium soy sauce

1 or 2 canned chipotle peppers in adobo, finely chopped

For Serving

6 pitas or fresh naan, warmed

Sliced avocado

6 fried eggs (optional)

Goat cheese

Arugula, baby kale, or microgreens

1. **MAKE THE BURGERS.** In a large bowl, combine the quinoa, cannellini beans, sunflower seeds, bread crumbs, carrots, egg, harissa, goat cheese, paprika, salt, and pepper. Mix well using your hands, then form into 6 patties, each using about ¼ cup of the mixture.

2. In a large skillet, heat the olive oil over medium. When it shimmers, add the patties, working in batches, and cook until golden and crisp on the bottom, about 5 minutes. Carefully flip and cook on the other side for 3 to 5 minutes, until golden and crisp.

3. **MAKE THE PEANUT SAUCE.** In a blender or food processor, combine the tahini, peanut butter, maple syrup, lemon juice, soy sauce, and chipotles to taste and pulse until smooth. Add water 1 tablespoon at a time until the sauce is thin enough to be drizzled.

4. To assemble, spread some of the tahini peanut sauce inside or on top of each warmed pita. Stuff a burger inside each pita (or just place on top). Top with sliced avocado, a fried egg (if using), goat cheese, and greens. Serve with the extra tahini sauce alongside.

NOTE
*To make these burgers vegan,
omit the egg and goat cheese
from the patty mixture and use
1 tablespoon of water
and 1 tablespoon of tahini
instead.*

NOTE

The crunchy apple and pomegranate salsa that goes with this dish is one of my favorites to make in the fall. It's great not only on these tacos, but also on salads or with chips. If apples and pomegranates aren't in season, I recommend using the mango salsa (page 83) or the pineapple salsa (page 82). Never enough salsa!

Chipotle-Roasted Sweet Potato and Quinoa Tacos

Serves: **4 to 6**

I went through a phase of trying to healthify all the food my family was eating, and during that phase, came up with the idea to swap the meat in our tacos for quinoa. Of course, I did this in the sneakiest of ways—if my brothers knew their tacos were not filled with meaty things, they'd freak. I pulled it off by preparing everyone's tacos for them, covering the tops with lots of cheese so that they couldn't see what was going on underneath. Later, after a good two days of everyone eating leftover quinoa tacos for lunch (and loving every bite), I finally told Creighton, my oldest brother and the biggest carnivore of the family, what was up. I kid you not, he LOST it. Now he finally admits that he loved them, and I've turned the rest of my family on to these epic quinoa tacos.

1 large sweet potato, chopped

4 tablespoons extra-virgin olive oil

2 canned chipotle peppers in adobo, chopped

Kosher salt and freshly ground pepper

1 cup uncooked quinoa

2 teaspoons chili powder

2 teaspoons smoked paprika

1 teaspoon ground cumin

½ teaspoon garlic powder

¼ teaspoon cayenne

1 (12-ounce) bottle beer (I like to use pumpkin or apple beer)

1 cup cooked black beans

½ cup shredded sharp cheddar cheese, plus more for serving

Handful of fresh cilantro, chopped

Juice of 1 lime

Corn or flour tortillas, warmed, for serving

Crumbled cotija cheese, for serving

Sliced avocado, for serving

Honeycrisp Apple and Pomegranate Salsa, (page 83), for serving

1. Preheat the oven to 425°F.

2. On a rimmed baking sheet, toss the sweet potatoes with 2 tablespoons of the olive oil, the chipotles, and salt and pepper to taste. Arrange in a single layer and bake for 15 to 20 minutes. Flip and bake for about 10 minutes more, until tender.

3. Meanwhile, in a large skillet, heat the remaining 2 tablespoons of olive oil over medium. When it shimmers, add the quinoa, chili powder, paprika, cumin, garlic powder, and cayenne. Stir to combine, then cook for 3 to 5 minutes, or until the quinoa is toasted. Slowly pour in the beer and ¾ cup of water. Cover and cook over low heat for about 20 minutes, until the quinoa is tender. Remove the lid and cook until all the liquid has been absorbed by the quinoa, 5 to 10 minutes more.

4. Stir in the roasted sweet potatoes, black beans, and cheddar cheese. Cook for about 5 minutes, until the cheese has melted. Remove from the heat and stir in the cilantro and lime juice.

5. Divide the quinoa among warmed tortillas and top with shredded cheddar, cotija cheese, sliced avocado, and the salsa.

15-Minute Thin-Crust Zucchini and Roasted Corn Pizza

Makes: **Two 8-inch pizzas**

Could there be anything more brilliant (or dangerous?) than a pizza that's ready in less than 15 minutes? I think not. This pizza was born on a July day out of hunger and the existing contents of my fridge. Typically, toward the end of the week, I have random veggies, hunks of cheese, and sauces left over from photo shoots, and that is how this came to be. I didn't have any of my pizza dough on hand, so I did what I do best and improvised with what I had. I put a bunch of random cheeses, veggies, and herbs on a flour tortilla, crisped it in a hot cast-iron skillet, finished cooking it in the oven, and called it a day. At the very first bite, I knew I had to share this pizza. The crispness was that of perfect thin-crust pizza, and the combo of provolone, Brie, and sweet chipotle honey was something made in cheese pizza heaven. Don't be afraid to come up with your own topping combos and have a little fun. As long as you have a tortilla, olive oil, and good cheese, you'll be making one killer pizza.

Extra-virgin olive oil

2 (8-inch) flour tortillas

⅓ cup chopped mixed fresh herbs (I like basil, oregano, and parsley)

2 cups shredded provolone cheese

2 small zucchini, thinly sliced

1 ear corn, kernels sliced from the cob (about 1 cup)

Kosher salt and freshly ground black pepper

4 ounces Brie cheese, cut into small wedges (rind on)

½ cup packed fresh basil leaves

Crushed red pepper flakes

Chipotle Honey (recipe follows)

1. Preheat the broiler to high with a rack in the top third.

2. In a large oven-safe skillet, heat a drizzle of olive oil over high. When it shimmers, add one tortilla to the skillet. Sprinkle with half the fresh herbs. Add half the shredded provolone cheese. Finish with half the zucchini and corn. Season the veggies lightly with salt and black pepper. Remove the skillet from the heat and add half the Brie wedges.

3. Transfer the skillet to the oven and broil for 1 to 2 minutes, or until the cheeses are melted and bubbling— watch closely, as this will cook fast! Remove from the broiler and carefully slide the pizza onto a plate. Tent with aluminum foil to keep warm.

4. Repeat to make a second pizza.

5. Top the broiled pizzas with fresh basil, red pepper flakes, and a drizzle of chipotle honey.

CHIPOTLE HONEY

Makes: **Just over ¼ cup**

¼ cup honey

2 canned chipotle peppers in adobo, chopped

Mix together the honey and chipotles in a glass jar. Store in a cool place for up to 1 month.

NOTE

If Taleggio is not available,
try using a soft Brie or a
white cheddar. You can really
use any cheese you have on
hand or love.

Perfect Potato Soup with Crunchy Kale

Serves: 4

Potatoes are pretty perfect. My grandpa has been saying for as long as I can remember: "Did you know the potato is the only food man can actually survive on alone?" Well, he's almost right—you would need to add a pat of butter or wash it down with a glass of milk, but then you'd be good to go. Potatoes are rich with every vital nutrient except calcium, vitamin A, and vitamin D (who knew?). So not only does this soup taste amazing, but between the potatoes, kale, porcinis, and cheese, you might just be able to call this Perfect Soup. It has all the major nutrients in one bowl, and it is delicious!

1 bunch curly kale, stemmed and leaves coarsely torn

2 tablespoons extra-virgin olive oil

2 tablespoons grated Parmesan cheese

¼ teaspoon kosher salt, plus more as needed

¼ teaspoon freshly ground pepper, plus more as needed

4 tablespoons (½ stick) unsalted butter

6 garlic cloves

2 cups low-sodium chicken broth or vegetable broth

6 Yukon Gold potatoes, peeled and diced

2 tablespoons chopped fresh thyme

6 ounces Taleggio cheese, cut into cubes

Porcini Oil (recipe follows)

1. Preheat the oven to 350°F.

2. In a large bowl, combine the kale, olive oil, Parmesan, salt, and pepper. Toss to coat. Using your hands, massage the kale for about 1 minute to soften. Spread onto a baking sheet and bake for 15 to 18 minutes, tossing once or twice during cooking, until crispy. Remove and set aside.

3. Meanwhile, in a large soup pot, melt the butter over medium-low heat. Add the garlic and cook, stirring often, until caramelized and golden, about 10 minutes. Slowly pour in the broth and 2½ cups of water. Add the potatoes and season with salt and pepper. Increase the heat to high and bring to a simmer. Cook for 15 to 20 minutes, or until the potatoes are fork-tender.

4. Remove the pot from the heat and let cool slightly. Transfer the soup to a blender or food processor and pulse until smooth. Return the soup to the pot and add the thyme and Taleggio. Stir until the cheese is melted and heated through.

5. Divide the soup among four bowls and top with the crunchy kale. Drizzle each bowl with porcini oil.

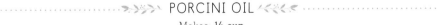

PORCINI OIL

Makes: ½ cup

½ ounce dried porcini mushrooms

½ cup extra-virgin olive oil

1. In a small saucepan, combine the mushrooms and olive oil. Bring to a gentle simmer over medium heat, then reduce the heat to low and cook for 15 minutes.

2. Pour the oil through a fine-mesh strainer and discard the mushrooms. Transfer to a glass jar and store in the fridge for up to 1 month.

Thai Coconut Veggie Curry with Crunchy Chickpeas

Serves: **4**

You can make this curry with any vegetables you have on hand, or even add chicken, beef, or seafood if you like, but the three super-important ingredients here are canned coconut milk (I highly recommend full-fat), Thai red curry paste, and fresh ginger. Honestly, if you have just those three ingredients, you can make a killer curry, and it's going to be totally healthy. It helps, of course, if you serve your curry over a bed of rice and top it with fresh ripe mango, with naan for dipping. Perfection in a bowl, I say. Oh, and about those crunchy chickpeas? They are just addicting. I could snack on these salty, crispy nuggets of goodness all day long. They're like a super-healthy potato chip, but with lots of protein and healthy fat. You can bake them ahead of time and then add them to the curry before serving.

Crunchy Chickpeas

1 (15-ounce) can chickpeas, drained and rinsed

1 cup raw peanuts and/or cashews

3 tablespoons extra-virgin olive oil

1 tablespoon honey

Cayenne

Kosher salt

Curry

2 tablespoons coconut oil

2 red bell peppers, sliced

2 or 3 carrots, chopped

1 cup broccoli florets

2 garlic cloves, minced or grated

1 tablespoon grated fresh ginger

1 tablespoon finely chopped fresh lemongrass (use only the pale inner core)

2 or 3 tablespoons Thai red curry paste

1 (14-ounce) can full-fat coconut milk

2 tablespoons fish sauce

1 tablespoon low-sodium soy sauce

1 tablespoon sambal oelek

½ cup chopped fresh cilantro or basil

Zest and juice of 1 lime

For Serving

Cooked rice

1 mango, diced, (see "How to Peel and Cut a Fresh Mango," page 38)

Seeds from 1 pomegranate

Fresh naan

1. **MAKE THE CHICKPEAS.** Preheat the oven to 425°F.

2. Spread the chickpeas out on a dish towel and pat them as dry as possible. Transfer to a rimmed baking sheet and toss with the nuts, olive oil, honey, and cayenne and salt to taste. Arrange in a single layer and roast for about 30 minutes, tossing halfway through, until browned and crunchy.

3. **MEANWHILE, MAKE THE CURRY.** Melt the coconut oil in a large saucepan over medium heat. Add the bell peppers, carrots (to taste), and broccoli and cook for 2 to 3 minutes, or until lightly charred on the edges. Add the garlic, ginger, lemongrass, and curry paste (to taste) and cook for 1 to 2 minutes, until fragrant.

4. Slowly pour in the coconut milk and 1 cup of water. Add the fish sauce, soy sauce, and sambal oelek. Stir to combine and then increase the heat to high and bring the mixture to a boil. Reduce the heat to low, cover, and simmer for 15 to 20 minutes, or until the curry has thickened slightly. Remove from the heat, then stir in the cilantro or basil, lime zest, and lime juice. If the curry is thick, add water, 1 tablespoon at a time, until the desired consistency is reached.

5. Ladle the curry over bowls of rice. Top with mango, pomegranate seeds, and crunchy chickpeas.

Broccoli, Cheddar, and Butternut Squash Galette

Serves: **4**

If you've yet to experience a savory galette, I am so excited to be the one to introduce you to it. How could the combo of broccoli and cheddar and flaky pastry dough not be good? What I love most about galettes (I mean aside from their buttery deliciousness) is that you don't have to worry about making them look perfect. Galettes are supposed to be rustic and free-formed, meaning mess-ups are okay. So don't worry—just enjoy!

2 tablespoons extra-virgin olive oil

½ sweet onion, finely chopped

2 cups cubed peeled butternut squash

1 head broccoli, cut into florets

2 garlic cloves, finely chopped or grated

1 tablespoon chopped fresh sage

1 tablespoon chopped fresh thyme

Kosher salt and freshly ground pepper

All-purpose flour, for dusting

1 sheet frozen puff pastry, thawed

1½ cups shredded cheddar cheese

1 large egg, beaten

½ cup grated Manchego cheese

Fresh thyme sprigs, for garnish

Flaky sea salt, for garnish

1. Preheat the oven to 375°F. Line a baking sheet with parchment paper.

2. In a large skillet, heat the olive oil over medium-high. When it shimmers, add the onion, squash, and cook, stirring often, until the squash has softened slightly, about 5 minutes. Stir in the broccoli and cook until the squash is fork-tender (but not mushy), about 10 minutes. Stir in the garlic, sage, and thyme. Cook for 30 seconds more, then season with kosher salt and pepper. Remove the skillet from the heat and set aside to cool slightly.

3. Flour your work surface and roll out the puff pastry to a 16 x 14-inch rectangle, about ⅛-inch thick. Transfer to the prepared baking sheet. Leaving a 3-inch border around the edges, sprinkle the dough with half the cheddar cheese, then add the broccoli and butternut squash mixture. Sprinkle with the remaining cheddar. Fold the edges of the dough over the filling. Brush the crust with the beaten egg and then sprinkle with the Manchego.

4. Bake for 45 to 55 minutes, or until the crust is golden. Let cool for 5 minutes, then slice and serve topped with fresh thyme and flaky sea salt.

Crispy Buffalo Quinoa Bites

Serves: 4

If there's one thing that my family loves as a united front, it's anything covered in buffalo sauce. There was a time, when I first started cooking, when I would make baked buffalo chicken bites for my family at least once a week. Actually, for a while, I was making buffalo-flavored everything. I have since found other flavors to play with, but these crispy bites made of quinoa and cannellini beans have remained a staple recipe for me. Dad and I agree that these are actually better than real-deal buffalo chicken bites, although he'll tell you that anything covered in my buffalo sauce is going to be good.

This recipe is great when all rolled up in naan, or equally great when served as a big salad in a bowl. They also make excellent game day appetizers, holiday party snacks, or toppings for a bowl of pasta!

Quinoa Bites

2 cups cooked quinoa

1 (15-ounce) can cannellini beans, drained and rinsed

½ cup panko bread crumbs

1 large egg

½ teaspoon kosher salt

½ teaspoon freshly ground pepper

Extra-virgin olive oil

1 cup buffalo sauce, store-bought or homemade (recipe follows)

Blue Cheese Yogurt

½ cup plain Greek yogurt

¼ cup buttermilk

1 tablespoon fresh lemon juice

1 tablespoon chopped fresh chives

Kosher salt and freshly ground pepper

2 to 4 ounces blue cheese, crumbled

For Serving

4 pieces fresh naan or other flatbread

1 or 2 heads romaine lettuce, chopped

4 carrots, shredded

2 celery stalks, sliced or shredded

1 cup cherry tomatoes, halved

1 avocado, sliced

⅓ cup fresh cilantro leaves, coarsely chopped

1. **MAKE THE QUINOA BITES.** Preheat the oven to 425°F. Line a baking sheet with parchment paper.

2. In a high-speed blender or food processor, combine the quinoa and cannellini beans and pulse until finely ground, about 3 minutes. Add the bread crumbs, egg, salt, and pepper. Pulse again until combined.

3. Using your hands, roll the mixture into balls a little smaller than a golf ball. Place the bites on the prepared baking sheet and brush the tops lightly with olive oil. Bake for 20 to 25 minutes, turning halfway through, until crisp. Let cool slightly, then gently toss in the buffalo sauce.

4. **MAKE THE YOGURT.** In a medium bowl, stir together the yogurt, buttermilk, lemon juice, chives, and salt and pepper to taste. Add the blue cheese and stir again. Taste and season with salt and pepper as needed.

5. To assemble, spread each piece of naan with blue cheese yogurt. Top with the lettuce, carrots, celery, tomatoes, avocado, and buffalo bites. Garnish with cilantro and an extra drizzle of buffalo sauce.

THE BEST BUFFALO SAUCE

Makes: ½ cup

2 tablespoons salted
butter, melted

2 tablespoons extra-virgin
olive oil

¼ cup hot sauce
(I like Frank's)

½ teaspoon seasoned salt

Stir together all the ingredients in a medium bowl. Store
in a glass jar in the fridge for up to 1 month. Warm in the
microwave before serving to liquefy the sauce.

NOTE

*You may not need all
the dressing, so use more
or less to your liking.*

Rainbow Veggie Pad Thai

Serves: 4 to 6

My version of pad thai is not crazy traditional, but it is delicious, colorful, and oh so healthy! While the base of my dish is noodles, I also use a mix of zucchini, beets, bell peppers, and carrots to really achieve that rainbow color. Fair warning: If you use a red beet, you are going to change the color of your noodles to one of the prettiest shades of pinkish-red you will ever see. It is the ultimate and instant mood booster. The sauce is the part that is not all that traditional—because it's soy-based, it's not as sweet as what you may have tasted before. That's why the mango and coconut are key to balancing out the saltiness.

8 ounces thick-cut rice noodles

5 tablespoons sesame oil

1 zucchini, thinly sliced or spiralized (see Note, page 199)

1 small red or yellow beet, thinly sliced or spiralized (see Note, page 199)

1 red or orange bell pepper, cut into matchsticks or spiralized (see Note, page 199)

1 mango, pitted, peeled, and cut into matchsticks (see "How to Peel and Cut a Fresh Mango," page 38)

2 cups coarsely chopped basil

¼ cup low-sodium soy sauce

2 tablespoons rice vinegar

2 tablespoons fish sauce (optional)

1 tablespoon honey

2 teaspoons grated fresh ginger

2 teaspoons sambal oelek or sriracha

Juice of 2 limes

¼ cup chopped fresh basil or cilantro

Soy-Toasted Coconut (recipe follows), for serving

4 to 6 soft- or hard-boiled or fried eggs, for serving

1. Bring a large pot of water to a boil over high heat. Add the rice noodles and cook until softened according to the package directions.

2. In a large skillet, heat 1 tablespoon of the sesame oil over medium-high. When it shimmers, add the zucchini, beet, and bell pepper. Cook for 2 to 3 minutes, or until tender-crisp, being careful not to overcook. Add the cooked rice noodles and cook for about 1 minute, until heated through. Remove the skillet from the heat and stir in the mango and basil.

3. In a small bowl, combine the remaining 4 tablespoons of sesame oil, the soy sauce, vinegar, fish sauce (if using), honey, ginger, sambal oelek, lime juice, and cilantro. Mix well, then pour the dressing over the pad thai (see Note). Toss well to coat.

4. Divide the pad thai among four to six plates and top each with the toasted coconut and an egg.

❯❯❯❯ SOY-TOASTED COCONUT ❮❮❮❮

Makes: 2¼ cups

1¼ cups unsweetened flaked coconut

1 cup raw peanuts or cashews

1 tablespoon coconut oil or extra-virgin olive oil

1 tablespoon honey

1 tablespoon low-sodium soy sauce

1. Preheat the oven to 425°F.

2. On a rimmed baking sheet, toss the coconut and nuts with the oil, honey, and soy sauce. Arrange them in a single layer, transfer to the oven, and roast for about 20 minutes, tossing halfway through, until the coconut is lightly toasted and crunchy. Let cool completely before transferring to an airtight container. Store at room temperature for up to 1 month.

Braised Mediterranean Lentils with Roasted Spaghetti Squash

Serves: 4

Lentils are one of my favorite foods. I love cooking them in a mix of Mediterranean spices and veggies for ample flavor, then serving them over a big bowl of roasted spaghetti squash. When spaghetti squash is at its best, in the fall and winter months, I love subbing it in for pasta. I adore its sweet, buttery flavor. Any leftover lentils are great warm or cold over a salad.

Spaghetti Squash

1 spaghetti squash, halved and seeds removed (see "Spaghetti Squash 101," opposite)

2 tablespoons extra-virgin olive oil

Kosher salt and freshly ground black pepper

6 rainbow or regular carrots, cut into 2-inch pieces

2 tablespoons honey

2 tablespoons chopped fresh thyme

Braised Lentils

2 tablespoons extra-virgin olive oil

½ sweet onion, finely chopped

2 garlic cloves, finely chopped or grated

1 tablespoon chopped fresh thyme

¾ cup green lentils

2 cups low-sodium vegetable broth

½ cup chopped fresh basil

½ cup pitted green and/or kalamata olives, chopped

1 (6-ounce) jar marinated artichoke hearts, drained

¼ cup pine nuts, toasted

Pinch of crushed red pepper flakes

Kosher salt and freshly ground black pepper

For Serving

1 cup cherry tomatoes, halved

4 ounces feta cheese, crumbled

1. MAKE THE SQUASH. Preheat the oven to 400°F.

2. Brush the cut sides of the squash with 1 tablespoon of the olive oil and season with salt and black pepper. Place cut-side up on a baking sheet and bake for 30 to 45 minutes, or until the squash is tender.

3. Meanwhile, on a separate rimmed baking sheet, toss the carrots with the remaining tablespoon of olive oil, the honey, thyme, and salt and black pepper to taste. Transfer to the oven and roast with the squash for 25 to 30 minutes, or until lightly charred and tender.

4. WHILE THE VEGGIES ROAST, MAKE THE LENTILS. In a large skillet, heat the olive oil over medium. When it shimmers, add the onion and cook until lightly charred and caramelized, 8 to 10 minutes. Add the garlic and thyme and cook for about 30 seconds, until fragrant. Add the lentils and toss to coat. Pour in the broth and stir to combine. Increase the heat to high and bring the mixture to a boil. Reduce the heat to low, cover, and simmer for 25 to 30 minutes, or until the lentils are tender. Stir in the basil, olives, artichokes, pine nuts, and red pepper flakes. Season with salt and black pepper and cook until warmed through, about 5 minutes.

5. Using a fork, scrape the roasted spaghetti squash into strands and divide among four plates or bowls. Add the roasted carrots and top with the braised lentils. Finish with the tomatoes and feta.

SPAGHETTI SQUASH 101

If cutting your squash in half proves too difficult, place the whole thing in the microwave and cook on high for 3 to 5 minutes to soften, then try again.

Spaghetti squash strands are arranged in a circular formation around the interior. Cutting the squash lengthwise results in shorter strands, while cutting crosswise keeps the whole strand intact. Both methods work equally well.

I prefer roasting my spaghetti squash in the oven, but sometimes time doesn't allow. Once you halve the squash and remove the seeds, microwave it on high for 10 to 15 minutes. Check for doneness after about 8 minutes, and every 2 minutes thereafter.

Creamy Curried Cauliflower and Goat Cheese Soup

Serves: 4

When it comes to soups, I like mine hearty, full of fun texture, and with lots of cheese (of course). This soup is no exception. It's super creamy thanks to the pureed cauliflower, coconut milk, and goat cheese. These tangy ingredients perfectly balance the spicy curry, creating the most incredible flavor.

1 large or 2 small heads cauliflower, cut into florets

6 garlic cloves, unpeeled

4 tablespoons extra-virgin olive oil

Kosher salt and freshly ground pepper

1 small sweet onion, chopped

1 tablespoon grated fresh ginger

2 to 3 tablespoons Thai red curry paste

1 teaspoon smoked paprika

½ teaspoon ground cinnamon

¼ to ½ teaspoon cayenne

1 (14-ounce) can full-fat coconut milk

3 to 4 cups low-sodium vegetable broth

4 ounces goat cheese, crumbled, plus more for topping

Juice of 1 lemon

3 tablespoons raw pumpkin seeds (pepitas)

3 tablespoons raw pistachios

2 tablespoons raw sesame seeds

1 teaspoon chili powder

Seeds from 1 pomegranate

Fresh cilantro

Fresh Thai basil

1. Preheat the oven to 425°F.

2. Arrange the cauliflower and garlic cloves on a rimmed baking sheet and toss with 2 tablespoons of the olive oil and a good pinch each of salt and pepper. Roast, tossing halfway through, for 20 to 25 minutes, or until the cauliflower is lightly golden and charred.

3. Meanwhile, in a large pot, heat 1 tablespoon of olive oil over medium. When it shimmers, add the onion and cook until fragrant and beginning to caramelize, about 8 minutes. Stir in the ginger, curry paste, paprika, cinnamon, and cayenne. Cook for about a minute more, until fragrant. Slowly pour in the coconut milk and 1 cup of broth. Cover and let simmer until the cauliflower and garlic are ready.

4. Remove the pot from the heat and let the mixture cool slightly. Transfer to a high-speed blender or food processor and add all but a ½ cup of the cauliflower. Squeeze the roasted garlic cloves out of their skins and add them all to the soup. Pulse until completely smooth and creamy.

5. Return the soup to the pot and add 2 cups of broth, or more as needed, until the desired consistency is reached. Simmer over medium heat until warmed through, about 15 minutes. Stir in the goat cheese until melted. Add the lemon juice and season the soup with salt and pepper.

6. Meanwhile, place a large skillet over medium heat. Add the pumpkin seeds, pistachios, sesame seeds, the remaining tablespoon of olive oil, the chili powder, and ½ teaspoon of salt and stir to combine. Cook, stirring, until the seeds are toasted, 5 to 7 minutes. Transfer the mixture to a plate.

7. Ladle the soup into bowls. Top with the toasted nuts and seeds, pomegranate seeds, cilantro, and Thai basil. Sprinkle with goat cheese and the remaining ½ cup of cauliflower.

Irish French Onion Soup

Serves: 4

I'm really not someone who loves onions—I actually use them rather sparingly in my cooking—but caramelized onions are a completely different story. I could put them in and on pretty much anything, and I guess that's why I love French onion soup. It's a rich, decadent, and cozy soup. I took the classic and put my own little Irish twist on it using Guinness beer and Irish soda bread. Even my mother (who hates onions) loves this soup, although I think she may just eat it for that cheesy bread on top. This is a great soup to make in advance and rewarm on the stove before serving. The longer it sits, the more flavor it develops!

6 tablespoons (¾ stick) salted butter, cubed

4 sweet onions, thinly sliced

2 garlic cloves, minced or grated

1 tablespoon light brown sugar

1½ cups Guinness stout

3 tablespoons all-purpose flour

2 quarts low-sodium beef broth

1 tablespoon Worcestershire sauce

2 bay leaves

3 or 4 sprigs fresh thyme, plus more leaves for garnish

Kosher salt

Pinch of freshly ground pepper

4 slices Irish soda bread

2 cups shredded sharp cheddar cheese

1. Preheat the broiler to high with a rack in the top third.

2. In a large pot, melt the butter over medium-high heat. Add the onions, garlic, and brown sugar and cook, stirring frequently, for about 10 minutes, until softened. Cook for 10 minutes more, stirring slightly less often, until the onions are deep golden in color and caramelized. Add ½ cup of the beer, letting it cook into the onions until the beer has evaporated, about 5 minutes.

3. Reduce the heat to low and sprinkle the flour over the onions, stirring to coat. Cook for about 5 minutes, until the raw flour taste has cooked off. Add the remaining cup of beer, the broth, Worcestershire, bay leaves, and thyme.

4. Increase the heat to medium-high and return the soup to a simmer. Cook until warmed through, about 10 minutes. Season with salt and pepper.

5. Meanwhile, arrange the soda bread slices on a baking sheet in a single layer. Sprinkle evenly with the cheddar and broil until the cheese is bubbling and golden brown, 3 to 5 minutes.

6. Remove the thyme sprigs and bay leaves from the soup. Ladle the soup into four bowls and place a cheesy bread slice on top of each. Sprinkle with thyme leaves. Eat!

NOTES

To make this more of a classic French onion soup, use your favorite red wine in place of the beer and swap the soda bread for a sliced baguette.

To make it vegetarian, use vegetable broth in place of the beef broth, but note that your soup will be lighter in both color and flavor.

The New Margherita Pizza

Serves: 2 to 3

I've made it no secret throughout the pages of this book that I live for carbs, cheese, and basil. So basically, I think Italy would really like me. No, wait, I would really like Italy. Either way, when it comes to pizza, my skills are on point. In the summer, there is nothing better than an heirloom tomato, ripe and perfect looking, drizzled with olive oil, topped with torn fresh basil, salt, and pepper. It just can't be beat . . . unless you add it to one heck of a cheesy pizza. Enter my version of a Margherita. It's simple as can be, but when that ball of burrata touches the warm crust and the aroma of basil hits your nose, you will quickly realize this is going to become your new favorite pizza. It's that good.

¼ cup plus 1 tablespoon extra-virgin olive oil, plus more for greasing

All-purpose flour, for dusting

½ pound pizza dough, store-bought or homemade (page 212), at room temperature

Pinch of crushed red pepper flakes

Kosher salt and freshly ground black pepper

1 cup chopped fresh basil, plus more for serving

2 tablespoons raw pine nuts

½ cup shredded fontina cheese

8 ounces burrata cheese

3 or 4 heirloom tomatoes, sliced

¼ cup balsamic vinegar

Handful of fresh arugula and/or chopped fresh chives, for garnish

1. Preheat the oven to 450°F. Grease a baking sheet with olive oil.

2. On a lightly floured surface, roll out the dough until it is very thin, about ¼ inch thick. Transfer to the prepared baking sheet. Drizzle lightly with 1 tablespoon of the olive oil. Sprinkle with the red pepper flakes and season with salt and black pepper. Add ¾ cup of the chopped basil and the pine nuts. Sprinkle evenly with the fontina.

3. Bake for about 10 minutes, until the cheese is melted and gooey. Remove from the oven and break the ball of burrata over the pizza. Bake for 3 to 4 minutes more, or until the burrata is just warmed through.

4. Remove the pizza from the oven and layer the fresh tomatoes over the cheese. Season lightly with salt and black pepper.

5. In a small bowl, whisk together the remaining ¼ cup of olive oil, remaining ¼ cup of chopped basil, the vinegar, and a pinch each of salt and black pepper. Drizzle the vinaigrette over the pizza. Top with arugula, basil, and/or chives.

HOW TO BAKE ON A PIZZA STONE

Preheat your oven to 500°F, or as high as it can possibly go, and set a pizza stone on the upper third rack. Let the stone sit in the hot oven for 1 hour prior to cooking your pizza. When ready to bake, slide the pizza directly onto the hot stone and bake for 7 to 8 minutes. Using a pizza peel, remove the pizza from the oven and break the ball of burrata on top. Return the pizza to the stone and bake for 2 to 3 minutes more, or until the burrata is warmed through. Continue as directed from step 4. Feel free to use this method for any of the pizzas in this book!

Chipotle Sweet Potato Noodles with Black Beans

Serves: 2 to 3

So there are zucchini noodles, aka zoodles, and then there are sweet potato noodles, aka swoodle poodles . . . nope, probably not. Sweet potato noodles definitely feel a little heartier than zucchini, and I love their pretty orange color. I gave them some Southwest flair here by using chipotle peppers for a smoky flavor, plus sweet corn, black beans, and spicy pumpkin seeds. You can spiralize the noodles up to a day in advance and store them in the fridge. Then just cook them right before dinner, turning this into the easiest, quickest meal ever. Well, um, okay.

6 tablespoons extra-virgin olive oil

3 medium sweet potatoes, spiralized (see Note, page 199)

3 ears corn, kernels sliced from the cob (about 3 cups)

1 red bell pepper, sliced

1 poblano chile pepper, sliced

1 jalapeño, seeded, if desired, and chopped

1 garlic clove, minced or grated

2 canned chipotle peppers in adobo, chopped

1 tablespoon honey

Kosher salt and freshly ground pepper

1 (14-ounce) can black beans, drained and rinsed

½ cup chopped fresh cilantro

Juice of 2 limes, plus lime wedges for serving

¾ cup raw pumpkin seeds (pepitas)

1 teaspoon smoked paprika

1 avocado, pitted, peeled, and sliced

½ cup crumbled cotija or feta cheese

1. In a large skillet, heat 2 tablespoons of the olive oil over medium. When it shimmers, add the sweet potatoes. Give everything a good toss and cook, stirring often, until the noodles have softened but are not mushy, 8 to 10 minutes.

2. Stir in the corn, bell pepper, and poblano and cook for 2 to 3 minutes more, until soft. Add the jalapeño and garlic and cook for 30 seconds to 1 minute more, until fragrant. Add 2 tablespoons of the olive oil, the chipotles, honey, and a good pinch each of salt and pepper. Toss to combine. Stir in the black beans, cilantro, and lime juice. Remove the skillet from the heat.

3. Meanwhile, in a small skillet, combine the remaining 2 tablespoons of olive oil, the pumpkin seeds, and the paprika. Toss to coat the seeds. Cook over medium heat, stirring often, until the seeds are lightly golden and toasted, 2 to 3 minutes. Remove from the heat and season with salt.

4. Divide the sweet potato noodles among two or three bowls and top each with some avocado, spiced pumpkin seeds, feta, and lime wedges.

Ginger-Miso Roasted Eggplant with Pomegranate

Serves: **4**

I have to tell you a secret: eggplant is not one of my favorite vegetables. It's not that I dislike it, but I typically wouldn't pick it up at the store and bring it home to cook . . . unless it was for this miso eggplant, which is absolutely delicious. This dish, salty with a hint of sweetness, has converted even the harshest of eggplant critics. The miso gives the eggplant a sweet, salty flavor, perfectly seasoning it. The pomegranate is equally important here—you'll be surprised how well it pairs with the eggplant! Plus, you really can't beat topping a dish with pomegranate seeds. They're so pretty and add a nice little crunch. This is great as a light main or side dish for the holidays with its festive colors. During the summer months, I love to grill the eggplant instead of broiling it. Grilling adds a really nice, smoky flavor. Simply grill the eggplant over medium-high heat about 10 minutes per side, until lightly charred. During the last 5 minutes of grilling, add the miso glaze. Finish and serve as directed.

6 medium Japanese or 3 small Italian eggplant

¼ cup sesame oil

Kosher salt and freshly ground pepper

⅓ cup rice vinegar

¼ cup white miso paste

2 tablespoons honey

1 tablespoon grated fresh ginger (from one 1-inch piece)

Toasted black or white sesame seeds, for garnish

Seeds from 1 pomegranate (about 1 cup), for garnish

1 cup microgreens (I use baby kale or beet greens), for serving

1. Preheat the oven to 425°F.

2. Slice the eggplants in half lengthwise, then, using your knife, make X marks in the flesh, being careful not to cut through the skin. Place on a baking sheet and rub the flesh all over with the sesame oil. Sprinkle lightly with salt and a little more heavily with pepper. Roast for about 20 minutes, or until tender.

3. Meanwhile, in a small saucepan, combine the vinegar, miso, honey, and ginger. Bring to a boil over high heat and cook, stirring, for about 5 minutes, until smooth and combined. Remove the pan from the heat.

4. Remove the eggplant from the oven and turn on the broiler; wearing oven mitts, set a rack in the top third of the oven. Brush the eggplant generously with three-quarters of the miso glaze; set aside the remainder. Broil for 2 to 3 minutes, watching closely to prevent burning, until the eggplant is lightly charred and caramelized. Sprinkle with the sesame and pomegranate seeds, top with the microgreens, and serve warm with the remaining glaze.

Apple and Brie Soup with Bacon and Pumpkin Seed Granola

Serves: 4

When the air turns crisp and the leaves begin to change colors, my apple obsession kicks into high gear, and I begin to focus all my creativity on cooking and baking with apples. Enter this soup! This is the ultimate in fall comfort food. If there's one recipe to make when the weather starts to change, this should be it. The Brie pairs so well with the sweet apples and autumn squash. Top off your bowl with savory pumpkin seed and bacon granola and this recipe will be one you return to year after year!

Apple and Brie Soup

2 tablespoons extra-virgin olive oil

1 small sweet onion, sliced

Kosher salt and freshly ground pepper

⅔ cup apple cider

2 Honeycrisp apples, cored and chopped

3 cups peeled and cubed butternut squash or pumpkin (about ½ medium)

2 teaspoons chopped fresh thyme

1 (12-ounce) bottle beer (I like to use pumpkin beer)

3 to 4 cups low-sodium chicken broth

¼ teaspoon cayenne

1 cup whole milk

1 cup shredded sharp cheddar cheese

8 ounces Brie cheese, rind removed, cut into cubes

Bacon and Pumpkin Seed Granola

4 thick-cut bacon slices

2 tablespoons salted butter

½ cup uncooked old-fashioned rolled oats

½ cup raw pumpkin seeds (pepitas)

Kosher salt

1. In a large stockpot, heat the oil over medium. When it shimmers, add the onion and season with a pinch each of salt and pepper. Cook, stirring frequently, for about 5 minutes, until softened. Slowly add ⅓ cup of the cider and let it cook into the onions. Repeat until all the cider has been added and the onions are caramelized, about 10 minutes total. Add the apples, squash, and thyme and cook over medium heat, stirring, until softened, about 8 minutes. Add the beer, 3 cups of the broth, and the cayenne. Increase the heat to high, bring to a simmer, and cook for 15 to 20 minutes, or until the apples and squash are tender.

2. MEANWHILE, MAKE THE GRANOLA. In a large skillet, cook the bacon over medium heat until crisp, 3 to 4 minutes per side. Drain on a paper towel–lined plate. When cool enough to handle, coarsely crumble the bacon.

3. In the same large skillet, melt the butter over medium heat and cook until just beginning to brown and smell toasted. Add the oats and pumpkin seeds and cook for 1 minute more. Remove the skillet from the heat and stir in the crumbled bacon. Season with salt.

4. When the apples and squash are tender, transfer the soup to a blender and pulse until smooth.

5. Return the soup to the pot and set over medium heat. Stir in the milk, then bring the soup to a low boil. Stir in the cheddar and Brie until melted and smooth. Add more broth to thin the soup, if desired. Simmer for about 5 minutes more, or until ready to serve.

6. Ladle the soup into bowls and top with the granola.

NOTE
*To make this recipe
vegetarian, omit the bacon
from the granola and use
vegetable broth instead of
chicken broth.*

Desserts

Peanut Butter–Dipped Cookies-and-Cream Cake

Serves: 10

Please tell me you love the movie *The Parent Trap* just as much as I do. I'm talking about the 1998 version with cute little Lindsay Lohan and her red hair and all those freckles. Do you remember the scene when Hallie and Annie are sitting in their cabin and they break out the package of Oreos, then bring out the big tub of Jif creamy peanut butter and proceed to dip the Oreos directly into the peanut butter? Oh my gosh! That right there is my childhood: peanut butter–dipped Oreos. I can't remember if I started dipping my Oreos in peanut butter before *The Parent Trap* or after, but either way, it's still one of my favorite sweet treats. This cake is that treat times ten. It's complete with three chocolate cake layers, peanut butter frosting, Oreo crumbs, Nutella buttercream (yes!), and chocolate-covered Oreos on top . . . you know, for good measure.

Chocolate Cake

Butter, for greasing

2¼ cups all-purpose flour

2¼ cups granulated sugar

1½ cups unsweetened cocoa powder

2¼ teaspoons baking soda

2¼ teaspoons baking powder

1½ teaspoons kosher salt

3 large eggs, at room temperature

1 cup plus 2 tablespoons buttermilk

¼ cup plus 2 tablespoons plain Greek yogurt

¾ cup canola oil

1½ tablespoons pure vanilla extract

1 cup plus 2 tablespoons strong brewed coffee, hot

8 Oreos

Nutella Buttercream

1 cup (2 sticks) unsalted butter, at room temperature

1 to 1½ cups confectioners' sugar

¾ cup Nutella

2 teaspoons pure vanilla extract

Pinch of kosher salt

1. **MAKE THE CAKE.** Preheat the oven to 350°F. Line three 8-inch round cake pans with parchment paper, then grease with butter.

2. In a medium bowl, combine the flour, granulated sugar, cocoa powder, baking soda, baking powder, and salt.

3. In the bowl of a stand mixer fitted with the paddle attachment, beat the eggs, buttermilk, yogurt, canola oil, and vanilla on medium speed until smooth, about 3 minutes. With the mixer on low speed, slowly add the dry ingredients and mix until there are no longer any lumps of flour. Add the coffee and beat to combine. The batter should be pourable but not super thin. Divide the batter evenly among the prepared pans. Arrange the Oreos flat on top of the batter in one of the pans.

4. Bake for 30 to 35 minutes, until the tops are just set and a tester inserted into the center of the cakes comes out clean. Remove and let cool in the pans for 5 minutes, then run a knife around the edges of each pan. Invert the cakes onto a wire rack. Remove the pans and let the cakes cool completely before frosting.

(recipe and ingredients continue)

Peanut Butter Frosting

2¼ cups creamy
peanut butter

1 cup (2 sticks) unsalted
butter, at room
temperature

1 tablespoon pure
vanilla extract

2 cups confectioners' sugar

1 cup crushed Oreos
(16 to 18 cookies)

5. MAKE THE NUTELLA BUTTERCREAM. In the bowl of a stand mixer fitted with the paddle attachment, beat the butter and 1 cup of the confectioners' sugar on medium-high speed until light and fluffy, about 3 minutes. Add the Nutella and vanilla and beat, scraping down the sides of the bowl as needed, for about 2 minutes more, until no streaks of white remain. Add a pinch of salt and whip the frosting for 2 to 4 minutes more, or until light and fluffy. Taste and add the remaining ½ cup confectioners' sugar if you like a sweeter or thicker buttercream.

6. MAKE THE PEANUT BUTTER FROSTING. In the bowl of a stand mixer fitted with the paddle attachment, beat the peanut butter and butter together on medium-high speed for about 3 minutes, until light and fluffy. Add the vanilla and confectioners' sugar and beat until combined and smooth.

7. ASSEMBLE THE CAKE. Place one of the plain cake layers flat-side up on a cake stand or plate. With a knife or offset spatula, spread the top with half the peanut butter frosting, then sprinkle with one-third of the Oreo crumbs. Set the Oreo cake layer on top, cookie-side up, and spread the remaining peanut butter frosting evenly over the top. Sprinkle on another third of the Oreo crumbs. Set the third layer on top, flat-side up, and frost the top and sides of the cake with the Nutella buttercream.

8. To finish the cake, sprinkle the top with the remaining Oreo crumbs. Chill the cake in the fridge for at least 2 hours.

9. Let stand at room temperature for 1 hour before serving.

Salted Treacle Butter Apple Pie

Makes: **One 8-inch pie**

I am so excited about this pie, and for more reasons than you'd probably think. Yes, it is insanely delicious, but perhaps more important, I want to chat about the fact that it has treacle butter. If you don't know what treacle butter is, you are obviously not as big a Harry Potter freak as I am. That's fine, but then I need to explain a bit. Treacle, also called golden syrup, is basically the British form of blackstrap molasses, and it happens to be one of Harry Potter's favorite flavors. I added flaky sea salt and butter to make salted treacle butter. Now, I fully realize that might not sound like the best thing ever, but I am here to tell you that it *is* the best thing ever. Slather the butter over the entire pie just as it comes out of the oven, and you will soon realize just how brilliant this combination is.

Butter or nonstick cooking spray, for greasing

All-purpose flour, for dusting

2 piecrust rounds, store-bought or homemade (recipe follows)

Treacle Butter

4 tablespoons (½ stick) unsalted butter, at room temperature

1 tablespoon blackstrap molasses

Pinch of flaky sea salt

Filling

3 pounds Honeycrisp and/ or Granny Smith apples, cored, and sliced ¼ inch thick

½ cup packed light brown sugar

¼ cup all-purpose flour

1 teaspoon ground cinnamon

¼ teaspoon freshly grated nutmeg

1 tablespoon fresh lemon juice

1 large egg, beaten

Coarse sugar, for sprinkling

Browned Butter Ice Cream (page 295), for serving

1. Grease an 8-inch pie plate with butter or cooking spray.

2. On a lightly floured surface, roll out the pie dough into two 12-inch rounds. Carefully transfer one round to the prepared pie plate, lifting up the edges and allowing the dough to sink down into the bottom of the dish—don't stretch it. Trim the edges if needed, then prick the bottom of the dough with a fork a few times.

3. MAKE THE TREACLE. Stir together the butter and molasses in a small bowl. Add the salt and stir to combine.

4. Pour half the treacle butter into a large bowl and set the remainder aside for serving. Add the apples, brown sugar, flour, cinnamon, nutmeg, and lemon juice. Toss until everything is evenly distributed. Spoon the mixture into the piecrust in the dish. Be sure to scrape in all the good juices from the bowl.

5. Place the second pie dough round on top of the apples. Push the edges of the top crust against the pie plate and crimp the edges of the bottom crust together with the top crust to seal the pie. Alternatively, roll out the top round, cut the dough into strips, and create a lattice top (see photograph, page 256).

6. Brush the top crust with the beaten egg. Using a sharp knife, cut four slits into the top crust to allow steam to escape. Cover with plastic wrap and chill in the fridge until the crust is firm, at least 1 hour.

(recipe continues)

7. Meanwhile, preheat the oven to 350°F.

8. Sprinkle the pie with coarse sugar, and then transfer it to the oven. Bake for 50 to 55 minutes, until the juices are bubbling and the crust is deep golden brown. If the crust is getting too brown, tent the pie with aluminum foil. Remove from the oven and brush the reserved treacle butter over the top crust. Transfer to a wire rack and let cool slightly, at least 15 minutes.

9. Slice and serve warm with a big scoop of Browned Butter Ice Cream.

PIECRUST

Makes: **Enough for one 8-inch double-crust pie**

2½ cups all-purpose flour, plus more for dusting

⅓ cup almond flour

1 teaspoon kosher salt

1 cup (2 sticks) cold unsalted butter, cut into pieces

1 large egg yolk

¼ cup cold buttermilk, plus more if needed

1. In a large bowl, combine the all-purpose flour, almond flour, and salt. Add the butter and use your fingers to break the butter into the flour until the mixture is the size of small peas.

2. In a small bowl, whisk the egg yolk and buttermilk, then add to the flour mixture. Blend with a wooden spoon, drizzling in more buttermilk as needed, 1 tablespoon at a time, until the dough just comes together (a few dry spots are okay).

3. Turn the dough out onto a lightly floured surface and knead until no dry spots remain, about 1 minute. Divide the dough in half and shape each piece into a ball, then flatten into a disk about 1 inch thick.

4. At this point you can wrap the dough in plastic wrap and place it in the fridge while you prepare the filling, or store it in the fridge for up to 1 week.

Chocolate Caramel Cake

Serves: 10

There are so many words I could use to describe this cake, but none of them seems good enough. It's over the top, but in the best way possible. It is sincerely the key to any chocolate lover's heart. It's just like a creamy, salted, chocolate-covered caramel, but in cake form. There is a chocolate cake base, a chocolate fudge center, and a sweet caramel buttercream frosting that's probably the best buttercream you will ever taste.

Cake

Butter or nonstick cooking spray, for greasing

2¼ cups all-purpose flour

2¼ cups granulated sugar

¾ cup unsweetened cocoa powder

2¼ teaspoons baking soda

2¼ teaspoons baking powder

1½ teaspoons kosher salt

3 large eggs, at room temperature

1 cup plus 2 tablespoons buttermilk

¼ cup plus 2 tablespoons plain Greek yogurt

¾ cup canola oil

4½ ounces dark chocolate, melted

1½ tablespoons pure vanilla extract

¾ cup strong brewed coffee, hot

Chocolate Fudge

12 ounces semisweet chocolate, chopped

½ cup heavy cream

3 tablespoons salted butter

Caramel Buttercream

1 cup (2 sticks) unsalted butter, at room temperature

4 ounces cream cheese, at room temperature

2 cups confectioners' sugar

1¼ cups caramel sauce, store-bought or homemade (recipe follows)

2 teaspoons pure vanilla extract

1. **MAKE THE CAKE.** Preheat the oven to 350°F. Line three 8-inch round cake pans with parchment paper, then grease with butter or cooking spray.

2. In a medium bowl, combine the flour, granulated sugar, cocoa powder, baking soda, baking powder, and salt.

3. In the bowl of a stand mixer fitted with the paddle attachment, beat the eggs, buttermilk, yogurt, canola oil, melted chocolate, and vanilla together on medium speed for about 3 minutes, until smooth. With the mixer on low speed, slowly add the dry ingredients and mix until there are no longer any clumps of flour. Add the coffee and beat to combine. The batter should be pourable but not super thin.

4. Divide the batter evenly among the prepared pans. Bake for 30 to 35 minutes, until the tops are just set and a tester inserted into the center of the cakes comes out clean. Remove and let cool in the pans for 5 minutes, then run a knife around the edges of each pan. Invert the cakes onto a wire rack. Remove the pans and let the cakes cool completely before frosting.

5. **MEANWHILE, MAKE THE FUDGE.** In a medium saucepan, combine the chocolate and cream. Cook over low heat, stirring often, for about 5 minutes, until melted and smooth. Remove from the heat and stir in the butter until melted and smooth. Let cool to room temperature.

6. **MAKE THE BUTTERCREAM.** In the bowl of a stand mixer fitted with the paddle attachment, beat the butter, cream cheese, and 1½ cups of the confectioners' sugar on medium-high speed for about 3 minutes, until light and

(recipe continues)

fluffy. Add ½ cup of the caramel sauce and the vanilla and beat, scraping down the sides of the bowl as needed, for about 2 minutes more, or until there are no streaks. Taste the frosting and add more of the confectioners' sugar if you like a sweeter or thicker buttercream.

7. **ASSEMBLE THE CAKE.** Place one layer of cake flat-side up on a cake stand or plate. With a knife or offset spatula, spread half the fudge over the top. Drizzle with ¼ cup of the caramel sauce so that it almost completely covers the fudge sauce. Set a second cake layer on top, rounded-side up, and repeat with the remaining fudge sauce and ¼ cup of the caramel sauce. Set the third layer on top, flat-side up, and frost the top and sides of the cake with the buttercream. Chill the cake in the fridge for at least 2 hours.

8. Let stand at room temperature for at least 30 minutes before serving. Just before slicing, drizzle the cake with the remaining ¼ cup caramel sauce, allowing some to drip down the sides.

CARAMEL SAUCE

Makes: **2 cups**

2 cups sugar

½ cup (1 stick) unsalted butter, diced, at room temperature

1½ cups heavy cream or canned full-fat coconut milk, at room temperature

2 tablespoons bourbon (optional)

1 teaspoon flaky sea salt

1. In a large skillet, cook the sugar over medium-high heat, stirring continuously, for 8 to 10 minutes, until the sugar has melted and turned a deep golden caramel color. Remove the skillet from the heat and add the pieces of butter one by one, whisking until combined—the caramel will bubble up. Slowly add the cream and whisk until combined.

2. Return the skillet to medium-high heat and cook, stirring, for 5 to 8 minutes, until the caramel has thickened and is deep amber in color. Remove the skillet from the heat. Add the bourbon (if using) and salt. Set the caramel aside to cool completely before using, at least 20 minutes. Store in the fridge for up to 2 weeks. Warm before using.

Surprise Tiramisu Cupcakes

Makes: 18 to 20 cupcakes

Soaked in coffee, then topped with the most luscious mascarpone buttercream—what's not to love about these tiramisu cupcakes? The only thing that could possibly make them better is stuffing them with a big spoonful of Nutella. Surprise!

2½ cups all-purpose flour

1 tablespoon baking powder

1 teaspoon kosher salt

¾ cup (1½ sticks) unsalted butter, melted

1 cup granulated sugar

2 large eggs

2 egg yolks

1 teaspoon pure vanilla extract

1 cup canned full-fat coconut milk

⅔ cup strong brewed coffee, hot

½ cup sweetened condensed milk

2 tablespoons Kahlúa (optional)

1 cup Nutella

Coconut Mascarpone Frosting

1 cup coconut cream or heavy cream

8 ounces mascarpone cheese

½ cup heavy cream

½ cup confectioners' sugar

1 tablespoon pure vanilla extract

Unsweetened cocoa powder and/or chopped chocolate, for dusting

1. Preheat the oven to 350°F with a rack in the center. Line 18 to 20 wells of two muffin tins with paper liners.

2. In a medium bowl, combine the flour, baking powder, and salt.

3. In the bowl of a stand mixer fitted with the paddle attachment, beat the melted butter, granulated sugar, eggs, egg yolks, and vanilla on medium speed until smooth and pale, 4 to 5 minutes. With the mixer on low speed, slowly add the dry ingredients and mix until there are no lumps of flour, about 2 minutes. Add the coconut milk and beat until combined.

4. Divide the batter evenly among the prepared muffin tins, filling each well three-quarters of the way. Bake for 18 to 20 minutes, until the tops are just set and a tester inserted into the center of a cupcake comes out clean. Remove the cupcakes from the tin and let cool for 10 minutes.

5. Meanwhile, in a small bowl, whisk together the hot coffee, condensed milk, and Kahlúa (if using) until smooth.

6. Use a small paring knife to cut a cone-shaped piece from the center of each cooled cupcake (which you can snack on!). Using the tines of a fork, carefully poke holes around the top of the cupcakes. Using a pastry brush or spoon, generously coat the cupcakes with the coffee mixture. Fill the center of each cupcake with 1 scant tablespoon of the Nutella. Cover the cupcakes with plastic wrap and refrigerate for at least 30 minutes.

7. MEANWHILE, MAKE THE FROSTING. In a large bowl using a handheld mixer, whip the coconut cream, mascarpone, and heavy cream until the mixture holds stiff peaks. Add the confectioners' sugar and vanilla and mix well until combined.

8. Spread or pipe the frosting onto each cupcake. Store in the fridge until ready to serve. Just before serving, dust the cupcakes with cocoa powder.

COFFEE TALK

You'll notice that with most of my rich chocolate desserts, I
like to include a little coffee in the recipe (see pages 252, 258,
262, and 276). Coffee accentuates the chocolate well, and, in
my opinion, it's what makes a great chocolate dessert. Even if
you don't drink coffee or don't like coffee, I still recommend
baking with it—you don't taste it when it's baked in with the
chocolate. It just adds something really special that makes you
say, "Mmm." With these molten cakes, pouring the coffee over
the cakes just before baking keeps them nice and moist, too.

Molten Chocolate Cakes with Whipped Vanilla Mascarpone

Makes: **4 individual cakes**

I truly believe you'd be hard-pressed to find a better-tasting molten cake than this one. Bold statement, I know, but I feel pretty confident in these cakes. I would even go so far as to say they make life worth living. You know what's so crazy about this recipe, though? You'd think something as amazing as this would be complicated and tricky to make. But if you follow the recipe as written, you'll get a cake that's soft on the outside, and oozing with milk chocolate once you dig in. To really finish this off properly, top with a dollop of whipped vanilla mascarpone, and you'll have what, in my eyes, is perfection.

Molten Cakes

Butter or nonstick cooking spray, for greasing

8 ounces dark chocolate, chopped

½ cup (1 stick) unsalted butter

3 large eggs

3 egg yolks

1 teaspoon pure vanilla extract

½ cup granulated sugar

¼ cup all-purpose flour

4 tablespoons strong brewed coffee, at room temperature

4 squares semisweet or milk chocolate, or ¼ cup chocolate chips

Whipped Mascarpone

1½ cups heavy cream

4 ounces mascarpone cheese

1 teaspoon pure vanilla extract

1 to 2 tablespoons confectioners' sugar

Unsweetened cocoa powder, for dusting

1. Preheat the oven to 375°F with a rack in the center. Grease four 8-ounce ramekins with butter or cooking spray.

2. In a small saucepan, melt the chocolate and butter over low heat, stirring often, until well combined and smooth, about 5 minutes.

3. In a medium bowl, whisk together the eggs, egg yolks, vanilla, sugar, and flour until combined. Stir in the melted chocolate mixture. Divide the batter evenly among the prepared ramekins. Stick 1 square of chocolate into the center of each ramekin and gently push it into the batter. Place the ramekins on a baking sheet. Spoon 1 tablespoon of the coffee over each cake. Bake for 18 to 20 minutes, or until the sides of the cake are set but the center is still slightly loose. Let the cakes cool in the ramekins for 1 minute, then run a thin knife around the sides and invert them onto plates. Remove the ramekins.

4. MEANWHILE, MAKE THE WHIPPED MASCARPONE. In a large bowl using a handheld mixer, whip the cream and mascarpone together until they hold soft peaks, about 5 minutes. Stir in the vanilla and confectioners' sugar. Taste and add more 1 tablespoon of the confectioners' sugar if you like a sweeter cream, but keep in mind that the cakes are sweet, so the cream doesn't need to be overly sweet.

5. Dollop each cake with a spoonful of whipped mascarpone and then dust with cocoa powder. Serve immediately.

Addictive Salted Caramel—Stuffed Chocolate Cookies

Makes: 24 to 28 cookies

My brother Malachi, or Kai, is probably one of the toughest critics when it comes to food, and especially cookies. He's all about the old-fashioned chocolate chip cookie, and who can blame him, really? But he'll be the first to tell you that these cookies are the best ever. And not a single person has ever argued that fact with him. Hello, soft chocolate cookie, stuffed with milk chocolate caramels, and sprinkled with flaky sea salt! And as a bonus, they're super easy to make! Warning: Addiction ahead.

6 tablespoons (¾ stick) unsalted butter

4 ounces bittersweet chocolate, chopped

2 cups semisweet chocolate chips

3 large eggs

½ cup granulated sugar

2 teaspoons pure vanilla extract

½ cup plus 2 tablespoons all-purpose flour

2 tablespoons unsweetened cocoa powder

¼ teaspoon baking soda

¼ teaspoon kosher salt

Canola oil or nonstick cooking spray, for greasing

24 to 28 milk chocolate caramels (I like Dove)

Flaky sea salt, for topping

1. Preheat the oven to 325°F. Line a baking sheet with parchment paper.

2. In a small saucepan, combine the butter, bittersweet chocolate, and chocolate chips. Cook over low heat, stirring often, until fully melted and combined—the chocolate will be thick. Remove the pan from the heat and let the chocolate cool slightly.

3. In a small bowl using a handheld mixer, beat the eggs and sugar together on high until light and fluffy, 2 to 3 minutes. Add the vanilla and the melted chocolate mixture and beat for 1 to 2 minutes more, until combined, scraping down the sides of the bowl as needed. Add the flour, cocoa powder, baking soda, and kosher salt and beat until fully combined and smooth, about 3 minutes. The batter should be thick but pourable. Cover the bowl and chill in the fridge for at least 1 hour or up to overnight.

4. Scoop out scant 2 tablespoons of dough and place them about 2 inches apart on the prepared baking sheet. Grease your hands with a little canola oil or cooking spray, then flatten the dough into small disks, about 2 inches in diameter, and place a caramel in the center. Scoop out a rounded teaspoon of dough and flatten into it into a disk. Place the disk over the caramel, pinching the layers of dough together.

5. Bake for 10 to 12 minutes, until just set on the edges. Remove from the oven and sprinkle each cookie with a little flaky salt. Let cool for at least 5 minutes on the baking sheet before serving.

Three-Milk Strawberry Shortcake

Makes: One 8-inch triple-layer cake

If you have ever had *tres leches* cake, this one will be very familiar. Essentially, you bake a cake, poke a bunch of holes in the top, and then pour a sweet milk mixture, consisting of whole milk, coconut milk, and sweetened condensed milk, over the cake. The cake soaks up all the milks, leaving you with a light, moist, and sweet cake. Once the cake is fully assembled, it needs to be served pretty much right away. The juices from the berries slowly seep into the cake and turn the whipped ricotta light pink—still edible, but not quite what you want to serve guests. I recommend preparing all the elements separately, then assembling just before serving.

Coconut Cake

Butter or nonstick cooking spray, for greasing

3¾ cup all-purpose flour

1½ tablespoons baking powder

1½ teaspoons salt

1¼ cups canola oil

¾ granulated sugar

½ cup honey

3 eggs

3 egg yolks

3 teaspoons pure vanilla extract

2 cups full-fat canned coconut milk

Zest of 1 lemon

Edible flowers, for decorating (optional)

½ cup goat's milk or regular whole milk

1 (14-ounce) can sweetened condensed milk

Strawberries

6 cups fresh strawberries, halved or quartered if large

¼ cup granulated sugar

2 teaspoons pure vanilla extract

Whipped Ricotta Cream

16 ounces whole-milk ricotta cheese

¾ cup heavy cream

2 tablespoons honey, plus more to taste

1. **MAKE THE CAKE.** Preheat the oven to 350°F. Line three 8-inch round cake pans with parchment paper, then grease with butter or cooking spray.

2. In a medium bowl, combine the flour, baking powder, and salt.

3. In the bowl of a stand mixer fitted with the paddle attachment, beat together the canola oil, sugar, honey, eggs, egg yolks, and 2 teaspoons vanilla until smooth, about 3 minutes. Slowly add the dry ingredients to the wet ingredients with the mixer on low and mix until there are no longer any clumps of flour. Add 1½ cups of the coconut milk and beat to combine. The batter should be pourable but not super thin. Fold in the lemon zest by hand.

4. Divide the batter evenly among the prepared pans. Bake for 20 to 25 minutes, until the tops are just set and a tester comes out clean. Remove and let cool 5 minutes, then run a knife around the edges of each pan. Invert the cakes onto a wire rack set inside a rimmed baking sheet. Using a skewer or the tines of a fork, poke holes all over the top of the cakes.

5. **MEANWHILE, MAKE THE GLAZE.** Whisk together the remaining ½ cup coconut milk, goat's milk, sweetened condensed milk, and remaining 1 teaspoon vanilla in a small bowl until combined. Pour the milk evenly over each cooled cake, dividing it evenly and making sure it gets down into

the cakes' nooks and crannies. You may not need all the glaze. Refrigerate for 1 hour or until the milk glaze has been absorbed. The cakes can sit covered in the fridge until ready to assemble, up to 1 day.

6. MAKE THE STRAWBERRIES. In a large bowl, combine the strawberries, sugar, and vanilla, tossing gently to combine. Allow the berries to macerate and release their juices, at least 20 minutes.

7. MAKE THE WHIPPED RICOTTA. In the bowl of a stand mixer fitted with the whisk attachment, whip the ricotta and heavy cream until the ricotta is smooth and the cream has fluffed, 5 to 6 minutes. Add the honey and whip until combined, about 1 minute.

8. To assemble, place one cake layer flat-side up on a cake stand or plate. With a knife or offset spatula, spread one-third of the whipped ricotta over the cake and then spoon over one-third of the strawberries. Repeat with the remaining cake layers, ricotta, and strawberries, layering one on top of the other. Be careful not to overfill the layers; otherwise the cake will be too hard to slice. If desired, decorate the cake with edible flowers. Serve immediately.

Ice Cream Banana Bread

Makes: **One 9 x 5-inch loaf**

Are you currently thinking to yourself, Wait, what? Ice cream banana bread? What the heck is that? It's actually exactly what it sounds like. Banana bread made out of melted ice cream—it's delicious and incredibly easy. Simply mix melted ice cream with self-rising flour and bake until golden and perfect. I like to use butter pecan ice cream because it's one of my favorite flavors, but anything works. Chocolate, peanut butter, caramel—whatever your heart desires. Just be sure not to skimp on the chocolate chips. Oh, and be sure to serve this warm, with a pat of salted butter and a scoop (or two) of frozen ice cream, of course. Whenever I have leftover banana bread, I use it to make French toast—it makes for some seriously decadent breakfast. You have to try it!

2 cups ice cream
(any flavor)

Butter or nonstick
cooking spray, for greasing

2½ cups self-rising
flour (see Note)

2 very ripe bananas,
mashed

2 teaspoons pure
vanilla extract

¾ cup semisweet
chocolate chips

6 tablespoons (¾ stick)
salted butter, cut into
½-tablespoon slices,
plus more for serving

Frozen ice cream
(any flavor), for serving

Fresh berries, for serving

Confectioners' sugar,
for serving

1. Let the ice cream stand at room temperature until softened and melty.

2. Preheat the oven to 350°F. Grease a 9 x 5-inch loaf pan with butter or cooking spray.

3. In a medium bowl, mix together the melted ice cream, flour, bananas, and vanilla until just combined. Fold in the chocolate chips. Spoon the batter into the prepared pan and smooth out the top. Scatter the slices of butter evenly over the dough.

4. Bake for 45 to 50 minutes, or until the bread is lightly golden on top and a tester inserted into the center comes out clean. Let cool for 5 minutes, then turn the bread out onto a cutting board. Slice and serve warm with a scoop of ice cream, berries, butter, and/or a dusting of confectioners' sugar.

NOTE
If you don't have self-rising flour on hand, you can use 2½ cups of all-purpose flour plus 1 tablespoon of baking powder.

Any Fruit Dump

Serves: 6 to 8

My Nonnie has a recipe for a peach dessert that entails dumping peaches, pits and all, into a baking dish with butter and brown sugar, and then baking it for an hour until the fruit is caramelized, soft, and all kinds of delicious. She then simply serves it with a scoop of vanilla ice cream. This is my triple-berry version of her peach dump; I just swapped the peaches for berries and added a crumble on top, you know, for good measure. As the title suggests, you can use an equal amount of any fruit.

6 cups mixed fresh berries (I like blueberries, blackberries, raspberries, and strawberries)

½ cup packed plus 1½ tablespoons light brown sugar

4 tablespoons (½ stick) cold unsalted butter, cut into cubes

2 tablespoons bourbon (optional)

1 tablespoon vanilla extract

4 tablespoons (½ stick) unsalted butter, melted

¾ cup all-purpose flour

1 teaspoon baking powder

Pinch of flaky sea salt

Vanilla ice cream, for serving

1. Preheat the oven to 350°F with the rack in the center.

2. In a 9 x 5-inch loaf pan or a 10-inch pie plate, combine the berries, ½ cup of the brown sugar, the cold butter cubes, bourbon (if using), and vanilla. Toss well to mix.

3. In a small bowl, stir together the melted butter, flour, baking powder, the remaining 1½ tablespoons brown sugar, and the flaky sea salt. Don't worry if the mixture seems dry. Crumble the topping over the berries.

4. Bake for 45 minutes, or until the berries are bubbling and the topping is golden brown.

5. Serve warm, with vanilla ice cream.

NOTE

When my mom was short on time, or didn't feel like rolling forty balls of cookie dough, she would bake these into cookie bars. To do so, grease a 9 x 13-inch baking dish and press the dough evenly into the dish. Bake in a preheated 350°F oven for 25 to 30 minutes. Let the bars cool in the pan for at least 30 minutes before slicing and serving. The bars are crumbly, so you may want to use a fork . . . my dad always does.

Mom's One-Bowl Oatmeal Chocolate Chip Cookies

Makes: **30 to 40 cookies**

Mom does many things incredibly well, but I've got to say, she is especially good at baking cookies. There's no doubt in my mind that she makes the best oatmeal chocolate chip cookie out there. Mom actually acquired this recipe from a close friend before I was born. The secret is one you might not expect, but makes all the difference: instead of butter, she uses oil. I know that might sound odd, but it works. A lot of people have asked if they can substitute butter for the oil, but this is one of the only times I have to say no to butter. This recipe does not fail. No matter where I am in the world, I can use this recipe and know it will always work. All you need is one bowl, a few simple ingredients, a billion and one chocolate chips, and about 25 minutes.

2½ cups old-fashioned rolled oats

2 cups all-purpose flour

1 cup packed light brown sugar

½ cup granulated sugar

1 teaspoon baking soda

1 teaspoon kosher salt

1 cup canola oil, or melted coconut oil, plus more if needed

2 large eggs

1 tablespoon pure vanilla extract

2 cups semisweet chocolate chips, plus more if desired

1. Preheat the oven to 350°F. Line a baking sheet with parchment paper.

2. In a large bowl, combine the oats, flour, brown sugar, granulated sugar, baking soda, salt, canola oil, eggs, and vanilla. Using a handheld mixer or a wooden spoon, mix until the dough is moist and all the ingredients are combined. The dough will be crumbly. Fold in the chocolate chips.

3. Using your hands, clump together about a tablespoon or so of dough at a time and squeeze into a ball. If the mixture is not holding, add 1 tablespoon more of oil to the dough. Place on the prepared baking sheet 2 inches apart. If the balls are a little crumbly, do not worry—they will come together while baking.

4. Bake for 15 to 20 minutes, or until set and golden. These are best right out of the oven, so eat up!

Bonfire Brownies

Makes: 16 brownies

Think of your favorite s'more: the marshmallow, all warm and toasty, sandwiched between two sheets of graham crackers, and multiple squares of melting Hershey's milk chocolate. Now add fudge brownies and salted pretzels. Oh, yes, I went there, and you are going to love it. My little sis and unofficial recipe tester, Asher, is declaring these brownies as one of the favorite desserts of her life. Granted, she is only seven, but the girl knows what's up when it comes to sweets. Here is how these brownies break down layer by layer: graham cracker, fudge brownie studded with salty pretzels, chocolate squares, and toasted marshmallow. Best part? You don't even need a bonfire.

4 or 5 whole graham cracker sheets

½ cup (1 stick) unsalted butter

2 ounces milk chocolate, chopped

¾ cup granulated sugar

1½ teaspoons pure vanilla extract

1 tablespoon high-quality instant coffee granules

1 tablespoon Kahlúa (optional)

2 large eggs

½ cup unsweetened cocoa powder

½ cup all-purpose flour

¼ teaspoon kosher salt

¼ cup smoked almonds, coarsely chopped

½ cup mini pretzel twists

1 or 2 (1.5-ounce) chocolate bars (I like Hershey's), broken into squares

2 cups large square marshmallows, store-bought or homemade (page 292)

1. Preheat the oven to 350°F. Line a 9-inch square baking dish with parchment paper or aluminum foil, letting some hang over the edges of the pan.

2. Arrange the graham crackers in a single layer on the bottom of the prepared baking dish, being sure the entire bottom is covered—you may need to break some to fit.

3. Put the butter and milk chocolate in a medium microwave-safe bowl. Microwave in 30-second intervals, stirring in between, until melted and smooth. Add the sugar and whisk until completely combined. Add the vanilla, coffee, Kahlúa (if using), and eggs and whisk until smooth. Stir in the cocoa powder, flour, and salt until smooth and just combined. Try not to overmix the batter; it will be thick. Fold in the almonds. Pour the batter over the graham crackers in the baking dish. Gently press the pretzels on top.

4. Bake for 25 to 30 minutes, until the brownies are set on top. Remove from the oven and immediately add the chocolate bar pieces to the top of the brownies—the chocolate will melt over the brownies. Add the marshmallows evenly over the chocolate and then return the brownies to the oven. After 5 minutes, turn on the broiler, and, wearing oven mitts, position a rack in the top third of the oven. Broil the brownies for 15 to 30 seconds, or until the tops of the marshmallow are just golden—watch closely, as they burn fast. Remove from the oven and let the brownies cool in the pan for about 30 minutes.

5. Lift the brownie block out of the pan using the overhanging parchment paper. Cut into squares.

WHAT ARE YOU, NUTS?

People either love nuts in their brownies or hate them. I can go either way; it just depends on the recipe. For these particular brownies, I love the addition of the smoked almonds. They really give you that "bonfire"-like feel. Of course, if you're opposed to nuts in your brownies or allergic to them, feel free to omit them.

Pumpkin Tart with Chai Cream and Maple-Glazed Pumpkin Seeds

Makes: **One 9-inch tart**

Come fall, everyone needs at least one go-to pumpkin recipe, and this is mine. What I love about this tart is that it's not overly sweet, which makes the light drizzle of maple syrup just before serving a must. If you prefer it sweeter, you can increase the maple syrup in the filling to ⅔ cup. However, if you are using a 9-inch tart pan, this will leave you with just a little too much filling. Either discard the excess or use an 11-inch tart pan. Alternatively, you can sweeten up the whipped cream, as opposed to the filling.

Crust

Butter, for greasing

2 cups raw pecans

2 tablespoons pure maple syrup

1 teaspoon pure vanilla extract

4 tablespoons (½ stick) unsalted butter, melted

¼ cup whole-wheat flour

¼ teaspoon kosher salt

Pumpkin Filling

1 (15-ounce) can pure pumpkin puree

½ cup canned full-fat coconut milk

2 large eggs

⅓ cup plus 3 tablespoons pure maple syrup

2 teaspoons pure vanilla extract

1 teaspoon ground cinnamon

½ teaspoon freshly grated nutmeg

½ teaspoon ground ginger

½ teaspoon kosher salt

⅓ cup raw pumpkin seeds (pepitas)

Chai Whipped Cream

1 cup heavy cream

¼ teaspoon ground cinnamon

⅛ teaspoon ground ginger

1 tablespoon pure maple syrup

1 vanilla bean, halved lengthwise and seeds scraped out

Pure maple syrup, for serving

Flaky sea salt, for sprinkling

1. **MAKE THE CRUST.** Preheat the oven to 350°F with a rack in the center. Grease a 9-inch tart pan with butter.

2. Pulse the pecans in a food processor until finely chopped. Add the maple syrup, vanilla, melted butter, flour, and kosher salt and pulse to combine. Press the mixture into the prepared pan. Set the pan on a rimmed baking sheet and bake for 10 to 15 minutes, until the crust is golden and the nuts smell toasted. Remove from the oven and set aside. Leave the oven on.

3. **MEANWHILE, MAKE THE FILLING.** In a large bowl using a handheld mixer, beat the pumpkin, coconut milk, eggs, ⅓ cup of the maple syrup, the vanilla, cinnamon, nutmeg, ginger, and kosher salt until combined. Pour the mixture into the baked crust—the filling is going to come up all the way to the top of the tart shell—it will sink during baking.

4. Bake the tart for 45 to 50 minutes, or until the center no longer jiggles. Let cool on the counter for 30 minutes and then place in the fridge to cool completely, about 1 hour.

5. While the tart bakes, toss together the pumpkin seeds and the remaining 3 tablespoons of maple syrup on a parchment paper–lined baking sheet. Add a sprinkle of flaky salt. Transfer to the oven and roast alongside the tart for 10 to 15 minutes, or until the pumpkin seeds are toasted and golden. Remove from the oven and sprinkle generously with sea salt.

6. **MAKE THE TOPPING.** In a large bowl using a handheld mixer, whip the cream until it holds soft peaks. Add the cinnamon, ginger, maple syrup, and vanilla bean seeds. Whip once more until combined and fluffy.

7. When ready to serve, top the tart with the chai whipped cream. Drizzle with a little maple syrup and top with the pumpkin seeds and some flaky salt.

Mom's Special K Bars

Makes: 18 to 20 bars

Sometimes it's the simplest of recipes that truly are the best. My mom's Special K bars will forever be one of my favorite desserts—and others feel the same way. My brother Malachi will jump through hoops just to get a K bar in his hand! These are without a doubt the most requested dessert Mom or I have ever made. Bring them to a party and they'll be the first dessert gone. I have no idea why my mom calls these "Special K" bars since she's always used cornflakes, but why change the name now? The only thing I changed from her original recipe was to replace the corn syrup with a combo of honey and maple syrup. No one can tell the difference, but Mom and I both feel a million times better serving and eating a slightly healthier version of our favorite dessert!

Nonstick cooking spray, for greasing

1 cup creamy peanut butter

½ cup honey

½ cup pure maple syrup

½ cup sugar

6 heaping cups cornflakes

3 or 4 cups semisweet chocolate chips, melted (see Note)

1. Grease a 9 x 13-inch pan with cooking spray.

2. In a large pot, combine the peanut butter, honey, maple syrup, and sugar. Cook over medium heat, stirring, until the mixture begins to bubble and the sugar has dissolved, about 5 minutes—be careful not to let the peanut butter burn. Remove the pot from the heat and immediately stir in the cornflakes. Spread the mixture into the prepared baking dish.

3. Put the chocolate chips in a medium microwave-safe bowl. Microwave in 30-second intervals, stirring in between, until melted and smooth. Spread the melted chocolate in an even layer over the peanut butter–corn flake mixture. Tap the pan against the counter to smooth if needed. Cover with plastic wrap and place in the fridge to harden for at least 2 hours.

4. Remove from the fridge 10 minutes before serving. Cut into bars and devour!

Towering Chocolate Banana Cream Pie

Makes: One 9-inch pie

If my dad were reading over your shoulder, he would tell you that you have now reached the most delicious pie recipe in the book. A picture's worth a thousand words, so take a look—but I should add that the chocolate truffle layer truly takes this pie over the top. I like to use canned full-fat coconut milk, as I think it adds incredible flavor and gives the pie an amazingly creamy texture. However, if you prefer, heavy cream can be used instead.

Crust

1 cup graham cracker crumbs

1 cup sweetened shredded coconut

6 tablespoons (¾ stick) salted butter, melted

Truffle Layer

6 ounces dark chocolate, chopped

½ cup canned full-fat coconut milk or heavy cream

1 teaspoon vanilla extract

Banana Layer

⅓ cup granulated sugar

¼ cup cornstarch

¼ teaspoon kosher salt

3 egg yolks

2 cups canned full-fat coconut milk or whole milk

1 vanilla bean, halved lengthwise and seeds scraped out

3 tablespoons unsalted butter, cut into cubes

8 ounces semisweet or milk chocolate, chopped

3 or 4 ripe but firm bananas, sliced

Topping

1½ cups heavy cream

Toasted coconut and/or shaved chocolate, for garnish (optional)

1. **MAKE THE CRUST.** In a medium bowl, stir together the graham cracker crumbs, shredded coconut, and melted butter until well combined. Pat the mixture into a 9-inch pie plate, pressing firmly into the bottom and up the sides.

2. **MAKE THE TRUFFLE LAYER.** Put the dark chocolate and coconut milk in a medium microwave-safe bowl. Microwave in 30-second intervals, stirring in between, until melted and smooth. Stir in the vanilla.

3. Pour the truffle filling into the piecrust. Smooth it out, then cover with plastic wrap and place it in the fridge.

4. **MAKE THE BANANA LAYER.** In a medium pan, whisk together the sugar, cornstarch, and salt. Add the egg yolks and whisk until smooth. Pour in the milk and whisk until fully combined. Add the vanilla bean seeds and set the pan over medium-high heat. Bring the mixture to a low boil. Cook, stirring continuously, until the mixture thickens and is puddinglike, about 8 minutes. Remove the pan from the heat and stir in the butter and chocolate until melted and smooth. Let cool for 10 minutes, then spoon the pudding over the truffle layer. Cover with plastic wrap and chill in the fridge for at least 4 hours.

5. In a large bowl using a handheld mixer, whip the cream until it holds stiff peaks.

6. Remove the pie from the fridge and arrange the sliced bananas on top. Top with the whipped cream. If desired, sprinkle with chocolate and/or toasted coconut. Slice and serve!

Mint Chocolate Chip Ice Cream Cake

Makes: One 8- to 9-inch ice cream cake

One of my favorite things to do on summer nights as a kid was to head over to Nonnie and Grandpa's for a slice of chocolate peanut butter ice cream cake. Nonnie would make it for many of our family parties, but she'd always send any leftovers home with Mom. Since moving to Colorado, I have been missing Nonnie's awesome cake back in Ohio. So I got to thinking one day about how I could put my own spin on it. It seemed obvious to me: mint chocolate chip was the only way to go. My favorite ice cream as a kid turned into an easy ice cream cake!

Nonstick cooking spray, for greasing

2 quarts mint chocolate chip ice cream

1 (9-ounce) box chocolate wafer cookies

½ cup (1 stick) unsalted butter, melted

1 cup semisweet chocolate chips

1 tablespoon coconut oil

1 cup roasted pistachios, chopped

1. Grease an 8- or 9-inch round springform pan with cooking spray.

2. Remove the ice cream from the freezer and let it sit on the counter for 10 to 12 minutes.

3. In a food processor, pulse the cookies into fine crumbs. Add the melted butter and pulse until combined. Dump the mixture out into the prepared pan and press the crumbs into the bottom to make a smooth, even crust.

4. Spread the ice cream on top of the crust and smooth into an even layer. Cover with plastic wrap, pressing the wrap directly against the cake to help prevent ice from forming. Freeze for 4 to 6 hours, or preferably overnight.

5. About 20 minutes before you plan to serve the cake, in a medium saucepan, combine the chocolate chips and coconut oil. Cook over medium heat, stirring frequently, until the chocolate is almost melted. Remove from the heat and continue stirring until completely melted and smooth. Let cool for 10 minutes before using.

6. Remove the cake from the freezer and pour the melted chocolate over the top, allowing some of it to drip over the sides. Immediately sprinkle with the chopped pistachios. Once the chocolate hardens into a shell, you can slice and serve the cake, or return it to the freezer until ready to serve. Just be sure to take the cake out of the freezer 10 minutes before cutting. This makes cutting it so much easier!

Pretzel and Honey Ice Cream in a Nutella-Lined Cone

Makes: **6 ice cream cones**

Thank you, Little Miss Asher, for dipping your pretzels in Nutella, and therefore inspiring me to make the most incredible ice cream. This is the best sweet-salty-chocolaty treat of all time. The Nutella-lined cone alone is something to be talked about, but then add the salty pretzel and honey ice cream? It's what I'd call a serious ice cream situation.

Ice Cream

5 egg yolks

2 tablespoons granulated sugar

2 (14-ounce) cans full-fat coconut milk

¾ cup honey

1 vanilla bean, halved lengthwise and seeds scraped out, or 2 teaspoons pure vanilla extract

¼ teaspoon flaky sea salt

1½ cups crushed pretzels

Nutella Cones

6 waffle cones

¾ cup Nutella

For Serving

Honey

Sprinkles

Crushed pretzels

Flaky sea salt

1. In a medium pot, whisk together the egg yolks and sugar until pale yellow. Add the coconut milk, ½ cup of the honey, the vanilla, and salt. Set the pot over medium-high heat and bring the mixture to a low boil. Cook, stirring continuously, until the mixture thickens and easily coats the back of a wooden spoon, 8 to 10 minutes. Remove from the heat. Place a fine-mesh sieve over a large heatproof bowl and immediately strain the custard into the bowl, discarding the solids. Let cool slightly, then cover with plastic wrap and chill in the fridge for 4 hours or up to overnight.

2. When the ice cream mixture is well chilled, transfer to an ice cream maker and churn according to the manufacturer's instructions. During the last few minutes of churning, add the pretzels and the remaining ¼ cup of honey. Transfer the ice cream to an airtight freezer-safe container. Freeze for 4 to 6 hours, or until firm—note that because of the honey in this recipe, the ice cream will be softer than most.

3. Spoon 2 to 3 tablespoons of the Nutella into each waffle cone and use a butter knife to spread it around the inside and outer edge of the cone. Roll the outer edge in sprinkles or crushed pretzels.

4. Place a couple of scoops of ice cream into each cone and serve immediately.

Death by Chocolate Icebox Cake

Makes: One 9-inch ice cream cake

Every Christmas Eve for as long as I can remember, my family has enjoyed Death by Chocolate. That sounds crazy—let me explain. Death by Chocolate is a trifle-style dessert made up of layers of Kahlúa-soaked chocolate cake, chocolate mousse, whipped cream, and crushed Snickers bars. Make more sense now? This dessert is my Christmas, and it's always fun helping Mom assemble it on Christmas Eve. Since it is a serious tradition to only eat Death by Chocolate on Christmas Eve (though leftovers are permitted for the next couple of nights), I've had to find ways to get my fix throughout the remainder of the year by making desserts with similar flavor profiles. Enter this icebox cake. It's just like Death by Chocolate, only simpler, and transformed into a frozen treat. It's equally perfect for easy entertaining or satisfying a critical craving.

Nonstick cooking spray

25 Oreos

¼ cup Kahlúa

6 cups heavy cream

¼ cup confectioners' sugar

2 teaspoons pure vanilla extract

½ teaspoon flaky sea salt

12 ounces semisweet chocolate, melted and cooled

6 regular-size Snickers bars, chopped

1. Grease an 8- to 9-inch round springform pan with cooking spray.

2. Put the Oreos in a food processor and pulse until you have fine crumbs. Add the Kahlúa and pulse until combined.

3. In a large bowl using a handheld mixer, whip 3 cups of the cream until it holds stiff peaks. Add the confectioners' sugar, 1 teaspoon of the vanilla, and the salt. Whip until just combined.

4. In a separate large bowl, whip the remaining 3 cups of cream. Add the melted chocolate and gently mix until the chocolate is fully incorporated into the cream. Stir the remaining 1 teaspoon of vanilla into the mousse.

5. To assemble, sprinkle half the cookie crumbs into the prepared pan to cover. Add half the mousse and then half the whipped cream. Sprinkle the whipped cream with one-third of the chopped Snickers. Repeat the layers one more time, ending with Snickers and a light sprinkle of cookie crumbs.

6. Cover with plastic wrap and freeze for at least 4 hours. Remove the cake 10 to 15 minutes before serving to allow it to soften slightly. Slice and serve!

NOTE
The Snickers can be
swapped out for
about 1 cup of chopped
roasted peanuts.

Gooey Chocolate Coconut Caramel Bars

Makes: **12 to 14 bars**

What's not to love here? Coconut, chocolate, and caramel—all of my favorites. Before you set out to make these bars, you should know this: the caramel is never going to firm up like a traditional caramel bar—it will always be gooey, runny, and all kinds of delicious! Therefore, I recommend storing the bars in the fridge at all times. When you're ready to serve, take them out and eat them rather quickly to avoid additional messiness, being sure to lick your fingers. Oh, and since these bars are reasonably healthy (. . . ish), I'm thinking they could be cool for breakfast, too! Okay, that may be a bit of a stretch . . .

12 ounces dark chocolate, chopped

4 heaping tablespoons creamy peanut butter or almond butter

2 cups unsweetened flaked coconut

1 cup roasted cashews

1 cup pitted Medjool dates

1 (14-ounce) can full-fat coconut milk

½ cup coconut sugar or packed light brown sugar

¼ cup honey

1 tablespoon coconut oil

1 teaspoon pure vanilla extract

¾ cup roasted peanuts

NOTE
Coconut sugar can be found at health food stores or purchased online.

1. Line a 9 x 13-inch baking dish with parchment paper.

2. Put 6 ounces of the chocolate and 2 rounded tablespoons of the peanut butter in a medium microwave-safe bowl. Microwave in 30-second intervals, stirring in between, until melted and smooth. Pour into the prepared baking dish and spread into an even layer. Place in the freezer for about 15 minutes to harden.

3. Meanwhile, in a food processor, pulse the coconut flakes and cashews until finely ground. Add the dates and pulse until the mixture comes together and forms a ball.

4. When the chocolate–peanut butter mixture has hardened, remove the pan from the freezer and, using your hands, press the coconut mixture into an even layer on top. Return to the fridge to chill.

5. In a medium saucepan, combine the coconut milk, coconut sugar, and honey. Bring the mixture to a boil over medium-high heat. Cook for about 10 minutes, until the caramel has thickened. Remove from the heat and let cool for 5 minutes, then stir in the coconut oil, vanilla, and peanuts. Remove the pan from the fridge and pour the caramel mixture over the top. Return to fridge to chill for at least 1 hour.

6. Put the remaining 6 ounces of chocolate and 2 tablespoons of peanut butter in a medium microwave-safe bowl. Microwave in 30-second intervals, stirring in between, until melted and smooth. Let cool for 5 minutes, then pour the chocolate over the caramel layer. Return the bars to the fridge until well chilled, at least 1 hour.

7. Cut the bars into squares. Store in the fridge for up to 1 week.

Santa's Hot Chocolate

Serves: **2**

I love nothing more than a cup of hot chocolate on a cold morning or a late afternoon. I inherited this trait from my mom, who I honestly don't think could survive without her daily cup. However, this hot chocolate is a little different from hers, and way more special than anything you've had before. I think of it as the ultimate cozy dessert, perfect for those colder months when you can get all snuggled in blankets and cozy up by the fire. Simply top each piping-hot cup with a generous dollop of salted whipped cream and a toasted marshmallow. I think even Santa and his elves would go crazy for this mug of hot chocolate. If you really want to impress him, serve it with a brownie or cookie for dunking.

4½ cups whole milk

¼ cup unsweetened cocoa powder

6 ounces milk chocolate, chopped

2 teaspoons high-quality instant coffee granules

1 tablespoon pure vanilla extract

Flaky sea salt

1 cup heavy cream

1 tablespoon confectioners' sugar

2 brownies, store-bought or homemade (page 276), for serving

2 large marshmallows, store-bought or homemade (recipe follows), toasted, for serving

1. In a large saucepan, combine the milk, cocoa powder, chocolate, instant coffee, vanilla, and a pinch of salt. Cook over medium-low heat until the milk is scalding, with bubbles forming just around the edges of the pan, 5 to 8 minutes. Stir often to ensure nothing is sticking to the bottom or burning.

2. Meanwhile, make the whipped cream. In a large bowl using a handheld mixer, whip the cream until it holds stiff peaks. Add the confectioners' sugar and a pinch of salt and whip until combined. Refrigerate until ready to serve.

3. When the hot chocolate is steaming, ladle it into two mugs and dollop with the whipped cream. Serve topped with a warm brownie and a toasted marshmallow. It's best to use a spoon for this one.

HOMEMADE VANILLA MARSHMALLOWS

Makes: **12 marshmallows**

Nonstick cooking spray

½ cup warm water

2 tablespoons powdered gelatin

1½ cups granulated sugar

⅔ cup honey

1 vanilla bean, halved lengthwise and seeds scraped out

Confectioners' sugar, for dusting

1. Line an 8-inch square baking pan with parchment paper and lightly spray with cooking spray.

2. In the bowl of a stand mixer, stir together the warm water and gelatin to combine.

3. In a medium saucepan, combine the granulated sugar, honey, and ½ cup water. Cook over medium heat, stirring often, until the sugar has fully dissolved, about 10 minutes. Increase the heat to high and bring the syrup to a boil. Cook until the temperature registers 240°F on a candy thermometer, 6 to 7 minutes. Remove the pan from the heat.

4. Fit the stand mixer with the whisk attachment. With the mixer on medium speed, slowly pour the hot syrup into the gelatin mixture. Add the vanilla bean seeds. Raise the mixer speed to high and beat for 4 to 5 minutes, or until the mixture is fluffy.

5. Working very quickly, use a greased spatula to transfer the marshmallow mixture to the prepared pan. Smooth the top into an even layer. Cover with plastic wrap and place in the fridge until set, 1 to 2 hours.

6. Generously dust the top of the marshmallow with confectioners' sugar and then invert it onto a clean cutting board. Dust that side with confectioners' sugar. Cut the marshmallow into squares. Store in an airtight container at room temperature for up to 1 month.

No-Churn Ice Cream, Three Ways

Makes: About 1½ quarts per recipe

Not much beats homemade ice cream, but let's be real: sometimes the process of making it is just too time-consuming. That's why I created these easy, no-churn ice cream recipes in three of my favorite flavors! Try pairing them with the other desserts in this book, or just enjoy them on their own.

Graham Cracker Crumble Ice Cream

1 sleeve graham crackers, crushed

½ cup (1 stick) salted butter, at room temperature

2 tablespoons light brown sugar

4 ounces mascarpone cheese

¾ cup sweetened condensed milk

1 tablespoon pure vanilla extract

2 cups heavy cream

1. Preheat the oven to 325°F. Line a rimmed baking sheet with parchment paper.

2. In a small bowl, combine the graham cracker crumbs, butter, and brown sugar. Using your hands, massage the butter into the graham crackers until the butter and sugar are evenly distributed. Spread the mixture over the prepared baking sheet and bake until light golden brown, about 10 minutes. Let cool to room temperature, 10 minutes.

3. Meanwhile, in the bowl of a stand mixer fitted with the whisk attachment, beat the mascarpone, condensed milk, and vanilla on medium speed until fully combined and smooth. Add the cream and whip until the mixture holds stiff peaks, 3 to 5 minutes. Fold in the cooled graham cracker crumble. Spoon the ice cream into a freezer-safe container and freeze for 4 hours or overnight before serving.

Browned Butter Ice Cream

6 tablespoons (¾ stick) unsalted butter

2 cups heavy cream

1 cup sweetened condensed milk

1 tablespoon pure vanilla extract

2 cups fresh raspberries, lightly mashed

1. In a medium saucepan, melt the butter over high heat. Cook, stirring often, until the butter is lightly browned and smells toasted, about 5 minutes—it will foam and then settle back down. Remove the pan from the heat and let cool slightly.

2. In the bowl of a stand mixer fitted with the whisk attachment, beat the cream, condensed milk, and vanilla on high speed until it holds stiff peaks, 3 to 5 minutes. Swirl in the browned butter and raspberries—it's okay if the butter starts to harden in the ice cream. Spoon the ice cream into a freezer-safe container and freeze for 4 hours or overnight before serving.

Chocolate Birthday Cake Ice Cream

2 cups heavy cream

1 cup sweetened condensed milk

2 teaspoons pure vanilla extract

½ cup unsweetened cocoa powder

1 cup crumbled chocolate cake, store-bought or homemade (page 252)

Pinch of flaky sea salt

In the bowl of a stand mixer fitted with the whisk attachment, beat the cream, condensed milk, vanilla, and cocoa powder on high speed until the mixture holds stiff peaks, 3 to 5 minutes. Gently fold in the cake crumbs and salt. Spoon the ice cream into a freezer-safe container and freeze for 4 hours or overnight before serving.

Mocha-Almond Streusel Doughnuts

Makes: 10 to 12 doughnuts

Deep-frying can be a pain and I tend to avoid doing it, but when it comes to doughnuts, I think you kind of have to. To me, a baked doughnut is just a cupcake in a different shape . . . yummy, but not authentic. Real doughnuts should be incredibly light and fluffy, with a slightly crisp, golden outer crust. Typically, I am all about classic doughnuts, but when making them at home, I always go for something a little more creative (duh). This mocha-almond streusel version is my favorite. While the dough is simple and delish, the stars of the show are the mocha glaze and the sweet, buttery almond streusel.

Doughnuts

1¼ cups milk, warmed

1½ tablespoons instant yeast

1 tablespoon light brown sugar

6 tablespoons (¾ stick) unsalted butter, melted

1 large egg

3½ cups all-purpose flour

1 teaspoon kosher salt

Nonstick cooking spray, for greasing

Canola oil, for frying

Almond Streusel

½ cup finely chopped raw almonds

½ cup unsweetened shredded coconut

6 tablespoons all-purpose flour

½ cup packed light brown sugar

¼ teaspoon ground cinnamon

1 teaspoon kosher salt

6 tablespoons (¾ stick) unsalted butter, at room temperature

Mocha Glaze

¼ cup milk

1 tablespoon instant espresso powder

1½ to 2 cups confectioners' sugar

⅓ cup unsweetened cocoa powder

2 teaspoons pure vanilla extract

Pinch of flaky sea salt

1. MAKE THE DOUGHNUT DOUGH. In the bowl of a stand mixer, stir together the warm milk, yeast, and brown sugar by hand to combine. Fit the mixer with the dough hook, add the melted butter and egg, and mix on medium speed. Add 3 cups of the flour and the kosher salt and mix until the dough comes together and is smooth, about 3 minutes. (Alternatively, knead the dough by hand for 5 to 10 minutes.) The dough should feel slightly sticky to touch. If it seems too sticky, add the remaining ½ cup flour, 1 tablespoon at a time. Grease a large bowl with cooking spray and add the dough. Cover the bowl with plastic wrap and let rise in a warm place until the dough has doubled in size, at least 30 minutes.

2. MEANWHILE, MAKE THE ALMOND STREUSEL. Preheat the oven to 325°F. Line a rimmed baking sheet with parchment paper.

3. On the prepared baking sheet, toss together the almonds, coconut, flour, brown sugar, cinnamon, and kosher salt. Add the butter and use your hand to incorporate it into the mixture, being sure all the dry ingredients have been coated in butter. Bake for 15 to 20 minutes, tossing halfway through, until golden and toasted. Remove from the oven and let cool.

4. FRY THE DOUGHNUTS. Line two baking sheets with parchment paper. Lightly flour a work surface and roll out the dough to ½-inch thickness. Using doughnut or circular cookie cutters, cut out rounds. Arrange the doughnuts on the prepared baking sheet, leaving at least 1 inch in between. Cover loosely with plastic wrap.

5. In a large pot or deep fryer, heat at least 2 inches of oil until a deep-fry thermometer registers 350°F or the oil sizzles when a wooden spoon is inserted. Working in batches, use a slotted spoon or spatula to carefully add two or three doughnuts to the hot oil; do not crowd the oil. Fry until light golden brown, 1 to 2 minutes per side. Transfer to a paper towel–lined plate to drain. Be sure to let the oil temperature return to 350°F between batches.

6. MAKE THE GLAZE. In a small saucepan, heat the milk over low until it begins to steam, 3 to 5 minutes. Remove the pan from the heat and stir in the instant espresso. Whisk in the confectioners' sugar, cocoa powder, vanilla, and flaky salt until smooth. If the glaze is too thin, add more confectioners' sugar until the desired thickness is reached. If the glaze is too thick, thin with more milk or water.

7. When the doughnuts have cooled, dip their tops into the glaze and let the excess drip off. Place on the prepared baking sheets. Sprinkle each doughnut generously with the almond streusel.

8. The doughnuts can be stored in an airtight container for 1 to 2 days, but are best enjoyed shortly after frying.

Strawberry-Peach Galette

Makes: One 12-inch galette

Certain fruity things just make me so happy that I stop dead in my tracks and do a little dance. One of those fruity things happens to be this galette. It is life-changing, all-over-the-place juicy, and delicious. It's perfection with vanilla ice cream, but let's be honest . . . what isn't? Finish this off with a good drizzle of butterscotch sauce and say hello to your new favorite fruity dessert. What I love most about this galette is that you can use the same base dough recipe, but simply swap out whatever fruits are currently in season, or whatever you have on hand. When fall arrives, I love to replace the peaches and berries with apples. Have fun here and use the fruits you love!

Crust

1½ cups all-purpose flour, plus more for dusting

½ cup pecans, toasted and finely ground

½ teaspoon kosher salt

½ cup (1 stick) cold unsalted butter, cut into ½-inch cubes

3 to 6 tablespoons cold water

Filling

3 ripe peaches, pitted and sliced

2 cups fresh strawberries, hulled and halved

¼ cup packed light brown sugar

1 tablespoon cornstarch

Juice of ½ lemon

1 large egg, beaten

Coarse sugar, for sprinkling

Ice cream, for serving

Butterscotch sauce, store-bought or homemade (recipe follows), for serving

1. In a large bowl, combine the flour, pecans, and salt. Add the butter and use your fingers to break it into the flour until the mixture is the size of small peas. Add 3 tablespoons of water and mix with a wooden spoon, drizzling in more water as needed, 1 tablespoon at a time, until the dough just comes together (a few dry spots are okay).

2. Turn the dough out onto a lightly floured surface and gently knead until no dry spots remain, about 1 minute. At this point, you can wrap the dough in plastic wrap and store it in the fridge while you prepare the filling, or for up to 1 week.

3. Flour your work surface and roll out the dough to about ⅛ inch thick. Transfer to a parchment paper–lined baking sheet.

4. In a large bowl, toss together the peaches, strawberries, brown sugar, cornstarch, and lemon juice. Arrange the fruit over the dough, leaving a 1-inch border around the edges. Pour any remaining juices from the bowl over the fruit. Fold the edges of the dough over the filling. Brush the crust with the beaten egg and sprinkle with the coarse sugar. Place in the fridge for at least 15 minutes or until ready to bake.

5. Preheat the oven to 400°F.

6. Bake the galette for 45 to 50 minutes, or until the crust is golden and the fruit is soft and caramelized. Serve warm or at room temperature with a large scoop of ice cream and a drizzle of butterscotch sauce.

EASY HOMEMADE BUTTERSCOTCH SAUCE

Makes: **1 cup**

4 tablespoons (½ stick) unsalted butter

½ cup packed dark brown sugar

½ cup heavy cream

1 teaspoon kosher salt

1 teaspoon pure vanilla extract

1 tablespoon scotch or other whiskey (optional)

In a medium saucepan, combine the butter, brown sugar, cream, and salt and bring to a boil over high heat. Cook for 5 minutes, then reduce the heat to medium and cook for about 5 minutes more, until the sauce has thickened slightly. Remove the pan from the heat and stir in the vanilla and scotch (if using). Let cool, then transfer to a glass jar and store in the fridge for up to 1 month.

Acknowledgments

A huge thank-you to Amanda Englander for putting up with me and dealing with my crazy Tieghan mind . . . and my grammar! Without you, this book would be the most chaotic piece of writing there ever was. Thank you for organizing my thoughts, taming my ideas, and teaching me that there is such a thing as too many exclamation points and overuse of all-capital letters. You made this book the best it could be, thank you times a million!!! Yes, three exclamation points are necessary.

I also would like to thank everyone at Clarkson Potter for helping to create a cookbook that I am beyond excited about. Stephanie Huntwork and Jen Wang, thank you for your impeccable taste and incredible designs. Thank you for coaching me through the photography process of shooting this book and for helping me to make every mouthwatering photo. Thank you to Terry Deal, Kim Tyner, Erica Gelbard, and Carly Gorga for bringing the book to life and for getting it out into the world!

Thank you to Peter Hoffman, my faithful recipe tester, for all of your invaluable feedback. You worked incredible hours and were even able to complete my last-minute recipe submissions. You helped to make the book what it is today.

Special thanks to Maeve Sheridan for packing up and shipping dozens of boxes of props and surfaces to Colorado. You are simply amazing and your taste in dishes is spot-on.

To my dad, without his help I could not have survived the process of writing this book. Thank you for being the best dishwasher a daughter could ask for . . . and for instilling in me at a very young age a love for cheese and fresh basil. You are the bestest!

To my mom, who taught me that kindness is the key to success, to never accept the word no, and that my only limit in life is me. Thank you for being my partner, my best friend . . . and for making the world's best oatmeal chocolate chip cookies. Never could I ever ask for a better mom.

To little Miss Asher, who no matter what can put a smile on my face, any time, any day. Thanks for being the world's most perfect gum-smacking, ice-cream-eating, "food holding" model I could ever ask for. I love you more than you know, little sis! You are such a little weirdo . . . don't ever change. To all my crazy brothers, friends, and anyone else who helped me taste-test all the recipes included in this cookbook. Thanks for the honest feedback and good times. Glad I was able to keep you guys full over the last year-plus while developing these recipes! You guys might drive me crazy, but I love you all!

To my kind, caring, and incredibly hardworking agent, Stacey Glick. I am still in awe of you and how much you do daily—you are awesome. Thank you for taking me in, showing me the ropes, and helping me through the process of writing this book. You were with me every step of the way and I can't wait to do it again.

Last, but certainly not least, to all my loyal halfbakedharvest .com, Instagram, Facebook, and Pinterest followers, this book would not have been possible without each and every one of you. I made this cookbook for you; my hope is that it will become a cookbook you turn to daily. Thank you for your frequent, kind as ever, comments and positive feedback. You guys will always be my favorite people and you are the bright spot in every day.

Index

Copyright © 2017 by Tieghan Gerard

All rights reserved.

Published in the United States by Clarkson Potter/Publishers, an imprint of the Crown Publishing Group, a division of Penguin Random House LLC, New York.

crownpublishing.com
clarksonpotter.com

CLARKSON POTTER is a trademark and POTTER with colophon is a registered trademark of Penguin Random House LLC.

Library of Congress Cataloging-in-Publication Data
Names: Gerard, Tieghan, author.
Title: Half baked harvest cookbook : recipes from my barn in the mountains / Tieghan Gerard; photographs by Tieghan Gerard.
Description: First edition. | New York : Clarkson Potter/Publishers, [2017]

Identifiers: LCCN 2016050905| ISBN 9780553496390 (hardcover/pob) | ISBN 9780553496406 (eISBN)
Subjects: LCSH: Cooking, American—Western style. | Cooking—Colorado. | LCGFT: Cookbooks.
Classification: LCC TX715.2.W47 G47 2017 | DDC 641.59788—dc23
LC record available at https://lccn.loc.gov/2016050905

ISBN 978-0-553-49639-0

Ebook ISBN 978-0-553-49640-6

Printed in China
Cover and book design by Jen Wang
Cover photography by Tieghan Gerard

10 9 8 7 6 5 4 3 2 1

First Edition